JAMES NORRIS AND THE DECLINE OF BOXING

JAMES NORRIS AND THE DECLINE OF BOXING

BARNEY NAGLER

THE **BOBBS-MERRILL** COMPANY, INC.
A SUBSIDIARY OF HOWARD W. SAMS & CO., INC.
Publishers • INDIANAPOLIS • NEW YORK

For BETTY

who takes a hell of a punch

First printing, 1964
Copyright © 1964 by Barney Nagler
All rights reserved
Library of Congress catalog card number 63-18999

Printed in the United States of America

Part One

Conspiracy

ONE

WEDNESDAY, DECEMBER 12, 1947, was cold and windy, with a clinging dampness that gripped walkers in the city. On Sugar Hill in Harlem, along Edgecombe Avenue, there was no sound but the puff and sough of the wind. In apartment 8E, at 555 Edgecombe Avenue, a man heard the wind and walked to a window and looked out over the city, and he was pleased to be warm. He wasn't well. Five nights before he had been in a fight downtown and had come away with his mocha chocolate face misshapen, his left eye closed, and his pride diminished, and now he was alone in a darkened room, reflective and moody. The telephone had rung many times; he had heard the bell and had started, as though he were still in the ring, between rounds and waiting for the bell to summon him. But he had not answered.

Joe Louis had been the world heavyweight champion since June 22, 1937, when he had knocked out James J. Braddock in the eighth round at Comiskey Park in Chicago. He had been startled in the first round when Braddock had put a hard right to his jaw, and he had gone down for a brief moment. There had been an immeasurable shout from the crowd and, later, when he had finished off Braddock with his own right hand, he had heard the same shout. Now, in his unhappiness, there was an immeasurable quiet.

Actually, Louis should have been downtown at Madison Square

Garden, where clamorous newspaper reporters were waiting to talk with him about the fight he had almost lost to "Jersey Joe" Walcott the past Friday night. Custom called for such a confrontation. In the old days, the day after a fight had been fun. Louis would go to the office of Promoter Mike Jacobs at the Garden, flop into a large chair upholstered in red leather, and attempt to explain to the reporters what it was all about—the overwhelming desire to win, which justified it all. He would glance at the comic pages while talking to them, and they would overlook his impoliteness because, they wrote, he was, after all, just a natural killer, born in a sharecropper's shack off a dirt road in red-clay country that runs between Lafayette and Cusetta in Chambers County, halfway down the map of Alabama where Georgia backs into it. Inwardly, he found the reporters' questions funnier than the comic pages, but his own sensitivity and inborn decency foreclosed laughter.

Now he was thirty-three years old, in the eleventh year of his time as heavyweight champion, but he felt older. His head had throbbed for hours after Walcott had finished hitting him, and when he looked into a mirror the image he saw was raw and unfamiliar. He sat in the dark and was worried. He was often happy and not usually worried; until the past few days he had not given any importance to what happened to himself. It was a new and terrible thing and, in the darkened room, he knew suddenly that he was about to make a decision. For most people it would have been a simple discovery; for Louis, it was the last moment of his innocence.

In the past, Promoter Mike Jacobs—the one he called "Uncle Mike"—and his managers, John Roxborough and Julian Black, had determined his course. Jacobs had had a severe cerebral stroke a year earlier and was no longer active, though his corporate image, the 20th Century Sporting Club, still held Louis in contractual bondage. Black had been dismissed as a manager the year before, when he had refused to lend Louis $25,000 which the heavyweight champion wanted to give to his wife, Marva, in fulfillment of a divorce agreement. Only Roxborough remained, but his influence on Louis had lessened since the champion had taken unto himself another co-manager to replace Black—a melancholy little man called Marshall Miles, who was more Louis's companion than Nestor.

Miles had been in the apartment on Edgecombe Avenue earlier in the day, but he hadn't stayed long. He had gone to the offices of the 20th Century Sporting Club in Madison Square Garden to check on Louis's earnings of $75,968 from the bout with Walcott. Then Mannie Seamon, Louis's trainer, had arrived to examine the champion's lacerated left cheek, which was marked by a vestigial scab. Louis's friend and court jester, Leonard Reed, had also visited the champion. He had tried to bring laughter into the apartment, but Louis had not laughed, and Reed had gone away, leaving the champion alone.

At two o'clock the telephone rang. Louis heard it ring four times and stiffened against a natural curiosity to know who was calling. The ringing stopped. Five minutes later it was heard again. This time Louis could not resist. A newspaper reporter had tracked him down despite the champion's unlisted telephone number.

"I ain't seein' nobody," Louis said.

"It won't take long."

"I'm tired," Louis said.

"I'll be right up," the reporter insisted.

"Okay," Louis said, grudgingly. "You know where it is."

"I've been there before."

"Don't bring any of them other fellows," Louis said.

"I will come alone."

Half an hour later the reporter sat across from Louis in the darkened room. The champion's daughter, Jacqueline, who was five years old, had returned from a walk in the park with a friend and ran through the living room. She was herded into the kitchen by her father. The reporter had seen Louis under happier circumstances, and he remembered the brightest moment of all, when the "Brown Bomber" had subdued Max Schmeling within two minutes and four seconds of the first round, to revenge himself on the German for an earlier humiliating defeat. Now, the heavyweight champion, who was unshaven, sat in a soft chair in an almost dark corner of the somber room. He was wearing a striped black-and-white bathrobe over pajamas. Only the right side of his face could be seen, and his eyes averted the gaze of his visitor.

"It was tough the other night," the reporter said.

"I made it tough," the champion said. "I saw openings I didn't use. Man gets old, he don't take advantage of them things as fast as he used to."

"How do you feel now?"

"Good."

"What will you do?"

"When?"

"About Walcott?"

"Fight him again."

"And beat him?"

"I beat him Friday. Next time I'll knock him out."

His voice was without firmness and his words lacked confidence. "I'll beat him and retire," he said.

"You're kidding, Joe."

"I mean it. I'm through after Walcott. It'll be my last fight."

"When'd you decide that?"

"Just now, sitting here alone, I come to think of it."

"It's a good story for me."

"It's true," the champion said.

The visitor sat back and was silent. He knew that Louis wanted to be alone, yet the champion had not made a move toward ending the interview. The reporter was eager to leave. He knew from experience how difficult it was to safeguard an exclusive story; it was more difficult to do this than to obtain such a story, even if you knew your way around.

Looking around apprehensively, as though he had just stolen the Kohinoor, he came off the chair and walked toward Louis. He extended his right hand and Louis shook it, and the reporter turned toward the door. On the way out he picked up his coat and hat from the chair on which he had dropped them. He said good-bye over his shoulder. The next day the *Bronx Home News* printed his story under a banner headline: LOUIS SAYS HE'LL RETIRE AFTER JUNE FIGHT. In other newspaper offices editors prodded their reporters to check the story. When they did Louis confirmed it. The news was printed in every major newspaper in the country. Millions read it and reflected on the impending finish of a glorious era in boxing. Louis, who had become the champion in the first year of the second administration of Franklin D. Roosevelt, had been regarded, like

FDR, as an everlasting symbol of a period that now, at last, was coming to a close.

In Chicago, James Dougan Norris read the story and thought about it at length. He was forty-one years old, tall and handsome and rich. Together with his father, James Norris, and his partner, Arthur M. Wirtz, he owned the Chicago Stadium, the Detroit Olympia, and the St. Louis Arena, and he held leases on the Indianapolis Coliseum and the Omaha Coliseum. He held stock in Madison Square Garden and, with his partners, owned and produced the Hollywood Ice Revue.

He owned thoroughbred horses and raced them at tracks throughout the country. His commercial interests held the ownership of the Detroit Red Wings of the National Hockey League. For many years, he had owned "pieces" of prize fighters and had even promoted boxing shows in the Chicago Stadium. He knew fighters and their managers, and he sought their company. Under black eyebrows, his eyes appeared to be piercing beacons lighting a path for an improbable assortment of companions. He knew gangsters and gamblers and stood out in their company because of his finely tailored clothes and proper manners. The story of Louis's plan to retire tickled his commercial imagination.

TWO

THE 20TH CENTURY SPORTING CLUB hastily scheduled a second meeting of Louis and Walcott for Yankee Stadium on June 23, 1948, and there were predictions of a million-dollar gate. Promoter Jacobs was still inactive in his business because of the cerebral stroke suffered on December 3, 1946. He would appear at the Garden occasionally, if only to check on his bank balance, but he was a semi-invalid and therefore unable to direct the corporation's activities. The business was being conducted by a regency composed of the two most improbable men in boxing: Sol Strauss, a hard-of-hearing Pickwickian lawyer, and Harry Markson, a lean, scholarly graduate of Union College, a fastidiously selective education plant at Schenectady, New York.

On the day Strauss and Markson were setting the price scale for the first meeting of Louis and Walcott, Jacobs shuffled into the promotorial corporation's office in Madison Square Garden. He had been in a coma for three days after his stroke, which had left his right arm paralyzed, but he was surprisingly alert when the price of tickets was the topic of conversation.

"We should make the top price twenty-five dollars," Markson said.

"I think so," Strauss agreed.

"Thirty," Mike growled. He was right. The bout drew a record gate of $216,497 at Madison Square Garden.

The day-by-day promotion of the second bout between Louis and Walcott was left to Markson and Strauss. Markson had been a sports writer for the *Bronx Home News* before taking a job as a publicity man for the 20th Century Sporting Club. At the time, he was just over thirty years old and addicted to culture, which brought him a measure of notoriety in the anti-intellectual field of boxing. He was accused by fight managers of visiting Carnegie Hall to hear the New York Philharmonic and was regarded as an infidel because he had expressed the opinion that Arturo Toscanini was a more compelling figure than Arturo Godoy, a heavyweight from Chile.

Strauss, the other half of the regency, was Jacobs' cousin. He had been retained as legal counsel for the 20th Century Sporting Club when it was organized in 1933 by Jacobs and a trinity of journalists who worked for William Randolph Hearst and who promoted boxing shows for Mrs. William Randolph Hearst's Free Milk Fund for Babies. They were Edward J. ("Ed") Frayne, sports editor of the New York *American*; Wilston S. ("Bill") Farnsworth, sports editor of the New York *Journal*, and Damon Runyon, who had been a Hearst columnist for three decades before his fictionalized Broadway characters became known wherever English was spoken and read.

Jacobs himself was a curmudgeonish product of the rough-and-tumble life of Broadway, along which he had achieved a reputation as the most resourceful ticket speculator in the theatrical district. He was hard-crusted and crafty and totally without formal education. When he was in need of a favor, he was charming and warm and obliging, almost to the point of sycophancy; otherwise, he was a ruthless predator who had struggled up from poverty on New York's lower West Side and had become the foremost promoter of boxing in the world.

Along with Frayne, Farnsworth, and Runyon, Jacobs had challenged Madison Square Garden's monopolistic hold on boxing. Outwardly they appeared to be motivated by an inexorable philanthropic compulsion to help Mrs. Hearst's Free Milk Fund. In reality they were an avid cabal of self-seekers.

For some years, the Milk Fund had benefited from boxing shows held in Madison Square Garden and other arenas controlled by the Garden, when James J. Johnston, a charming man known as "The Boy Bandit" though he was long past his nonage, was the nominal promoter of boxing. He was an aggressive veteran of many promotional wars and chose to criticize Frayne, Farnsworth, and Runyon as opportunistic villains. They used the Hearst press to assail Johnston as an inept promoter whose deficiencies cost the Garden a great deal of money. In 1933, Colonel John Reed Kilpatrick, who was president of the Garden, informed the Milk Fund that he had raised the rental fee for its next boxing show at the Garden. Frayne, Farnsworth, and Runyon cloaked themselves in the garb of charitable men. They accused the Garden of depriving helpless infants of free milk and implemented their campaign by prevailing upon Jacobs to join them in the organization of a new promotional corporation, the 20th Century Sporting Club.

Laying philanthrophy aside, Jacobs joined the schemers. As a ticket scalper, he had held commercial hands with George L. (Tex) Rickard, who had raised the game to lofty million-dollar heights during the time of Jack Dempsey and Gene Tunney. Jacobs had never promoted a fight, but his devotion to tickets as a commodity and his willingness to invest in the new company appealed to the Hearst troika. They met secretly, in the Forrest Hotel in West 49th Street, off Broadway, across the street from Jacobs' ticket brokerage office, and plotted their campaign. The stock in the new corporation was held in Jacobs' name because none of the others could acknowl-

edge their involvement publicly. Only Frayne received a covering
letter from Jacobs to certify his partnership in the new corporation.
Farnsworth and Runyon took Jacobs at his word, and together the
four dragon-killers went forth to battle Madison Square Garden,
which had monopolized the promotion of boxing for years.

Their success was instantaneous. Frayne and Farnsworth could
"deliver" the support of the Hearst press in New York, and Runyon,
in his column, indicated that any promotion by the 20th Century
Sporting Club was the second coming of the First Punic War. In
January, 1935, Jacobs went to Miami Beach to promote a bout between Barney Ross, the junior welterweight champion and Frankie
Klick, a San Franciscan. At Miami Beach, Ross's co-managers, Sam
Pian and Art Winch, delivered unto Jacobs a recommendation that
sealed the Garden's fate.

"Mike, I got something good for you," Pian said.

"Listen, Mike, this is good," Winch said.

"I got 'nuff troubles with the fight," Jacobs scowled. "I don't
need nothing more."

"Mike, there's a kid fighting around Chicago name of Joe Louis
you should get," Pian said.

"He's a heavyweight," Winch said. "He'll be a champ."

"We'll see about it," Jacobs said.

Jacobs did not forget. Upon his return to New York, Jacobs called
Detroit and talked to John Roxborough, Louis's co-manager. Jacobs
stressed his alliance with the Hearst triad by way of supporting his
application to become Louis's exclusive promoter.

"We can help the boy along," Jacobs said.

"I got other offers," Roxborough said.

"None come better than mine," Jacobs said.

Frayne, Farnsworth, and Runyon used their editorial influence to
seal the deal. Louis signed to fight exclusively for the 20th Century
Sporting Club. At Madison Square Garden there was no sign of
panic. The Garden went about the business of promoting a world's
heavyweight championship bout between Max Baer and James J.
Braddock, which took place on June 13, 1935, at the Madison
Square Garden Bowl in Long Island City, across the East River from
Manhattan. It drew only $205,366 at the box office and, of all things,

Braddock outpointed Baer in fifteen rounds although he had been in betting disfavor at odds of 10 to 1. Twelve days later, Louis fought his first bout in New York City. He opposed Primo Carnera, a ponderous Italian from whom Baer had won the heavyweight title in 1934. Louis was twenty-one years old and superbly conditioned. His earthen-tinted body was a figure of subtle strength and attractiveness. The Hearst press had presented him as a gloved god, and there had been an imaginative publicity campaign in his behalf. He was greeted at City Hall by Mayor Fiorello H. LaGuardia, and the "Little Flower" felt his biceps for newspaper photographers. Louis had shown surprising agility while performing with dancing girls at the Harlem Opera House and had moved just as gracefully against Carnera. In the sixth round, Louis put a left and right to the Italian's jaw and knocked him out. The bout, at Yankee Stadium, drew $328,655, surpassing by more than $100,000 the gross receipts for the heavyweight championship bout between Braddock and Baer. The newspapers said Louis was the touchstone of boxing's resurgence, and Mike Jacobs had cause to smile.

Three months later, Jacobs' avidity was fulfilled once again. Louis went back to Yankee Stadium, where he had knocked out Carnera, to fight still another former heavyweight champion, Max Baer, who had relinquished the title to Braddock. By now Louis was being called the "Brown Bomber." Baer was a quavering victim; he was knocked out in the fourth round, and the 88,150 persons in the arena rose to cheer Louis. Jacobs counted $1,000,832 in the till. The million-dollar gate was back in boxing, although economic blight still lay on the land, despite the New Deal of Franklin D. Roosevelt.

Jacobs now saw a straight line to the heavyweight championship for Louis. Although it was true that Braddock, the title holder, was under contractual obligation to fight only for Madison Square Garden, Jacobs was warmed by the promotorial fact that the most profitable bout for all concerned would be one between the champion and Louis. Braddock was managed by Joe Gould, a slender bundle of mingled rancor and charm, though it was rumored that Owney Madden, a delicately turned out Prohibition mobster, had a "piece" of the champion.

Gould chose to stand aside with Braddock, while Louis continued his campaign to establish himself as the leading challenger for the title. Jacobs matched him to fight Max Schmeling, a beetle-browed German who had won the heavyweight championship on a foul in a bout with Jack Sharkey in 1930 and had lost it to Sharkey by decision the next year. The bout was set for Yankee Stadium, June 19, 1936. Louis switched his training camp from one part of New Jersey to another—he went from Pompton Lakes to Lakewood, a pine-protected resort made famous by John D. Rockefeller years before.

At Lakewood there was gaiety. By now Louis was married to the former Marva Trotter of Chicago and, in defiance of all training precepts, he invited her to spend time at the camp. He learned to play golf and spent many hours on the course under a hot sun. Nights were time for fun instead of relaxation. Even the sparring sessions were marked by indifference, and when Louis went into the ring at the Stadium against Schmeling he was unprepared. The German was a sharpshooter with his right fist and kept up a fusillade. His left cheek was cut in the fourth round, but he responded by flooring Louis with a right to the jaw in the same round. Louis's jaw was swollen when he came out for the fifth round, and Schmeling hit him repeatedly. Louis was groggy and did not hear the bell at the end of the round. Schmeling smashed still another right to Louis's face. Louis went down, and when he finally returned to his corner he was groggy and sore. Schmeling finished Louis off in the twelfth round with a bombardment of right hands. The people at Madison Square Garden were pleased; Jacobs went about planning the revival of Louis's prestige.

There is a technique of ballyhoo in boxing that is infallible: match a young fighter against former champions and his prestige soars in direct ratio with triumph. Aware of this immutable law, Jacobs sought the services of Jack Sharkey, another former heavyweight champion. On August 18, 1936, Louis knocked Sharkey out in three rounds at Yankee Stadium. Somehow, the public was made to forget the disgrace of the knockout by Schmeling. Louis went on tour and was seen in rings in Philadelphia and South Bend, in New Orleans and Cleveland, in Madison Square Garden and Kansas City. He was his old devastating self.

Meanwhile, Madison Square Garden had matched Braddock to fight Schmeling at the Madison Square Garden Bowl on June 3, 1937. Rather than accept this as a fact of fistic history, Jacobs chose to subvert Braddock's contract with Madison Square Garden. By stealth and cunning he convinced Braddock's manager, Joe Gould, that there was more to be gained from a bout between Braddock and Louis than between Braddock and Schmeling. In return for their willingness to breach their agreement with the Garden, Braddock and Gould were guaranteed 10 per cent of Jacobs' profits from all world's heavyweight championship bouts for the next ten years. Years later, Braddock and Gould would sue Jacobs in court in an attempt to collect their swag, but in 1937, the time of the plotted subversion, all was harmony among the schemers. History was on their side.

Remember back to the climate of international politics of the time. Nazi tyranny and savagery were bestirring men of good will all over the world. In New York, the Anti-Nazi League to Champion Human Rights was abundantly active in a movement to boycott all German products, including Max Schmeling. The League's leaders presented the thesis that if Schmeling were allowed to fight Braddock for the championship and were to win, he would serve the cause of Nazi propaganda and its chief minister, Dr. Joseph Goebbels.

Boxing historians were asked by Gould to join in a poll to determine whether a meeting of Louis and Braddock would bring more money into the box office than a bout between Schmeling and Braddock. They were overwhelmingly of the opinion that Louis's magnetism would attract more money than Schmeling's pan-Germanism. Gould knew the answer in advance, but he took the course in order to present a brightly washed face to the public. He smiled, and so did promoter Jacobs, who now offered Braddock a guarantee of $400,-000 to fight Louis. It was a bait of a beautiful hue, all green.

In Germany, Schmeling huffed and puffed, but not without a certain smugness. After all, he had been named the outstanding challenger for Braddock's title by the New York State Athletic Commission. Furthermore, he remembered that Braddock already had signed a contract for a defense against him under the promotion of Madison Square Garden.

One day, Gould received a transatlantic telephone call from Schmeling. The German heavyweight said he was in the office of Herr Goebbels, Reichsminister of National Enlightenment and Propaganda. The conversation, as reported by Budd Schulberg in *Collier's* magazine, May 6, 1950, went:

"Joe, I am speaking from the office of one of the most important people in Germany—in the world," he corrected. "Reichsminister Goebbels wants to talk to you personally."

"Mr. Gould," Goebbels began in broken but understandable English, "we are ready to make you a very interesting offer to bring your champion to Germany to fight Max."

Said Gould, "Just a minute, Mr. Goebbels. Has Max told you the kind of deal we want?"

"He has given me a general idea," Goebbels answered. "But let me hear exactly what you want. The match will be very popular in Germany and I feel sure we can meet your terms."

"All right," Gould said, "I've got three conditions. If you can agree to them I will bring Braddock to Germany."

"Excellent," Goebbels said. "I feel sure I can arrange everything to your satisfaction. Now your three conditions please."

"In the first place," said Gould, "I want $500,000 in real money —I mean American dollars—deposited in my name in a New Jersey bank before we get on the boat."

"I can promise you that will be done," Goebbels said without hesitation. "Go on, Mr. Gould."

"Second, I want to bring over an American referee, and one of the two judges must be an Englishman. We don't mind if the other's a German," Gould continued.

"One minute, please," Goebbels said. Apparently after conferring with Schmeling he told Gould, "Yes, we will agree to that also. And now, please, the third point."

"The third point," Gould said matter-of-factly, "is that you get Hitler to stop kicking the Jews around. Unless he gives them back full citizenship and property rights, you know what you and Max can do with your fight."

Later, Schmeling came to the United States to fulfill his contract

with Madison Square Garden to fight Braddock. He knew that Braddock, through Gould, was committed to fight Louis for Jacobs, but
he was determined to get it on the record that he was ready to go
through with the bout. The Garden concurred in the legalistic fiction,
even to the point of having the State Athletic Commission weigh in
Schmeling at noon on June 3, 1937. That night Schmeling went out
to the Garden Bowl and, silhouetted in moonlight, strode toward the
ring. Braddock was not there. He was at Grand Beach Michigan, a
summer resort on the southeastern shore of Lake Michigan, where
the Wolverine State rests on Indiana. While Braddock was in training at Grand Beach, Louis was flexing his muscles at Kenosha,
Wisconsin.

In Chicago, Jacobs was selling tickets for the meeting of Braddock
and Louis. Each night, the promoter carried away the day's receipts,
secretly. He was worried because Madison Square Garden was
seeking an injunction in Federal Court to prevent the fight from taking place. Jacobs' lawyer, Strauss, was in the forefront of the battle.
He pored over the exclusive service contract between Braddock and
Madison Square Garden. He found a chink: the contract was
legally deficient because there was no mutuality. While Braddock
guaranteed his services to the Garden, the contract in no wise set a
time limit on Braddock's indenture. On May 14, 1937, a federal
judge in Newark, New Jersey, denied the Garden's application for a
temporary injunction that would restrain Braddock from fighting
Louis. He was named Guy L. Fake, and sports writers throughout
the country had great sport with his name. Four weeks later, the
District Court of Appeals in Philadelphia upheld Judge Fake's decision by a vote of 2 to 1. Unfettered, Braddock was now free to be
knocked out by Louis, legally.

The night of June 22, 1937, was bright and starry, and 45,500
persons were there in Comiskey Park, Chicago. This was something
you *had* to see, like *Of Thee I Sing* or the Mona Lisa. Braddock was
in betting disfavor at 5 to 2, but he did not surrender without a
touch of dignity. He came out swinging and, in the first round,
floored Louis with a right to the jaw. Louis was startled. He arose
hurriedly and later, when he went back to his corner, his trainer,

Jack Blackburn, a saturnine, balding Negro, scowled at him and said, "Chappie, you can't get up fast enough so them people don't know you was down."

At the end, which came at one minute and ten seconds of the eighth round, Braddock's face was a pulpy mask. A severed artery in his upper lip spurted blood, one eye was closed and the other puffed, and there was blood coming from his left ear. He had gone down proudly. Mike Jacobs rose and shouted with glee; it was inevitable that he should become premier promoter of boxing in the world. Inevitably, Jacobs' 20th Century Sporting Club was invited by Madison Square Garden to take over the promotion of boxing in the famous arena.

There was trickery to be done. Jacobs was still at the mercy of the Hearst triplets, Frayne, Farnsworth, and Runyon, who cut into his profits while he did all the work. He resented their fiscal presence. Then, from a surprising source, there was help. In the very week in which Louis became the heavyweight champion, the Hearst organization decided, in the interest of economy, to combine the New York *Journal*, an evening paper, with the New York *American*, a morning paper. Frayne was named sports editor of the hypenated *Journal-American*; Farnsworth was out of a job. Jacobs smiled.

A year later, on June 22, 1938, Louis and Schmeling fought for the world heavyweight championship at Yankee Stadium. Schmeling was a symbol of Germany's racist policies; Louis was represented as a warrior in the mail of democracy. It was, in fact, just another fist fight, although the public refused to accept it as such. There was even talk that President Roosevelt had summoned Louis to the White House to say that the heavyweight champion had to beat Schmeling for him; Louis knew he had to knock out Schmeling to heal the mental stigmata inflicted by the beating he had taken two years earlier.

The Brown Bomber knocked out Schmeling within two minutes and four seconds of the first round. A crowd of 70,043 huddled under a cloudless sky to see the Hessian humiliated and bruised. Jacobs counted gross receipts of $1,015,012 and managed another smile.

That August he leaked a story to Harry Grayson, sports editor of the *Newspaper Enterprise Association*. Grayson was covering horse racing at Saratoga when he encountered Jacobs in the clubhouse.

"What's new?" Grayson asked.

"I got a story for you," the promoter replied.

"Let's go," Grayson said.

On Saturday, August 13, 1938, the New York *World-Telegram* printed Grayson's story under a black headline—MIKE JACOBS ADMITS HEARST WRITERS SHARE IN BOXING SWAG. In his story, Grayson wrote:

In closing a new five-year tieup with Madison Square Garden for sixteen boxing shows a season and exclusive privileges at its Bowl in Queens, Michael Strauss Jacobs makes it very emphatic that he is through with the "Hearst Athletic Club."

By this action, the old Broadway ticket scalper remains unquestionably the nation's mitt monopolist.

The Hearst A. C. which grew out of boxing shows sponsored by the Free Milk Fund for Babies during Tex Rickard's days, was composed of three New York Hearst writers—Damon Runyon, Bill Farnsworth, and Ed Frayne. These three, with Jacobs, became partners in the 20th Century Sporting Club, when the Hearst A. C. named Mike as its head man. The 20th Century Sporting Club has promoted every important fight during the last two years.

The break came after Jacobs kept his partners waiting for a month for their share of the profits of the second Louis-Schmeling fight in June, which grossed $1,015,012, including radio and film revenue. It seemed there was a squabble about the deduction of losses on two other shows. Also, Jacobs said "No" when the three directors of the Hearst A. C. suggested he promote an outdoor show in September for the Free Milk Fund for Babies, long sponsored by the Hearst newspapers. Jacobs claims lack of appreciation for the $80,000 given the fund in the last two years.

Jacobs wound up paying one of the newspapermen $25,000 for his 25 per cent interest in the 20th Century Sporting Club after the three partners drew down five-figure amounts as their share of the return match between Louis and Schmeling.

By the time the story was published, Runyon had already severed his connections with Jacobs in exchange for $25,000. Only Frayne among the trio had testimony in writing of his affiliation with Jacobs. It was in the form of the letter of understanding written by Jacobs to Frayne when the 20th Century Sporting Club was organized. Farnsworth, who had been let out by Hearst when the *Journal* and the *American* had been hypenated, was now a captive employee of the 20th Century Sporting Club. Jacobs insisted that Farnsworth report to his office daily and accept the assignment of such tasks as opening the morning mail and ordering coffee. In Jacobs' hand, humiliation was a weapon leading to separation. Frayne was still a Hearst sports editor, but his days were numbered and his fate sealed by Grayson's story. Jacobs was lord of the flies.

THREE

THE NEXT TEN YEARS were raucous ones in boxing. Jacobs prospered until and right through World War II; he withstood libel, slander, and founded accusation on all sides. He was a ruthless and arrogant dictator, perhaps the most ruthless and arrogant the business of sports promotion has known. From 1937 through 1947, he promoted sixty-one world championship bouts and more than fifteen hundred boxing cards. His promotions involving Louis had gross receipts in excess of $10 million, and during his thirteen years as a promoter he sold ten million tickets worth $30 million at face value. He was accused of scalping working-press tickets, creating a monopoly in which he alone decided which fighters were to fight for world championships, and of holding hands with assorted underworld overlords, including Paul John Carbo, alias Frankie Carbo, alias Paul Carbo, alias Frank Carbo, alias Paul John, alias Frank Russo, alias John Paul Carbo.

In December, 1960, the subcommittee on Antitrust and Monopoly of the Committee on the Judiciary of the United States Senate, happily known as the "Kefauver Committee," held a series of hearings on what it chose to describe as "the monopoly aspects of boxing." Among those who testified was Detective Frank Marrone, of

the New York City Police Department. He obviously qualified as an
expert on the life and times of Frankie Carbo. Under questioning
by John G. Bonomi, an assistant counsel to the committee, his testimony ran as follows.

Paul John Carbo, also known as Frankie Carbo, was born in New
York City, August 10, 1904. His New York City Police Department
Number is B-95838. Mr. Carbo's first conflict with the law came in
1915, when at the age of twelve he was sent to the Catholic Protectory. Since that time, Mr. Carbo's police record shows seventeen
arrests for vagrancy, suspicious character, felonious assaults, grand
larceny, robbery, violation of New York boxing laws, and five for
murder.

Mr. Carbo's first homicide charge occurred in 1924 when he was
indicted for the killing of a taxicab driver in the Bronx. He subsequently took a plea to the charge of manslaughter and was sentenced
two to four years in Sing Sing. Mr. Carbo was a fugitive in this case
for four years before being apprehended.

Carbo was also arrested for homicide in September, 1931, for the
killing of a Philadelphia beer baron in his room in an Atlantic City
hotel. Again in July, 1936, he was arrested in Madison Square Garden for the underworld murders of Max Hassel and Max Greenberg,
henchmen of Waxey Gordon.

On Thanksgiving Day in 1939, Harry Shachter, alias Harry Greenberg, also known as "Big Greeney," a member of Murder, Inc., was
assassinated outside his home in Hollywood, California. Indicted for
this murder was the notorious New York gangster, Louie ("Lepke")
Buchalter, and the following: Benjamin ("Bugsy") Seigel, Emanuel
Mendy Weiss, Harry ("Champ") Segal, Frank Carbo.

Al Tannenbaum, a member of Murder, Inc., subsequently testified
in the murder trial of the above, that "Bugsy Seigel and Frank Carbo
killed "Big Greeney." He testified that Carbo fired five bullets into
Shachter, and that "Bugsy" Siegel drove the getaway car. This trial
resulted in a hung jury and Abe "Kid Twist" Reles, a witness who was
to testify against Carbo in the second trial, fell or was pushed from
a hotel window in Coney Island. Carbo was not retried for this homicide.

Carbo's arrogance was great in Jacobs' days. He held court in
the dining room of the Forrest Hotel, on 49th Street, down the block
from Madison Square Garden. To his cronies he openly proclaimed

his suzerainty over boxing and let it be known that his fighters—he controlled at least half a dozen headliners—could get all the work they wanted in Madison Square Garden.

He was surrounded at all times by a circle of stooges who rendered unto him the things that were theirs. The terror he imposed was subtle and meaningful, although there was at least one instance when Carbo knocked to the pavement a courtier who had spoken out of turn regarding a match Carbo was trying to impose on Madison Square Garden.

He dressed somberly, in dark suiting and white-on-white shirting, and his high-priced shoes were spit polished to a luster in which groveling foot-wipers cast their reflections. His hair was gray and contrasted with the deep blackness of his eyes, which were piercingly alert and challenging. He resembled nothing so much as a Madagascan aye-aye whose nocturnal habits he surpassed with a determination bordering on a total abhorrence of daylight. The place of his home was known only to his muscular cronies. For a time he lived in a penthouse in the high-rent area of Sutton Place, overlooking the East River, and there were reports that he had taken a bride. On September 5, 1956, Carbo, under the name of Paul John Carbo, applied for a marriage license at Palm Beach County, Florida. While asking permission to marry Viola Masters, of 10010 West Broadview Drive, Miami Beach, he said he had been previously married and divorced. He gave his age as fifty-two and his address as the Balmoral Hotel in Miami Beach. Five days later, a license was granted. Thereafter, Viola Masters was known in social circles as Mrs. Frankie Carbo.

It is easy to describe the face and form of Carbo and achieve a good likeness, but it is impossible to get a perfect image of him as overlord of boxing in the United States. Of necessity, his labors were hidden under a black cloak and not even the other mobsters who were in conspiracy with him to control boxing in the United States can, each of himself, offer a total picture. Carbo spoke in circles, rambling on by design to give the impression of uncertainty, and nobody ever came away from a conversation with him certain of what he had heard. He was more than one-dimensional.

He was, for one, a sort of Broadway Robin Hood, and in this

guise he handed out alms and largesse to needy serfs. He was a soft touch for anybody with a tale of sorrow and melted in the presence of a guy who was down on his luck and in need of room rent. When he was drunk he ran a rambling verbal course, from sentiment to cruelty and arrogance, and mumbled words intended to convey the impression that he was a misunderstood adult who, as a boy, had stolen an apple and had never been forgiven by society. He was gallant in the presence of women, who were charmed by his soft voice and good manners, and he regarded motherhood as being more sacred than money.

By 1947, he had achieved widespread notoriety as the underworld's commissioner of boxing. Yet he walked openly in the game's marketplace. While newspaper columnists and reporters made continual references to Carbo's role in boxing, state and city boxing commissions throughout the country reacted as if he were a folk myth, existing only in the addled brains of journalists. Then, suddenly, there was an unexpected outburst of official concern with gangsterism in boxing—all in New York State.

Rocco Barbella, alias Rocky Graziano, was a middleweight fighter. Into his twenty-six years he had compressed a history of terror that cavalcaded penal names like the Catholic Protectory, where Carbo had also taken lessons in his youth, the New York City Penitentiary on Rikers Island, the Tombs, and Leavenworth Barracks in Kansas. He had been in trouble as an irascible juvenile, as a burglar, and as a deserter from the United States Army. In boxing, somehow, he had found an outlet for his antagonism and antisocial vigor. He was a smashing puncher and a swashbuckling competitor, and the public came to regard him as a representation of anger harnessed purposefully.

On Saturday afternoon, January 25, 1947, Graziano left his home at 1357 Ocean Parkway, Brooklyn, in his new Cadillac. He was alone and reflective, as he stepped on the gas. A few blocks from his home he was overtaken by a black sedan and forced to park at the curb. He took one look at the men in the other car and knew the police were on hand.

"The DA wants to talk to you," a detective said, coming toward Graziano's car.

"What's up?" Graziano asked.

"Drive back to your house and come with us."

Graziano complied with the order. On the way to Manhattan in the police car, Graziano talked with the detectives about his recent bout with Tony Zale for the world middleweight championship, promoted by the 20th Century Sporting Club. It had taken place at Yankee Stadium the previous September 27. Graziano had been knocked out in the sixth round but he had achieved the verisimilitude of a champion and the forty thousand persons who had purchased $342,000 worth of tickets had cheered him.

In the District Attorney's office there was no talk of Graziano's bout with Zale, nor of the impending return bout with the middleweight champion. Instead, Chief Assistant District Attorney Alfred J. Scotti was concerned about a fight that had not happened.

"Why'd you call off your bout with Ruben Shank?" Scotti demanded.

"I had a bad back, like the papers said."

"Wasn't it because you were offered a bribe to throw the fight and didn't want to take a dive?"

"Aw, that was fun," Graziano said.

He told Scotti that a man he did not know by name had offered him $100,000 to take a dive for Shank.

"Where'd it happen?" Scotti asked.

"In the gym. In Stillman's gym."

"You didn't want to take it, so you faked a bad back and didn't go through with the fight. Is that right?"

"It was nothing like that. The gymnasium is full of characters all the time coming around offering guys dough to go into the tank. It's a gag. Who cares?"

The District Attorney did. Graziano was held for questioning for the next eighteen hours, until 5 A.M. Sunday morning. He was not permitted to call his lawyer, but he was unswerving in his story: the bribe offer was a joke, nothing more. Yet he was on the spot and he knew it. Although his manager of record was a small, sallow-complexioned former lingerie salesman named Irving Cohen, there were two others sharing in his earnings: Edward Coco, alias Eddie Coco, alias Ettore Coco; and Jack Healy, an old friend of Graziano.

Healy was, for the most part, above suspicion, but Coco was a police character. At the time, his record included twelve arrests for crimes ranging from felonious assault through robbery and rape. Coco was a man just over five feet tall, with dark, forbidding eyes and sable hair, and he was given to outbursts of temper. Once, during an argument with Jimmy White, a fight manager, in the dining room of the Forrest Hotel frequented by Carbo, Coco threw a wineglass in the direction of White's face. The police were not informed of the incident. Nobody talked, least of all Cohen, who was meek and soft-voiced and entirely respectable in a most singular way.

There is a wide gap between rumor and gossip in boxing and facts available to law-enforcement officials. While Coco was known to be Carbo's pal, it was the District Attorney's belief that their friendship was based on a commercial alliance, perhaps involving Graziano. The interrogation of Graziano did not uncover such a relationship. Angrily, District Attorney Frank S. Hogan berated Graziano to newspaper reporters.

"There's more to the story than Graziano has told us," Hogan insisted vigo. ously. "He was apparently afraid of the characters— gangsters and gamblers—he's been associating with, so he does not tell us the truth. I want to tell you one thing. The $100,000 bribe was offered not at Stillman's gym, but at a bar—and not in jest, as Graziano said."

"The only thing I know," Cohen said, "is the kid don't frequent no bars."

Several days later, the District Attorney's office forwarded all its information in the Graziano case to Edward P. F. Eagan, chairman of the New York State Athletic Commission. Eagan had been appointed to head the boxing board by Governor Thomas E. Dewey, who had expressed vigorous confidence in the former Olympic boxing champion and Yale graduate. In office, Eagan had been dragging his feet, but now, confronted with the District Attorney's activity, he was forced to run.

Within days, Eagan ordered a hearing to be held by the Commission in connection with the bribe offered to Graziano. Chief Assistant District Attorney Scotti testified that Graziano had feigned a back injury in order to get out of the bout with Shank. "He realized,"

Scotti said, "that he would be double-crossing persons who had bet on his opponent if he went through with the bout without taking the bribe to lose."

Graziano was harassed throughout the hearing. He repeated his story ingenuously, apparently as it had happened, and heard himself branded a liar by Scotti. Sports columnists defended Graziano in print, charging he was being hounded back to the life of crime from which boxing had saved him. The Commission announced its decision on February 7, 1947. Graziano was adjudged guilty of violating Rule 64 of the Commission's laws, which made it incumbent on boxers to report bribe offers. Eagan read the decision to about a hundred reporters and officials packed into a room large enough to hold half that number comfortably. "Rocky Graziano," he said, "is guilty of acts detrimental to the best interests of boxing. His license as a boxer is hereby revoked."

Three months later, on April 11, Graziano asked the Commission to change its mind. His request was denied. In Illinois, the State Athletic Commission was asked to license him as a fighter and his application was accepted. On July 16, 1947, in 100° temperature in the ring of the Chicago Stadium, Graziano faced Zale in a return bout. Blood-smeared and arm weary, Rocky came off the canvas to knock out Zale in the sixth round. He was the world middleweight champion everywhere but in his native New York State. Twenty thousand sweating fans rose to cheer the new champion, and when he returned to his hotel suite many important mobsters in America, including Frankie Carbo, were there to greet him.

In New York meanwhile, the District Attorney's office had been engaged in a program aimed at chasing hoodlums out of boxing. Fifty witnesses were paraded before a grand jury to testify in connection with the underworld's control of boxing. Among those who appeared in the jury room were Johnny Greco, a Canadian welterweight who was managed by Carbo; Jimmy Plumeri, alias Jimmy Doyle, a mobster who had been sent to Sing Sing years before by Dewey as a garment district racketeer; and, briefly, Carbo himself.

Ten days after Graziano had become world's champion, the minutes of the grand jury hearings were turned over to the New York State Athletic Commission. Rumor now had the support of testimony given under oath. What had been hinted at in the press time after time now appeared in the official record and Eagan was provoked to action.

He summoned Sol Strauss, Jacobs' stand-in as boss of the 20th Century Sporting Club, to the offices of the Commission in Worth Street, Manhattan, and, flanked by Leon Swears and Dr. Clilan B. Powell, his co-commissioners, read the Commission's decision.

The 20th Century Sporting Club, Eagan pronounced, was guilty of dealing with individuals with criminal records "regarding certain contests which were held in Madison Square Garden." Eagan made it plain that these dealings took place before Strauss had stepped into Jacobs' shoes, but he was no less bitter in his comments, even while failing to name the criminals involved or their fighters.

"Prior to your direction," Eagan told Strauss, "the 20th Century Sporting Club had dealings with unlicensed persons with criminal records." He then directed the 20th Century Sporting Club to pay a fine of $2,500.

The next day, at least one sports writer on a metropolitan daily commented: "The $2,500 fine was a slap on the wrist for the 20th Century Sporting Club."

The New York State Athletic Commission held its meetings on Friday afternoons because, at the time, the Garden ran its boxing shows on Friday nights. Accommodation was the Commission's watchword. The matchmaker of the 20th Century Sporting Club was Nat Rogers, a bespectacled, balding little man given to mild protests against the harshness of life and its problems. Rogers knew all the dark pathways in boxing's jungle, but as a mere hired carrier on safari he was led always by Jacobs. He was, at best, almost totally motivated by a need to make Jacobs' commercial life comfortable. He loaded the matchmaking guns for Jacobs, who did all the firing. As Jacobs' nominal matchmaker, he had contractually dragged the carcasses of numerous warriors into the ring at Madison Square Garden and was therefore culpable.

On Friday, October 3, 1947, Rogers went before the State Athletic Commission to ask for renewal of his license as a matchmaker. The application was rejected and a stern rebuke delivered. Rogers was charged with "acts detrimental to the best interests of boxing."

In essence, the Commission adjudged Rogers guilty of doing business with assorted hoodlums who controlled sundry prize fighters. Unlike Graziano's, Rogers' retirement from boxing in New York State was final; Graziano's lasted until September, 1949, when his license was restored and he was again granted the privilege of slugging other young men in gloved combat in New York. Muckrakers were taken in by the Commission's apparent sternness vis-à-vis Rogers. They hailed a new deal in boxing and foresaw the departure of the mobsters from the arena.

At that very moment a covey of hoodlums were planning to fix a main-event bout in Madison Square Garden, no doubt laughing as they went at those naïve enough to believe they had surrendered to mere name-calling by the District Attorney, a Grand Jury, and the New York State Athletic Commission.

FOUR

FRANK PALERMO, a sharp-eyed Philadelphia hustler, had cause to laugh the day the 20th Century Sporting Club was fined. And laugh he did, his gimlet eyes narrowing and his large irregular nose winging out over thick, heavy lips. His friends called him "Blinky" because of his peering manner, although his rasping voice was a more striking feature of his personality. Little more than five feet tall, he preferred to think of himself as a man of physical prowess. His police record included two arrests for assault and other less muscular crimes like larceny of an auto, operating a lottery, and the ownership of a disorderly club in violation of the liquor control law of Pennsylvania.

In 1947, Palermo was forty-two years old. Even then he could look back on a busy life of turmoil. His first difficulty with the law happened when he was twenty-three—an arrest for assault and battery. He was fined $200 and sentenced to six months in jail. Before long the sentence was reconsidered; he was fined $500, and the jail term was wiped out. Later, Palermo was to demonstrate an even more impressive and unexplained ability to persuade public officials that he was not as bad as he seemed. He was twice pardoned by the State of Pennsylvania, once after he was found guilty of running a disorderly club and the second time after he had been sentenced to six months in jail as a lottery operator. His charm was pervasive and reached even into the chambers of the New York Athletic Commission, which licensed him as a manager despite his reputation as the "numbers king" of Philadelphia.

Palermo was the manager of Ike Williams, who was, in 1947, the world lightweight champion. He also was the guide and preceptor of Billy Fox, a light-heavyweight boxer from Philadelphia who had, amazingly, knocked out forty-nine of the fifty fighters he had encountered in the ring. The only time Fox had failed to win was when he himself had been knocked out by Gus Lesnevich, the world light-heavyweight champion. Only the black eyebrows of Frank Palermo and Frank Carbo were not arched in disbelief as Fox went along flattening the opposition. They—the two men named Frank—were partners in crime. Indeed, Palermo was a crony of Harry Stromberg, alias Nig Rosen, with whom Carbo operated a bookmaking establishment in Camden, New Jersey.

The afternoon of September 26, 1947, was a busy one for Sol Strauss in his capacity as viceroy of the 20th Century Sporting Club. After hearing the State Athletic Commission brand the boxing club as a corporate miscreant for doing business with unlicensed managers with criminal records, he returned to his office in Madison Square Garden. Palermo was waiting for him, all done up in a dark suit, a red tie, a white-on-white shirt, and a contract in hand.

The contract called for Billy Fox to fight Jake LaMotta, a bole of a man, in the Garden on Friday, November 14, 1947. It was signed by Fox, as the boxer, and Palermo, as the manager, and was certified by Rogers, as the matchmaker. It prescribed payment of 20 per cent of the net receipts for Fox. LaMotta's purse was to come to 30 per cent of the net receipts.

LaMotta was an outstanding middleweight renowned for his incredible stamina. He was less than five feet seven inches tall, but his torso was constructed along the lines of a tank. He was relentless in attack and apparently impervious to pain. He had not been knocked down in seventy-eight bouts and had been the first professional fighter to defeat "Sugar Ray" Robinson, who was regarded as a peerless pugilist. When he was sixteen years old, LaMotta had been sentenced to the New York State Vocational Institution after his arrest and conviction for burglary. He had been in difficulty with the law earlier and had spent more time in police stations than in schools. He was clever in the way a gamin becomes clever, and within him there was a restless eagerness to be accepted as a community-minded individual who had achieved success against all odds.

He had earned large sums as a fighter and had invested a substantial part of his money in two boxing clubs: one called Jerome Stadium, an outdoor arena directly across the street from the Yankee Stadium in the Bronx, where he lived, and the other the Park Arena, a renovated movie house in a rundown neighborhood in the East Bronx. Because the rules of the New York State Athletic Commission forbid a licensed boxer to have a financial interest in a boxing club, the stock in LaMotta's clubs was held by members of his family.

Boxing shows at the Park Arena took place on Tuesday nights, when LaMotta would be seen playing the role of an entrepreneur. He would stand in the lobby leading from the main entrance and greet his customers, signing autographs for some, shaking the hands of others. His tongue was etched with a soupçon of charm, and he smiled smugly. He was especially charming on Tuesday night, November 11, 1947, four nights before his bout with Fox. He was a one-man receiving line when two visitors entered the arena. They were Blinky Palermo and Frankie Carbo.

LaMotta picked at his teeth with a toothpick on which he had been chewing. First Palermo and then Carbo shook LaMotta's right hand, which he made available by shifting the toothpick to his other hand. For several minutes there was earnest conversation, but it faltered when LaMotta, Carbo, and Palermo were joined by three other men.

Jake's brother, Joey, was one of the newcomers. A rugged young man built along the same functional lines as his brother, he had been a middleweight fighter until the year before, when he retired from the ring after losing three bouts in succession. Jake LaMotta's stock in the Park Arena was held in Joey's name.

The others who had joined the circle were William Phillip Daly, a fight manager who was known, tongue in cheek, as "Honest Bill" Daly, and Billy Stevens, a part-time press agent and boxing writer. In the years ahead, Daly's name would come up in almost every investigation of boxing by athletic commissions, legislative committees, and the federal government, but on this night he was all charm in the company of his fraternity brothers.

Jake LaMotta, Carbo, and Palermo soon edged away from the others, moving toward a flight of stairs at the opposite end of the lobby. The stairs led to a basement, where the fighters' unbelievably bare and dank dressing rooms were located. Beyond the dressing rooms, in a shadowy corner of the catacomb, Jake and Carbo and Palermo found refuge from the eyes and ears of boxing hangers-on who had gaped when the two hoodlums had entered the fight club. Brazenness was not unknown in boxing, but its display was restricted generally to a scattering of reasonably honest men in the game. Having little to hide, they were gaudily openhanded. The mobsters in the business usually were as cozy as dope pushers about their activities in boxing, but Carbo and Palermo had chosen to consort with Jake LaMotta in a public fight club, on a fight night, when officials of the New York State Athletic Commission were near enough to smell them. Apparently, the odor did not evoke an olfactory response; doing nothing, the boxing board reacted as though the fight world was redolent of wine and roses.

The next day, bookmakers, usually more sensitive to odors than boxing officials, gave no indication that they had been more responsive in this instance. They held LaMotta as the favorite over Fox at odds of 8 to 5. Within twenty-four hours, there was an apparent shift in the wind. Noses caught a whiff of the Bronx bouquet, and the betting went to even money. In Pittsburgh, a bookmaker who specialized in bets on horseracing got word that the outcome of the bout between LaMotta and Fox was prearranged. He checked with Broadway: Fox had become the favorite at odds of 7 to 5.

At four o'clock on the afternoon of November 14, 1947, six

hours before LaMotta and Fox were to enter the ring at Madison Square Garden, an increased outpouring of venture capital in behalf of Fox sent the odds to 11 to 5, causing panic among bookmakers. Ordinarily, a bookmaker who finds himself overloaded with bets on one fighter attempts to walk a narrow crest by laying off some of the bets with other bookmakers. The sudden shift in the odds favoring Fox caught all major bookmakers imbalanced and surprised. At the last minute, they scurried across the land in search of relief. None came their way, and all they could do was to take the fight "off the boards," which meant they would only accept bets supporting La-Motta. They cried tears of red ink in anticipation of a deficit.

Madison Square Garden was packed when the fighters left their dressing rooms in the half-lit corridors and followed their handlers into the ring. Officially, the attendance was put at 18,340 persons, but those who knew their way around the arena were aware that the crowd was larger. Some years before, the New York City Fire Department had imposed a ceiling on the number of persons permitted in the Garden at one time. Somehow, the announcement of the size of a sellout crowd always seemed to coincide with the Fire Department's maximum.

In the lobby, the trade assembled. Fight managers whispered to other fight managers about the trend of the betting odds. Reporters heard the whispers and went to their typewriters to write first-edition stories suggesting that a betting coup was in the wind. Only the State Athletic Commission sailed blithely on a calm sea.

When the fighters were called to the center of the ring to receive instructions from the referee, LaMotta came dancing out of his corner, his body squirming inside his robe, his arms working as though he were preparing to reach for the moon. Fox was more than six feet tall and towered over LaMotta, who averted his angular gaze by glaring at Palermo, in contrast with the bonhomie of their earlier confrontation. The referee was Frank Fullam, a credulous former fighter who capsuled the rules obtaining in the bout in about twenty seconds.

Now the fighters were back in their corners. LaMotta doffed his synthetic leopard skin robe and awaited the bell. At its toll, he rushed across the ring and opened a body attack that had the verisimilitude of fury. His punches appeared purposeful, delivered as they were with seeming vigor, but Fox was undaunted and unhurt. Those who concerned themselves with such things made a judgment after the first round: LaMotta had won it by a considerable and putative margin. It indicated a total victory for him.

Abruptly, in the second round, LaMotta went on the defensive. Fox moved aggressively and smashed LaMotta into the ropes by flailing away with both fists. His punches were sharply delivered and when they reached their target, LaMotta took them without firing back, retreating in apparent dismay, drawing a great shout from the crowd.

So it went in the third round, and when the fourth started LaMotta made a display of pugnacity that was both brief and insincere. In the face of his tormentor's counter-assault, LaMotta went into a shell. Once, for an instant, his right knee almost touched the canvas, but he came erect swiftly because, he said later, he was proud of the fact that he had not been on the floor once in seventy-eight previous bouts.

Three days later, in the office of the State Athletic Commission in downtown Manhattan, Fullam, the referee, offered quaint testimony on the flow of battle:

In the fourth round when I stopped the fight, it was one-sided from the start. Fox rushed LaMotta all over the ring, throwing both left and right hooks to the body and head without any return from LaMotta. I only stopped the contest after it was evident to me that LaMotta was unable to defend himself. The contest was stopped in mid-ring. I also felt that any further punishment might bring serious injury to LaMotta.

I want to state that during the course of the three rounds and two minutes and twenty-six seconds in the fourth round when I stopped the contest, during that time LaMotta could have gone down from several hard blows he received from Fox, but refused to do so especially when he was in the corner and one of his knees nearly touched the canvas. As a referee of many contests, I thought that LaMotta showed great durability to survive the punishment that he took. If I didn't stop the fight, it would have been a tragedy and perhaps the fellow might have been killed. As a representative of the Commission, I am there to see that it is an honest fair fight and to see that the boys are not hurt.

The setting for the referee's testimony was the hearing room of the State Athletic Commission, where LaMotta also took the stand. He insisted for the first time that he had received a spleen injury in a sparring match a month before the bout with Fox. He said the injury justified his knockout; he was smugly pleased with the explanation.

The next day, Jake's brother Joey also testified under oath. Chairman Eagan asked him whether he had known about the large bets made on the outcome of the bout. "Yes," he said, he had, adding boldly, "yes, all the time, all day people came over to me, and different people asked me 'There's a rumor going around your brother is going to throw the fight.' I said, 'My brother never threw a fight, he never intends to throw a fight.' "

Eagan asked whether anybody had given out information that LaMotta had injured his spleen in training. Joey LaMotta said, "Well, that was supposed to be a secret that my brother injured his side."

Blinky Palermo was a witness. Eagan asked him whether he had been in the Park Arena *the week* before the fight. "I don't know," Blinky said, "I have been in quite a few different places." Had Blinky seen Jake LaMotta when he was at the Park Arena? "No, I didn't see Jake at all," he replied. Had he seen Jake's brother Joey, or Jake's father? "No, never, Commissioner," Blinky replied, contrition lighting his pasty face. "I don't know his father. I know his brother when I see him because he looks like Jake."

Sparring partners were questioned and so was Al Silvani, who was handsome and muscular and, at the time, Frank Sinatra's private masseur. The entire cast was paraded before the Commission, and while the Commission was hearing a dull story, District Attorney Hogan's staff was working on the case. Palermo was brought in for questioning. So was Carbo. He sauntered into Room 701, at 155 Leonard Street, New York City—the District Attorney's office—

after rushing past newspaper photographers and ducking the questions of reporters. Assistant District Attorney Scotti learned nothing from him.

Eventually, six days after the bout, Jake LaMotta himself went to the District Attorney's office. At first he was most cordial. He denied he had ever borrowed money from Carbo and conceded that he had invested $10,000 in the Park Arena. Where had it come from? From his ring earnings, he said, while insisting he could not remember whether he had withdrawn the money from a bank account or had found it in his pants pocket one morning. He did concede that he had invested $60,000 in the Jerome Stadium and that the money had come from a safety deposit box in a bank.

"Where did you get that money?" the Assistant District Attorney asked LaMotta.

"Boxing."

"Boxing?"

"That's right."

"What did you do, every time you earned money, you put it in a vault?"

"I like to keep my money in cash," the fighter insisted.

Some $20,000 was due him from the 20th Century Sporting Club, but he had to wait several weeks before he could translate it into cash, and then it cost him $1,000 in the process. That was the amount of the fine levied against him by the State Athletic Commission—not because he had been involved in a fixed fight, but because he had failed to report the spleen injury to the Commission.

"Such concealment for personal gain the Commission holds to be against the best interest of boxing," the Commission ruling said. "Therefore, the withholding of the payment of the purses and indefinite suspension of LaMotta is herewith ordered. A final determination will be made after public investigative agencies have advised this Commission of the facts disclosed by their investigations. At that time the Commission will take into consideration all the facts adduced."

The District Attorney came up with nothing. LaMotta paid the $1,000 fine, the purses were released to both LaMotta and Fox, and the loser was suspended indefinitely. Seven months later, under pressure from LaMotta's lawyer, one Irving Tell, the Commission lifted the suspension.

It was, in effect, the worst of times and the best of times in boxing. Louis and Walcott were on the verge of their second bout, which was scheduled for Yankee Stadium, June 23, 1948, and Promoter Jacobs, who could smell box-office profits at a mile and upward, was semi-active once again in the 20th Century Sporting Club, though the actual work was still being done by the lawyer Strauss and the press agent Markson.

After the first bout with Walcott, Louis had gone off to Europe with a retinue comprising Marva Louis, Mannie Seamon, Leonard Reed, Marshall Miles, Eddie Green, who had become Louis's friend in the Army, Nelson Sykes, who owned a bar and grill on the South Side of Chicago, and Irwin Rosee, Louis's press agent and friend. With Louis laughing the loudest, the happy group sailed on the *Queen Mary*. Before sailing, Louis had asked Jack Dempsey to purchase 1,000 pounds of prime steaks for him. Dempsey stored the meat in his restaurant on Broadway and had it delivered to the ship just before the *Queen Mary* pulled away from Pier 90 into the North River on its way to Southampton, where Louis learned that the meat had to be "smuggled" into England in contravention of food import laws. Meat was still being rationed in England, and possession of the rare commodity without justification was regarded as outlandish.

Friends of Louis solved the problem. They caused a hearse to be drawn up to the wharf. When the ship was unloaded, half a ton of steak was carted away in the hearse. In London, Louis found he could not eat the steak while knowing others were being deprived of it. He distributed it among friends.

Together with his retinue, Louis lived in a large house in the fashionable Chelsea section of London. He boxed in exhibitions at the Health and Holiday Exposition in Earl's Court. He visited Commons and received a standing ovation from the members. From England, Louis and his cronies went on to Paris and Brussels. In April he came home on the *Queen Elizabeth* and went into training at Pompton Lakes, his favorite camp. He worked hard because he had, in his own mind, been disgraced in the first bout with Walcott, which he had approached with disarming confidence. This time he would be ready for Walcott. Because he believed he might have to go the full fifteen rounds to win, he trained for the distance.

The price of a ringside ticket was $50, which some critics considered exhorbitant, but the 20th Century Sporting Club encountered no resistance. Although he was still encumbered by the physical effects of the stroke he had suffered eighteen months earlier, Promoter Jacobs came to his office in Madison Square Garden occasionally to learn how his proconsuls were doing. Expectedly, he arrogated control of the working-press tickets. His left hand still hung uselessly by his side, but with his right he peddled working-press tickets to "safe-and-sane" customers.

One afternoon he was seen working his nice little racket just outside the door of his office. A veteran sports columnist from Cleveland bought six working-press tickets for $200 each. It was estimated that Jacobs made a minimum of $25,000 in this manner. It was to be his last windfall.

At noon on Wednesday, June 23, 1948, Louis and Walcott weighed in at Madison Square Garden for their fight at Yankee Stadium. When Louis stepped on the scale in the main lobby of the arena he weighed 213½ pounds, two and a half pounds more than he had for the first bout with Walcott. Walcott was 194¾ pounds. It rained that afternoon, and the fight was postponed until the next night.

Thursday, June 24, was a day of warmth and sunshine. Louis awaited the bout eagerly. So did Promoter Jacobs and his proconsuls, who counted about $950,000 in the cash box. That evening, at 7:05, a localized cloudburst hit Yankee Stadium. The rain turned the outfield grass into a green river and the ring, which was pitched where great Yankee infielders had trod the sod and sand, was a sodden stage. So was the thirty-foot-high platform constructed on the field for the television cameras, which were obtruding on an outdoor world's heavyweight championship bout for the first time.

Somehow, Jacobs was not around to make a decision about another postponement; Strauss and Markson were.

"Let's put it off until tomorrow," the press agent Markson said.

"Let's wait," the lawyer Strauss said.

"We can't. You're making a mistake. Call it off or we'll murder the gate sale."

Strauss finally acceded to Markson's proposal. The fight was postponed until the next night and ticket holders who wanted refunds were told they could obtain these at the 20th Century Sporting Club's box office in Madison Square Garden. About $150,000 worth of tickets were honored for refunds. Yet, when Louis and Walcott entered the ring at the Stadium the next night, there was $841,739 in the till. The postponement had deprived the 20th Century Sporting Club of another million-dollar gate. Some months later, Louis described the bout with Walcott in an article in *Life*:

> We hooked and jabbed a lot in the first rounds. He kept backing away. I knew what he was after. He was going to try to get in a few hard ones every now and then and play for points. In the third round he got me with a left and a right to the face and I went down. I got up without a count. He got another hard right to my jaw in the fifth. He was tired in the eighth and I went to work on him. We traded punches in the ninth. I got some hard ones to the head. He tried backing away in the tent. I knew then I would take him. I put a real hard right to his jaw in the eleventh. It shook him good. I followed with hard rights and lefts. He tried to back away, but I kept right on him. He was hurt. He tried to cover his face. I hit right through his guard. I rocked his head with right and left. His arms came down and I got a hard right through. He went down on his face. He rolled onto his back. I could see by his mouth he wasn't going to come up. He was on his knees by the seven count, but he couldn't get up. That was my last fight.

The reporters would not believe Louis meant to retire. When the article appeared in *Life* he wrote a short note to the editors of the magazine which he signed and they printed:

> There's a lot of talk about my fighting again. I haven't signed any papers to fight. I haven't discussed any terms or opponents with anybody. Nobody has done this for me. So far as I'm concerned now, I'm through with fighting except for exhibitions. If some new sensation comes along—and there aren't any around now—and if the public

wants to see me fight again, I'll reconsider my decision. In the meantime, I stand by what I said after the last Walcott fight: "This is the
last one."

Nobody in sports believed Louis, but this brief statement confirming the one he had given to the reporter from the *Bronx Home News*
after the first bout with Walcott would be borne out later.

FIVE

E ARLY IN Louis's ring career he had become friendly with a New
Jersey press agent and promoter named Harry Mendel. Jacobs
had brought the two together when he had hired Mendel to work as
a publicity man in one of Louis's training camps, and there had been
an outburst of friendship.

Mendel stood about five feet two inches in silk socks and weighed
about two hundred pounds. He was a completely extroverted individual who devoured food in huge quantities. When he laughed,
which was often, his huge belly shook in rippling rhythm. The effect
on Louis was catalytic: the champion would break up in waves of
booming laughter. Mendel had learned his way around in speakeasy
society and, in earlier times, had worked as a press agent at six-day
bike races in Madison Square Garden. He had assumed the role of
a warm host whenever he was on a promoter's payroll, and sports
writers and columnists flocked around him because of his freewheel-
ing attitude toward pleasure.

In the months after the second Walcott bout, Mendel took Louis
on an exhibition tour of the United States. The tour started in September, 1948, and it took Louis to the South in the early months of
1949. While he was on tour, there were consistent reports that Louis
would announce his retirement formally from the ring.

At Madison Square Garden, there was disbelief. Strauss and
Markson were locked in a bitter promotorial conflict with an organ-

ization called the Tournament of Champions, and they had lost touch with Louis's plans. In the past, Jacobs had dealt directly with Louis, but he was in semi-retirement and spent most of his time sunning himself on the lawn of his home on Normandy Isle in Miami Beach.

The Tournament of Champions had been organized in May, 1947, by seven nonboxing enterpreneurs who saw in boxing a broad avenue leading into the marketplace of television. Among the seven incorporators of the organization were Lawrence Lowman, of the Columbia Broadcasting System, and Charles Miller, of the Music Corporation of America. In its brief history, the Tournament of Champions had promoted two important bouts, both involving the world middleweight championship. One was the third meeting of Graziano and Zale, which Zale won, and the other was Zale's title loss to Marcel Cerdan, the charming Frenchman from Afrique du Nord who was to lose his life in a plane disaster in the Azores.

In addition, the Tournament of Champions had been promoting a series of Wednesday night bouts that had been televised by the Columbia Broadcasting System in competition with the 20th Century Sporting Club's Friday night series on the National Broadcasting Company's network.

Whenever the 20th Century Sporting Club would attempt to match two boxers in an important bout, the Tournament of Champions would offer the fighters a better deal, thus raising the cost of ring labor. It was uneconomic, and the fighters and their managers used one organization against the other to enrich themselves.

One day Sugar Ray Robinson visited the offices of the Tournament of Champions in Broadway and assured one of the officers, George Kletz, that he would take a bout with a middleweight from the Bronx named Steve Belloise if he could borrow $5,000. A check was hastily drawn in his name. At the same moment, Robinson's associate, George Gainford, was in the offices of the 20th Century Sporting Club in Madison Square Garden borrowing $2,000 on the condition that Robinson's next bout would take place in the Garden ring.

Louis was not unaware of the existence of the Tournament of Champions. Nor was he of a mind simply to resign his championship without turning it into cash, which he sorely needed. The federal government was pressing him for tardy income taxes in a case that would eventually burden him with a federal lien in excess of $1,250,-000. He was, in a phrase, dead broke, yet he tried to keep on fighting in defense of the heavyweight championship he still owned.

Perhaps the easiest source of money had dried up. Jacobs no longer was willing to dig into the corporate vault, as he had in the past, in order to maintain his hold on the heavyweight championship. Louis could take another bout, but it was rather obvious to him and those around him that his ring skill and power had diminished. Fighting, he could lose the one major asset he still owned—the title. He wanted a deal that would give him an income over a long period.

Along the way, Louis had become acquainted with Truman K. Gibson, Jr., a lawyer who was an impressive member of the Negro community in Chicago. Gibson was a graduate of the University of Chicago Law School and had served, during World War II, as a civilian adviser on Negro affairs with the War Department. In the course of this work he met Louis and later became his attorney.

Until this time, Louis had almost always surrounded himself with Negroes who had made their way in nether pursuits. Both John Roxborough and Julian Black, his first managers, were lottery operators. Jack Blackburn, his first trainer, had served a prison term for murder. Now along came Gibson, who was sophisticated and presentable, and, above all, possessed of a keen and searching intelligence.

While he was not at that time as versed in the trickery of the boxing business as he would become, Gibson was cunning enough to know that general commercial acumen pointed the way to success in the shadowy fight game as elsewhere. Mendel was to supply the *modus vivendi* that Gibson would put in motion.

SIX

THE "MENDEL PLAN," as it was later called, was startlingly simple in concept. It invoked in boxing the principle of royal prerogative. During its period of gestation it took real form, but in conception in Mendel's agile mind it went like this:

1. Joe Louis Enterprises, Inc., would obtain by contract the exclusive services of four leading contenders for the heavyweight championship.

2. Louis would resign as heavyweight champion.

3. Joe Louis Enterprises, Inc., would assign the four exclusivity contracts to an individual or corporation willing to pay a price for the right to promote world's heavyweight championship bouts.

Even before the Mendel Plan was proposed, Louis and Gibson had, between them, hatched a plan of their own for the future control of the heavyweight championship. It was formless and seemingly without direction, and involved a Florida hotel owner named Harry Voiler, who had been on the fringe of boxing in the past.

Voiler had a reputation as a romantic. Once, years before, his name had appeared in the newspapers when Mae West had been the victim of jewel thieves. He had been her friend. Voiler and Gibson had lunch at Voiler's DeWitt Hotel in Miami one day. They discussed the possibility of the formation of a promotorial firm and even a nebulous plan by which Joe and Voiler could obtain and maintain control of the heavyweight championship after Louis's retirement.

In its bare state, the program called for Voiler to put $100,000 into a corporation. Louis would own 51 per cent of the stock, with Voiler holding 49 per cent. Furthermore, Louis was to be permitted to withdraw immediately $60,000 from the corporation's funds.

There were many meetings between Voiler and Gibson. Later, Gibson was to tell a Federal District Court in New York:

Voiler was actively pushed by the executives of one of the large newspaper publishing companies in the country. I had several conversations in New York with the publishing people and with Voiler's lawyer, a New York lawyer. We had several meetings, and in late 1948 —in December of 1948—I expressed to Louis the feeling that the offer did not have any substance whatever because whenever we got down to discussing when the $100,000 would be turned over, it was on the mortgage of a hotel in Florida or the sale of a hotel, and it became evident to me, and so I stated to Louis, that the $100,000 was not readily available.

By this time Louis was eager, even anxious, to make some sort of deal. He was determined to retire. He put pressure on Gibson, who went to New York from Chicago and called David Charnay, one of several partners in the Tournament of Champions. He asked Charnay if the Tournament of Champions would be interested in joining Louis in the promotion of boxing, with emphasis on heavy-weight championship bouts.

Charnay expressed disinterest. Gibson pressed on by disclosing the nature of a two-ply alternate plan: Louis would defend his title for the Tournament of Champions, after a two-bout elimination series to determine a leading challenger. The fighters who would be involved in the elimination tournament were Ezzard Charles, Joe Walcott, Lee Savold, and either Gus Lesnevich or Joey Maxim.

Gibson told Charnay that these contenders already had been told to stand by and had indicated interest in any proposal to be made by Louis. The alternate proposal called for Louis to resign his championship and to deliver the contracts with the four contenders to the Tournament of Champions. In each instance, Louis wanted a down payment of $100,000 plus a guaranteed salary of $10,000 annually to be paid by the Tournament of Champions.

At the time, the Music Corporation of America and the Columbia Broadcasting System had become disenchanted with their participation in boxing. They had each contributed $25,000 toward the formation of the Tournament of Champions in the hope that participation in the promotional firm would involve them in the televising of championship boxing bouts. The only title bouts they had obtained were the Zale-Graziano and the Zale-Cerdan middleweight championship matches.

Beyond that, the Columbia Broadcasting System had, beginning in January, 1949, obtained the rights to a series of Wednesday night bouts. The telecasts of these bouts, sponsored by a New Jersey brewery, were not all that the Columbia Broadcasting System had anticipated; no championship bouts were included in the series, and this omission tended to diminish the series' attractiveness.

By way of repairs, the Tournament of Champions attempted to sign two world championship matches: Sugar Ray Robinson versus Kid Gavilan for the welterweight title and Marcel Cerdan versus Tony Zale for the middleweight title. In furtherance of this project, the corporation entered into negotiations to lease the Polo Grounds as the scene of these bouts.

It was at this juncture that Gibson came to see Charnay and was rebuffed in his attempt to make a deal in behalf of Louis.

In January, 1949, Louis was scheduled to box Elmer ("Violent") Ray in an exhibition bout in Miami. Gibson had returned to Chicago from New York after seeing Charnay. He received a phone call from Louis.

"How 'bout comin' down to let me know what's happenin'?" he said to Gibson. "Man, the sun's good."

Gibson flew down to Miami and checked in at the Mary Elizabeth Hotel, which was at the time the only first-class Negro hotel in Miami.

That night Gibson sat down with Louis and Mendel and told them that the projected deal with Voiler was dead. "He doesn't have the money," Gibson said, "and let's forget him. Forget Charnay and the Tournament of Champions. They're not interested."

"I've got a guy I know who'd be right for the deal," Mendel said.

"Who?" Truman asked.

"Jim Norris in Chicago," Mendel said. "I got to know him when I was doing publicity for those six-day bike races. He's down here, living in Coral Gables. I'll call him."

"Call him," Louis said.

Mendel phoned Norris the next day and made an appointment to see him —alone. Gibson was furious. Later he would say, "It was

Florida, remember, and a fellow didn't like to have Negroes around with him in those days."

Norris and Mendel spent forty-five minutes together. Mendel outlined the plan of action, including the deal calling for exclusive service contracts Louis was about to sign with the four foremost heavyweight contenders. Norris immediately expressed interest.

"I think what I had better do," Norris said, "is call my partner, Arthur Wirtz, in Chicago, tell him about it and have him meet with Louis or his representatives and, if he feels the same way as I did about it, then possibly we could make a deal on it."

Norris proceeded in accordance with his suggestion, but not until after he had checked by phone with Louis and Gibson. They substantiated Mendel's outline, whereupon Norris expressed some disappointment because, he said, Wirtz had been in Miami until a few days ago and had returned to Chicago.

"Go up and talk with him," Norris suggested.

Gibson and Mendel flew to Chicago and made an appointment to meet Wirtz in the office of his attorney, Charles Watson. At the meeting, Gibson unrolled his charm. He was then, as now, a strikingly handsome man whose light brown complexion and straight black hair set off alert eyes, a slender nose, and a delicately drawn mouth. He was slender and of medium height, in contrast with Wirtz, who stood more than six feet and weighed perhaps 225 pounds.

At the outset, Gibson flattered Wirtz. He explained that Mendel had praised both Wirtz and Norris and had described them as men of affluence and influence. At the time, Norris and Wirtz owned or had controlling interest in the Chicago Stadium, the Detroit Olympia and the St. Louis Arena. They also had an investment of $125,000 in the Cincinnati Gardens. They held leases on the Omaha Coliseum and the Indianapolis Arena, and they owned a considerable number of shares in the Madison Square Garden Corporation. By April, 1955, they were to increase their joint holdings in Madison Square Garden to 219,450 shares, or 38 per cent of the shares outstanding.

For the first time, Gibson disclosed that he had been talking with Ben Lindheimer, the owner of several race tracks in Chicago, and that Lindheimer had expressed an interest in the deal he was about to propose to Wirtz. The response was typical of Wirtz's stolidity.

Wirtz was a graduate of the University of Michigan who had made a fortune in Chicago real estate and had, along the way, become Norris's partner. He presented a formidable, austere front at all times, though he could be rather charming when the pressure of business ebbed. He was a shrewd dealer in real estate and, together with Norris, he had gained control of the Chicago Stadium after it had gone into bankruptcy. He scrutinized Gibson and his proposition.

Gibson told Wirtz the same story Mendel had told Norris, except that there was flesh added to the skeleton. He said Louis was "in a position to deliver contracts with leading heavyweight title contenders" and that when the contracts were accepted by the Norris-Wirtz group, Louis would abdicate.

In return for that resignation, Gibson said, Norris and Wirtz would be required to pay Louis $250,000, plus 51 per cent of the stock of the promotorial organization. He also specified that Louis would take an active part in the business.

"Not interested," Wirtz said. He explained that the amount Louis wanted was too large, that the stock interest demanded by Louis was too great, and that he was not convinced that the course outlined by Gibson was the proper one. The meeting broke up when Wirtz agreed to let Norris make the final decision.

Four days later there was another meeting, this one in Wirtz's office at 3180 Sheridan Road, Chicago. The cast of characters had changed slightly. This time Norris and Louis were present. No holds were barred. Louis and Gibson admitted frankly that they had already obtained the sanction of the National Boxing Association for their course of action.

This meant that the National Boxing Association, which was a loosely joined organization of State boxing commissions, had, in effect, granted Louis permission to sign up the four contenders—Charles, Walcott, Savold, and Lesnevich—and had sanctioned them as the ones who would fight for Louis's title if he retired.

By now, Louis had altered his demands. He was willing to go along with Norris and Wirtz on a greatly reduced scale. He would accept $150,000 instead of the $250,000 demanded earlier. He would accept only 20 per cent of the stock in the projected promotorial corporation instead of the 51 per cent he had demanded earlier, and he would accept an annual salary of $15,000.

"One more thing," Gibson said.

"What's that?" Norris asked.

"We need $15,000 to bind Savold and Lesnevich."

"How come?"

"We've promised Lesnevich $10,000 and Savold $5,000."

Norris agreed to advance the $15,000 in return for a promissory note signed either by Louis or Gibson. There was agreement that the first bout in the heavyweight tournament would take place in Chicago, and there was further agreement that the meeting would be kept secret.

There were several reasons for the pledge to secrecy. Louis still was tied to Promoter Jacobs contractually, although Gibson had expressed the opinion that Jacobs could no longer carry out the terms of the agreement because of his illness. In addition, there was the matter of making certain that the four challengers were signed up before the newspapers were informed of the new organization.

Louis had been in Jacobs' palm for many years, but had, during their association, developed an affection for the old man. He had seen Jacobs in Miami Beach on January 24, about a week before the Chicago conference, and had walked on the beach with him. Photographers had snapped the two together, and the pictures had been published in papers all over the country over captions that spelled out loyalty and long friendship.

From Chicago the planners returned to Miami, where Abe J. Greene, who was Commissioner of the National Boxing Association, was vacationing. Wirtz insisted on meeting with Greene in order to get assurance that the National Boxing Association had indeed placed its cachet on Louis's program for the development of a successor to the title. Greene gave his assurances, but there still remained one drawback: Charles was scheduled to fight Maxim in the Cincinnati Gardens on February 28, 1949. If he were to lose to Maxim, there would have to be a change in the plot. For one thing, Louis had to wait until after the meeting of Charles and Maxim to make a public and formal declaration of his retirement.

By now, rumors of Louis's impending announcement were being whispered in boxing circles. They finally came to the ears of Jacobs' proconsuls in the 20th Century Sporting Club, which still had a two-year lease on boxing in Madison Square Garden. The lawyer Strauss and the press agent Markson decided to go to Cincinnati on the day of the bout between Charles and Maxim.

In Cincinnati, they went to the Terrace Plaza Hotel. During the afternoon, they invited Jake Mintz to visit with them in their suite. Mintz was a veteran manager of fighters. Some years before, he had been associated with Jacobs in the promotion of a light-heavyweight championship bout in Pittsburgh between Billy Conn and Melio Bettina. Now he was Charles's co-manager. He was on friendly terms with both Strauss and Markson and accepted their invitation.

When he entered their suite, Mintz was immediately badgered for information. He cringed in a way only he could: whining and squealing alternately, saying he was pledged to secrecy and would not utter a word.

"Jake, is it true?" Markson demanded to know.

"Is what true?"

"Are you signed up with Louis?" Strauss asked.

"I can't talk. I said I wouldn't talk."

"We have the right to know," Markson insisted.

"You shouldn't ask me, Harry," Mintz pleaded.

"If you're a friend, you'll tell us," Strauss said.

Mintz broke down. He detailed the entire program. He recited chapter and verse, and for the first time Strauss and Markson heard the names of Norris and Wirtz linked with Louis and Gibson.

Mintz said, "Please, I told you, but don't tell nobody I told you."

That night, Charles outpointed Maxim in fifteen rounds. Strauss and Markson were at the fight, but they rushed to the airport in a blizzard to board a plane for Miami. The flight was a nightmare. The plane was tossed by thermal drafts and challenging headwinds. In Miami the next morning, the weary travelers rushed to Jacobs' home on Normandy Isle to tell him of their discovery.

They found an unlistening ear. Jacobs wouldn't believe that Louis, who had walked with him on the sandy beach only weeks before, would involve himself in a plot to destroy the 20th Century Sporting Club. He had been Louis's friend and banker and benefactor, and it was difficult for him, in his infirmity, to accept the facts of life in the boxing jungle in which he himself had been a predator for so long.

"It's true, Mike," Markson insisted.

"Don'tcha believe it," the promoter growled.

Jacobs' wife Josie came into the living room and overheard the conversation. She had been around boxing long enough to know that loyalty ran as deep as the ink on a dollar bill. She was a realistic woman of considerable discernment in matters of business.

"Sure it's true, Mike!" she screamed when her husband asserted his confidence in Louis's loyalty. "I told you it was going to happen."

Jacobs broke out in a fit of temper. "What the hell do you know?" he shouted.

"You wouldn't know it if a truck hit you," Mrs. Jacobs screeched.

Strauss, who was a cousin to Jacobs and a loyal counsel for many years, cowered. Markson tried to hide in the soft comfort of the couch on which he was seated. It was time for them to leave. When they went away, it was the end of an era in boxing. New people had come in to take Mike Jacobs' place.

SEVEN

D AMON RUNYON had a knack for quick labels. He could pinpoint a place or a mood or a time with few words. He was at his best one day in the spring of 1934 while strolling through West 49th Street on his way from Broadway to Madison Square Garden, on the corner of Eighth Avenue. Going past Mike Jacobs' theater-ticket store, he came upon several fight managers seated on brightly colored chairs, "taking the sun." "Is this Jacobs Beach?" he asked. The name stuck.

When word of the deal between Louis and Norris reached Jacobs Beach in the winter of 1949, no sunbathers warmed themselves on its gentle strand of pavement. They huddled against the cold in the lobby of the Forrest Hotel and were warmed by the thought that a millionaire was on the verge of taking over boxing.

They knew all about Norris and Wirtz, dating back to 1935 when a pair of promoters named Nate Lewis and Jim Mullen ran fights in the Chicago Stadium. Lewis and Mullen had rented the Stadium from the Norris group, and the arrangement proved to be happier for them than for the landlord. More often than not, there was not enough left over after the fight promotion for rent. Other boxing promoters succeeded Lewis and Mullen, but none achieved wealth even this side of their wildest dreams.

Norris was also known as the co-owner with his father, also named James Norris, of the Detroit Red Wings, a team which came regularly to Madison Square Garden to challenge the New York Rangers on the hockey rink. And, the better-informed fight managers knew, Norris and Wirtz were major stockholders in the Garden itself.

So Norris needed no introduction, although he did need time to put together the pieces of his new organization.

By the third week in February, Gibson had succeeded in obtaining the signatures of Charles, Walcott, Savold, and Lesnevich on contracts binding them to fight for Joe Louis Enterprises, Inc., or "any corporation, partnership or association to which Enterprises shall hereafter assign this agreement by the terms hereof."

The contract with Savold was signed during the first week in February at LaGuardia Airport, where Savold and his manager, Bill Daly, were departing for London. In the hit-and-run fashion of boxing, Savold wrote his name on the agreement at a restaurant table.

Gibson went over to New Jersey to get Lesnevich's name on an exclusive service contract. It was countersigned by Joe Vella, Lesnevich's manager, in the presence of NBA Commissioner Greene.

Walcott wrote his name on a contract in Camden, New Jersey, and Charles came to Gibson's law office in Chicago to sign his agreement with Joe Louis Enterprises, Inc.

Thus armed, Gibson was able to go to Norris and Wirtz in Florida to inform them that all was in readiness for the announcement of Louis's retirement and the formation of the International Boxing Club. That announcement was to come on March 1, but the day before, Louis and Gibson went to Jacobs' home in Miami Beach to inform him finally and legally that Louis was retiring as world's heavyweight champion.

The physical deterioration of Jacobs was later described by Gibson as "shocking." Perhaps the word was harsh, but it had validity as a physiological and psychological appraisal. In health, Jacobs would have stormed about the living room in which he greeted Gibson and Louis. In decline, he listened to Louis and Gibson, and said, "Well, champ, when you go out, I'm going out, too. If you aren't going to fight, I'm going to quit, too."

If a major commercial corporation wants to make an announcement to the press, it generally does so in a most formal setting, perhaps in an oak-paneled conference room or in an auditorium acoustically accurate and decoratively acceptable. In boxing, announcements of importance generally are made on the run, winging.

The retirement of Joe Louis and the consequent birth of the International Boxing Club were announced officially in the old airport building at Miami. Norris and Wirtz flanked Louis as he told an assemblage of reporters that he was hanging up his gloves. Wirtz was introduced and so was Greene, who, by his presence in his role as Commissioner of the National Boxing Association, sanctioned the departure of Louis from the ring and the arrival of the International Boxing Club.

The announcement at the airport had not been scheduled; it just happened. In Chicago, the newspapers had learned of the developments and had published strong hints of Louis's retirement and the organization of the new promotional group. Under pressure, the announcement was made officially.

In Chicago, the International Boxing Club was incorporated under the laws of the state of Illinois. The board of directors, in the mysterious ways of the commercial world, were Charles Watson, the lawyer in whose office Gibson had first met with Wirtz, and two of Watson's employees, Leland P. Broehl and A. L. Kriz. Thus did Watson, Broehl, and Kriz make fight history, standing for a moment in the center of the ring, as it were, only to be forgotten within twenty-four days, when Norris, Louis, and Wirtz succeeded them as members of the board of directors.

The change in the board of directors was accomplished at a meeting on March 24 in Chicago. At the meeting the exclusive service contracts binding Charles, Walcott, Savold, and Lesnevich to Joe Louis Enterprises, Inc., were formally assigned to the International Boxing Club, Inc. In return, the IBC was to pay $150,000 to Louis's corporation. Louis also was named director of boxing and matchmaker for the IBC. It was, at best, a token gesture. History does not record a single instance in which the former champion acted in such a capacity with the IBC.

Elsewhere, the fat was in the fire. Madison Square Garden was on the hook with Jacobs. The older promoter's boxing lease had two more years to run, and although it was inevitable that Norris's stock holdings in the Garden would open a clear path for the introduction of the IBC to New York, the legal fact remained that Jacobs was still a fistic flower in the Garden.

The president of Madison Square Garden was Brigadier General John Reed Kilpatrick, a tall and imposing man in a blue suit. Kilpatrick had been an All-America football player at Yale in 1909, and although weight had come upon him he was still ramrod straight forty years later. He had been president of the Garden at the time Jacobs had virtually forced his way in as a tenant by "stealing" control of the heavyweight championship from the Madison Square Garden Corporation, and had been less than friendly with the old promoter.

During the twelve years of Jacobs' association with Kilpatrick they had come to understand each other and to achieve a mutual respect. Kilpatrick was loathe to make a move toward the sacrificing of Jacobs for the benefit of the IBC without first assuring the old promoter of a square deal.

On March 13, 1948, Wirtz was at the Roney Plaza Hotel in Miami Beach. Never one to let pleasure interfere with work, he wrote a long letter to Kilpatrick that struck the general with such force he filed it away for safekeeping. Eight years later he would have cause to regret his devotion to Wirtz's epistolary talents. The priceless letter said:

> Early last summer I spoke to you about the boxing situation when I had information that the Tournament of Champions, which is owned

jointly by CBS, Music Corp., and Allied Syndicates were going to make a strong bid to tie up the various boxing champions so they could control the television and broadcasting of the major boxing events with the long range of controlling boxing in the Garden.

I mentioned to you at this time it looked as if Mike Jacobs was losing his hold on boxing and suggested a program of getting together on an agreement of our respective buildings and trying to work out mutual protective agreements that might save this situation.

Later in the summer when there was further evidence of a general breakdown of the Twentieth Century organization Jim [Norris] had a conversation with you in your office at the Garden and outlined practically the same program. You advised both Jim and myself that you recognized the merits of our suggestions but with your agreement with Jacobs and the Twentieth Century having approximately two years to run you could do nothing except leave the matter in Jacobs' hand.

Last Fall when I was in New York I met a top executive of CBS who, not knowing of my close association with you and the Garden, told me that CBS was prepared to lose a substantial sum of money backing the Tournament of Champions, hoping to eventually control the televising of major fights. He further advised that Columbia had bought a substantial block of Madison Square Garden stock and that some day I might have to negotiate with them for a lease for the Sonja Henie show in the Garden.

Fights have not been a major promotion of ours in either Detroit or Chicago in the past. It was difficult, or practically impossible, for us to obtain popular talent and we, therefore, tried to develop good local fights at reasonable prices rather than bid against New York.

We would have been content to continue along these lines except for the development of television and the new coast-to-coast cable. The Friday on which you had the Pep vs. Saddler championship fight in the Garden, we were also running a fight in Detroit and in Chicago. We were caught completely unaware that the Pep vs. Saddler fight was being televised on a national hookup and it seriously affected our attendance because a great many people preferred to see your world's championship fight on television.

Shortly before I came to Florida, Jim and I were reliably informed that Joe Louis was definitely going to retire and accept one of two substantial offers from interests closely aligned with radio and television, completely competitive both to the Garden and ourselves. We were always led to believe that the Twentieth Century had the exclusive for fights both at the Yankee Stadium and the Polo Grounds and were surprised to learn that the Polo Grounds was available for outside fight promotions.

Music Corp., which is part owner of the Tournament of Champions, has been very successful in the booking field. There was a time when they controlled the leading name bands of the country but they finally charged so much for their talent that a great many places who formerly used name bands had to change their policies. It is apparent that they are trying to tie up boxing in this same manner and if we don't do something now we will find ourselves renting our buildings at a low figure and their controlling the television rights. Boxing is the leader of all television sports shows and it would be a major prestige blow to lose control of boxing television. Under the circumstances, we could not idly stand by and see television and broadcasting interests try to grab control of one of our major prestige attractions.

A few days before we made our deal, Joe Louis called on Mike Jacobs at his home in Miami and told him that he had several substantial offers and had decided to resign the heavyweight title. We understand that Jacobs made no attempt to interest Louis with any kind of offer. We further understand he wished him well in his new venture and told him that he thought he himself would retire. Later, conflicting statements attributed to Mike Jacobs appeared in the papers.

We had hoped that had you been able to come down this weekend, that we could acquaint you with the moves of the Tournament of Champions to stage two world's championship fights in the Polo Grounds this summer. We had the manager of one of these champions here in Florida and we feel that we have the inside track on this fight, which would leave the Tournament of Champions with only one major fight this summer.

We have been approached with an interesting proposition from one of the top radio-television networks but we are hesitant to consider this proposition because it might create a very competitive situation.

I have tried to outline in this letter the steps that led to the formation of the International Boxing Club. As stated before, we were satisfied that the Twentieth Century was not on top of the situation and that the Tournament of Champions with their television hookup would control fights unless we stepped into the situation quickly.

You must realize that Jim, his father, James Norris, and myself have interests in stadia and arenas representing an investment in excess of ten million dollars, plus long term leases on two other arenas, exclusive of our stock interests in the Garden.

Mr. Norris, Jim's father, felt that he should not be connected with International Boxing Club in any capacity, but felt he could not stand in the way of our making this deal when we convinced him that Twentieth Century had no chance.

We have always felt very close to everyone connected with the Garden and in the past I doubt if we were ever competitive in any of our attractions. We had hoped that television would be a large added source of revenue for us. Our experience to date indicates that television on certain events is harmful . . .

I would appreciate your explaining the contents of this letter to your board so they will fully understand our position.

When General Kilpatrick had finished reading the letter from Wirtz, he gulped. He knew now that the steamroller was heading his way, and that there was need for swift action regarding Jacobs' boxing lease at the Garden.

At the time, the Garden was mostly concerned with the contract the 20th Century Sporting Club had with the Gillette Safety Razor Company for the radio broadcasting and telecasting of the Friday night fights. This needed to be protected, looking toward the time when the 20th Century Sporting Club's lease was up and the Garden wanted to promote boxing on its own. There was a challenging question: was it prudent for the Garden to retain its lease with Jacobs in the face of the Norris group's seeming control of the world's heavyweight championship and the stock interests held by Norris, his father, and Wirtz in the Garden?

Within three weeks, General Kilpatrick, the habitual collector of documents and data, wrote himself a note. It was labeled: MEMO-RANDUM REGARDING BOXING SETUP. The date on it was April 5, 1949, and it comes before us now as the first bit of evidence that the Garden was about to surrender to Norris:

It is proposed to set up under the International Boxing Club an Illinois and a New York corporation to conduct boxing in Madison Square Garden and the ballparks in New York, and in the Chicago Stadium and the Chicago ballparks. The Illinois corporation may handle boxing in the Detroit Olympia.

From the gross receipts (less admission taxes) in each building, 10 per cent plus the cost of personnel, setup, cleaning, insurance, etc., will go to the building as rent. The balance shall be divided two-thirds and one-third, the two-thirds (less certain expenses for the local corporation) shall go to the building in which the match is held. The one-third shall go to International.

It is possible that, due to arrangements with Louis, all profits (less expenses for the local corporation) may have to go to International but a formula will be arrived at under which two-thirds of such profits (less necessary expenses) will go back to the building in which match is held.

It is contemplated that indoor fights will be allocated two-thirds to New York, one-third to Detroit-Chicago groups, and that championship bouts will be allocated on the same basis, i.e., two-thirds New York, one-third Detroit-Chicago group.

Control and participation in earnings of International to be joint between New York and Detroit-Chicago group with some form of voting trust. Exclusive contracts with boxers to be held by International. Mike Jacobs to be Chairman or Honorary Chairman of International at a fixed salary for five years. Actual direction of International to be through an executive committee of Norris and [Edward S. "Ned"] Irish with such other additions as may be advisable.

New York corporation to handle New York bouts under supervision of International and Illinois corporation to handle Chicago and Detroit bouts under International's supervision.

Possible bouts in other cities to be handled by such local corporations as International may determine or by International itself.

The division on profits of outdoor fights and the allocation of outdoor fights as between cities to be worked out. The allocation of receipts from radio and television to be discussed separately.

Some days later, on April 11, General Kilpatrick wrote a letter to Stanton Griffis, a member of the Garden's board of directors and former United States ambassador to Spain. He informed Griffis that Jacobs had agreed to terminate his agreement with the Garden and had given the Garden permission to negotiate with the International Boxing Club.

Jacobs was adamant on one point. He would not turn over to the Garden the personal service contracts he held with Louis. "We have not pushed this particular point and Mike has definitely refused to

turn this over, but we felt it bad judgment at this state of the proceedings to stress this point as he is a trifle bitter toward Louis."

Kilpatrick outlined another proposed financial split-up between
the Garden and the International Boxing Club and said, "These
figures indicate clearly that Joe Louis would receive far too much
money and when I indicated these figures to Wirtz he agreed, and
the object of a meeting scheduled with Truman Gibson this afternoon is to break down Louis's position."

Louis, it was obvious, had fallen among lions.

EIGHT

FOR A TIME the Madison Square Garden Corporation and General Kilpatrick, in their eagerness to get rid of Jacobs, considered going to court to have the promoter declared incompetent.
In this way, the 20th Century Sporting Club's lease on Garden boxing, with its two years still to run, could be broken.

A smidgen of sensitivity and a measure of practical concern forced
the Garden to take another course. The Garden itself, apart from
Jacobs' 20th Century Sporting Club, had never been popular with
newspapermen.

General Kilpatrick would concede later, ". . . I knew that if we
were unfair to Jacobs we would be very, very severely criticized in
the press. All of the newspapermen were friendly toward him. In
fact, more friendly than they were toward us. . . ."

The realization that the Garden and Jacobs would have to part
did not occur suddenly. General Kilpatrick had been aware that
Jacobs was no longer fully functional in the boxing business. Mid-
way in 1948 Jacobs cut the salaries of his staff at the 20th Century
Sporting Club arbitrarily. This bothered General Kirkpatrick, who
took it as an indication that Jacobs was losing control of the situation.

At one point, Norris came to see the General in his office at the

Garden and recommended coordination of the Garden's and the Chicago Stadium's modest boxing operations. The General refused to discuss the subject with Norris because the contract with Jacobs' 20th Century Sporting Club was still in effect.

By Sunday night, April 10, 1949, General Kilpatrick knew all about the organization of the International Boxing Club of Illinois and the deal for the payment of $150,000 to Louis for the delivery of Charles and Walcott, among others, into the clutches of the IBC. At a meeting with Norris, Wirtz, Gibson, and Irish, there was a discussion of the future setup of boxing in the United States. The IBC would, in effect, take over the 20th Century Sporting Club's role, with Louis sharing in the proceeds.

There were other meetings on the following Monday and Tuesday, April 11 and April 12, and on April 15, General Kilpatrick, still pursuing his arch role as America's foremost diarist, wrote a memorandum which said in part:

> Wirtz, Norris are obligated to Joe Louis in the amount of $150,000 for having made available to them the NBA heavyweight championship through the Walcott-Charles match which they with Louis's help have signed on a 25 per cent-25 per cent basis. The winner of this bout is signed to meet Savold or Lesnevich in the fall on a 25 per cent basis. They have advanced Savold $10,000 and . . . they have advanced Lesnevich $5,000. . . . Wirtz and Norris intend to devote the net profits from the Walcott-Charles fight to the liquidation of the $165,000 advanced to Louis, Savold, Lesnevich, and Louis's interest in the profits does not begin until this amount has been liquidated. It would be expected that any monies paid Mike Jacobs would be handled in the same manner.

General Kilpatrick assembled the breathless press at Madison Square Garden on May 5, 1949, and announced that Jacobs' days at the Garden were over. The old promoter came to the conference, but only the ashes of his fiery personality remained. Runyon, Frayne, and Farnsworth were dead. Louis had walked out on him. Jacobs wore a flamboyant tie of flowered design, a gray suit, and a wan smile. A reporter asked if he was heartsick over the way things had turned out. He said, "I just want to get better."

On Jacobs' old desk on the first floor of the Garden—a desk at which Jim Norris would soon sit—there was a letter from General Kilpatrick. It was without warmth and said:

This will confirm that, as of June 1, 1949, you will cancel and surrender to us that certain lease dated November 17, 1943, between the undersigned as lessor and yourselves as lessees, as extended and supplemented by agreements dated January 22, 1946, and presently expiring on May 31, 1951, in consideration of the payment by us to Mr. Michael S. Jacobs, his heirs, executors, administrators or assigns, of the sum of $100,000 in installments as follows:

$20,000 upon execution of this agreement, the receipt of which is hereby acknowledged;

$10,000 on the first day of December, 1949, and a like sum of $10,000 on the first days of June and December in each and every year thereafter until said sum of $100,000 shall have been fully paid.

On or before June 1, 1949, you shall deliver to us and we shall deliver to you general releases of and from all claims whatsoever pursuant to the aforesaid lease except as to claims for money hereafter received as a result of boxing matches heretofore promoted by you pursuant to said lease, which moneys shall be accounted for hereafter as if said lease had not been canceled. We shall also deliver to you prior to June 1, 1949, duly certified resolutions of our Board of Directors authorizing this agreement and you shall simultaneously furnish us with duly certified resolutions of Twentieth Century Sporting Club, Inc., authorizing this agreement.

Your signature on the carbon copy of this letter enclosed herewith shall constitute an agreement between us.

Jacobs' right hand had been immobilized by the stroke he had suffered thirty months earlier. With his left hand he made his mark on the contract. It was a large X.

There remained only the Tournament of Champions, Inc., to be removed from the field before the Garden and Norris's group could join hands and dance around the corporate maypole.

By May 27, 1949, this detail had been taken care of, at a cost of $100,000 and other minor expenditures. The $100,000 was turned over to the various principals in the Tournament of Champions and, in return, the Garden obtained several contracts owned by the Tournament of Champions. One was an agreement guaranteeing the exclusive services of Marcel Cerdan, the world middleweight champion. Another was a lease on the Polo Grounds in New York City, running from March 15, 1949 through July 1, 1950.

The Columbia Broadcasting System, which had contributed $25,000 toward the organization of the Tournament of Champions, received an important consideration in return for the sale of the boxing organization to Madison Square Garden. The Garden granted CBS the right to broadcast or telecast a new series of Wednesday night bouts in competition with the Friday night series already promoted by the Garden and broadcast and telecast by the National Broadcasting Company.

Joe Louis celebrated his thirty-fifth birthday on May 13, 1949, in the Chicago Stadium. Norris, Wirtz, and Kilpatrick gathered around the former world's heavyweight champion and sang birthday greetings around a *papier-mâché* cake surmounted by miniature outlines of two fighters and a referee, and Louis used a knife to simulate the slicing of the synthetic cake. The International Boxing Club of Illinois, Inc., the International Boxing Club of Michigan, Inc., the International Boxing Club of Missouri, Inc., and the International Boxing Club of New York, Inc., were now in business.

The membership of the board of directors of the New York organization was of particular interest. When it had been formed the first board of directors comprised three employees of The Corporation Trust Company, 120 Broadway, New York City. They were succeeded by "three individuals" associated with Simpson, Thacher & Bartlett, a law firm which numbered Madison Square Garden among its clients.

On July 8, 1949, a new board of directors was named: Norris, Wirtz, Louis, Kilpatrick, and Irish. Shortly thereafter, Joe Louis resigned as a member of the board of directors. The vacancy was filled by the election of Truman K. Gibson, Jr., who was also named the corporation's secretary. He was on his way. Mendel, the little fat man who had started the whole deal, was almost forgotten.

Mendel had been promised $4,000 as a reward. Instead, he was paid $135 a week to work as an assistant in the new boxing organization's publicity department. When he complained to Louis, the former champion said, "Harry, all you did was make a phone call."

Two years later, Mendel finally received $2,000 from the International Boxing Club. He wrote a receipt on a sheet of flimsy paper. It was dated August 6, 1951. It said:

Received from IBC $2,000 as ½ Settlement of Agreement.

It was signed *H. Mendel.*

NINE

HARRY MARKSON was in the dark. In the midst of the arcane maneuverings leading to the formation of the International Boxing Club, he had been told nothing by the Garden brass. He did not know, for example, that boxing at the Garden would be run by the International Boxing Club of New York, while boxing in the Midwest—at the Chicago Stadium and the Detroit Olympia, both owned by the Norris interests—would be operated by the International Boxing Club of Illinois and the International Boxing Club of Michigan. He was an employee only of the 20th Century Sporting Club, which was about to die, and he was realistic about his future. It was nebulous.

One afternoon he was summoned to General Kilpatrick's office on the sixth floor of the Garden. Eileen McKay, the General's secretary, ushered him into the inner office, where he found Kilpatrick, Irish, and Benjamin C. Milner, a lawyer from the firm of Simpson, Thacher & Bartlett.

"We want to bring you up to date," Kilpatrick said.

"What we want you to do," Irish said, "is to keep things going as they are. You will be retained by the new organization. Keep anybody you think you need down there and continue doing the things you have been doing."

"I'd like to make one change," Markson said.

"What is that?" asked Milner, who was secretary of the Madison Square Garden Corporation.

"As you know, we are now operating with Tex Sullivan as our matchmaker. I would like to recommend that we replace him with Al Weill. I believe Weill is the best matchmaker in the country for our business."

"If you want him, get him," Kilpatrick said.

There was further discussion. In the early days of the 20th Century Sporting Club, Weill had been Jacobs' matchmaker. He was a crafty manager of fighters who had once forced Jacobs to pay $82,000 for the services of Lou Ambers, a world lightweight champion owned and operated by Weill. Jacobs had never forgiven him for the "holdup," and it was inevitable, when they were associated in the 20th Century Sporting Club, that they should clash. They did, and Weill "took a walk."

Now Markson was determined to have him in the new organization. He said, "Weill knows more about boxing styles than anybody in the business. He will make good fights for us and will not toss away our money doing it."

Weill was hired, but even before he came to work for the International Boxing Club Markson was operating as the overseer in the Garden. He had known of Norris as a result of Norris's connection with the Detroit Red Wings and had been told by hockey writers that the new boxing man was a "stand-up guy" of great charm and enthusiasm. But he had never seen him or even talked with him on the phone.

One afternoon, Markson was at his desk in his office in the Garden. He looked up and found a man he knew well staring down at him.

"Hi, Lew," he said.

"Hi, Harry," Lew said.

The visitor was Lew Burston, a man who was a rarity among fight managers, a charming and articulate person. He could discuss politics, the manufacture of kewpie dolls, and the price of *pâté de foie gras* on the Champs Élysées, which he had trod on many trips to France. He had managed European fighters and, in 1949, was the

American representative with a man named Sammy Richman of Marcel Cerdan, the world middleweight champion.

"Harry, how'd you like to have a fight between Cerdan and Jake LaMotta?" Burston asked.

"Don't bother about it," Markson said. "I'd never get the New York commission to approve it."

"Who's talking about New York?"

"Where then?"

"Detroit, Chicago."

"Are you sure we can get it?"

"Would I be talking if I weren't?"

"Let me call Ned Irish," Markson said, "and ask him about it."

Irish was delighted, but conceded he was without authority to give Markson a green light.

"Tell you what, Harry," Irish said, "why don't you and Burston go and see Jim Norris. He's at the Delmonico. Call him."

"Ned, I don't even know the guy," Markson said.

"He's easy to know," Ned said, "You'll have to get to know him sooner or later. Give him a ring."

Markson did. Norris was affable on the phone. He said he had been meaning to get in touch with Markson, but hadn't done so because of the pressure of getting the International Boxing Club organized. He said he had heard many nice things about Markson and was pleased to have him on the team. When Markson told him the reason for his call, Norris invited him to come right over to the Delmonico, on Park Avenue, across Manhattan from the grubby section in which Madison Square Garden is located.

A taxi ride from Madison Square Garden to the Delmonico should take about ten minutes under medium traffic conditions. This day traffic was heavy. The ride took more than twenty minutes because of traffic in 50th Street. By the time the taxi pulled up in front of the Delmonico Hotel, at Park Avenue and 59th Street, Markson was at the edge of his seat. Usually nervous, he was doubly so this day in his eagerness, even anxiety, to meet Norris. He had worked for Mike Jacobs for twelve years and had grown accustomed to the promoter's irascibility. Now he was about to confront a new boss. He went to a house phone and called Norris's apartment.

"Come on up, Harry," Norris said, warmly.

"Let's go," he said to Burston. "Might as well meet him now as later."

In the elevator, Markson thought, "Well, I'm bringing something big to him, a fight between Cerdan and LaMotta. It's certainly a good beginning and a surprise to him."

When they reached their floor, they went to the door of Norris's apartment and knocked. Norris himself opened the door. He was wearing a dark red silk bathrobe and a smile. In person he was attractive—a large man more than six feet tall and weighing 210 pounds, a graceful man with a richness of black hair, pleasant dark eyes which sometimes, after a tough night, looked muddy, and an engulfing smile. They were caught by that smile, and Markson thought. "I'm going to like this guy."

Markson explained the purpose of the visit, telling his story as though he were delivering an apple to the teacher. He expected Norris to be both surprised and pleased by the offer of a big match for the International Boxing Club. He almost fell off the couch on which he was seated when Norris said, "Harry, let me call Jake and talk to him."

Without having to refer to any source, Norris asked the telephone operator for a number in the Bronx. It was LaMotta's private number.

"Jake, Harry Markson and Lew Burston are here," Norris told the fighter, after saying hello. "Lew tells me the fight with Cerdan is all right. I know you'll be glad to hear this."

They talked for a few minutes and when he had hung up, Norris said, "That'll be all right. Jake has two fights booked, but we'll try to get him out of those."

One of these bouts was to be against Joe Taylor in Binghamton, New York, and the other against Joey DeJohn in Syracuse, New York. LaMotta bought his way out of the Binghamton match; he was forced to fight DeJohn, and knocked him out in the eighth round.

On the way back to the Garden from the meeting with Norris, Markson kept thinking of his artlessness. He had been taken in. Although he was aware that Norris, in his capacity as landlord of the Chicago Stadium, had had dealings with fight managers and promoters, he did not realize for a moment that the man knew his way in the boxing jungle. He had expected surprise on Norris's part; instead, he had found his own embarrassment. The deal for the La-Motta-Cerdan fight had been arranged elsewhere, out of Markson's sight and hearing, and he was simply a dupe. It was to happen again and again in the ten years that lay before him.

TEN

NORRIS WAS TWENTY-FOUR YEARS OLD in the summer of 1930 when he went to the racetrack in Chicago one day. It was rather early in his time as an owner of thoroughbreds, and he attended the races frequently. He knew everybody around the track and was known, despite his family's wealth and social position, as a regular guy. He was handsome and quiet-spoken. He had no snobbishness and was rather contemptuous of convention.

When the races were over that afternoon, he got into his car and began driving back to the North Side, where he lived. Just as he got out of the car in front of his home, a man holding a revolver and wearing a handkerchief to mask his face forced Norris back behind the steering wheel.

"I want your money," the gunman said.

"I don't have any," Norris said.

The gunman pressed the revolver in Norris's right leg. "Where's your money?" he demanded.

Norris now saw that the gunman was not alone. Two other men were with him, one standing near the door opposite the driver's seat, the other at the rear of the car.

"I don't have any money," Norris insisted.

"Blow his head off," one of the other robbers growled.

Finally, the robber with the gun turned Norris's pockets inside out. No money. The revolver was pressed harder against Norris's leg. "Let's see what you have in your socks," he demanded. Norris turned down his socks. No money.

Finally, the holdup man spotted a golf bag on the back seat. They pulled out some of the clubs and found $1,100 in the bag. Stunned, Norris remembered that one of the clubs in the bag was a prize he he had won at a tournament. "Can I have that club?" he pleaded.

The one with the revolver handed the club to Norris. "Are you broke?" he asked.

"Yes," Norris said.

The gunman gave Norris ten dollars. "Don't move or turn around for five minutes," he said.

Norris was frightened. He waited a reasonable period and then drove his car to the nearest police station, where he reported the holdup. He was told to go to police headquarters the next morning to check the lineup of persons arrested during the past twenty-four hours. It was a waste of time. He could not identify any of the men in the lineup as the three robbers who had taken $1,100 from him.

That afternoon, at the track, he was approached by a tall, slender, bespectacled man with the mien of a minister and the voice of a confessor.

"What happened, kid?" the man asked.

Norris told him.

"How much did they get you for?"

"About eleven hundred," Norris said.

"Okay, kid," the man said.

That was all, until a few days later, when the man walked up to Norris at the track and handed him $1,100.

"Your money, kid," the man said.

"Thanks," Norris said.

It was the beginning of a long friendship between Norris and "Golfbag" Sam Hunt, a notorious killer in the Al Capone days in Chicago.

The nickname of Golfbag was given him because of his quaint custom of carrying his murderous machine-gun in a golf bag. Ghouls said, "He always shouted 'fore' before firing."

"I was very friendly with him," Norris would say later. "If he would want fight tickets, I would leave him fight tickets. If he wanted hockey tickets, I would leave him hockey tickets, and I had a very friendly feeling for Hunt. To me he was not the type of individual that he has been portrayed, and it was hard for me to believe that he did the things that he has been charged with."

Norris's sense of social justice was more authentic than his syntax. There were to be other instances later of his strange devotion to ruffians who were beneath his economic and social level. He chose his companions as he found them, without regard to their antecedents or their criminality, and in the rowdy world of sports he was unto himself as the arch democrat. For him, the mobster held a fascination not easily explained in the mumbo-jumbo of this age of free-wheeling psychoanalysis.

He possessed a safety valve of humor and knew how to laugh at himself. Once, while riding on a train from New York to Baltimore to see Joe Louis box a fighter named Jimmy Bivins, he passed a huge grain elevator completely covered by a painted sign: NORRIS GRAIN COMPANY.

He turned to Markson, who was seated alongside him, and fairly shouted. "See, Harry, you didn't believe I was rich. Look at that. That proves it."

"Jim, who built the family fortune, you, your father, or your grandfather?"

"Hell, I hope you don't think it was me. I'm doing my best to dissipate it."

In truth, Norris added considerably to the family fortune once his father had given him enough financial credit to get started on his own. On April 26, 1957, while testifying in the United States District Court for the Southern District of New York, Norris identified himself as the chairman of the board of the Norris Grain Company, senior partner in the Chicago stock brokerage house of Norris & Kenly, director of the American Furniture Mart in Chicago, director of the Upper Lakes Transportation Company, and director of the West Indies Sugar Company, among others. He had no cause to identify himself as the owner of Spring Hill Farm, a horse-breeding establishment in Kentucky, nor as the primate in the world of boxing. These were taken for granted.

Norris's father was the son of a Montreal grain dealer who came to

Chicago in the early years of the twentieth century to establish the Norris Grain Company in a city bristling with rowdies and opportunists. He could take care of himself against both breeds. There was about him the muscle and manner of an athlete, both developed as a high-sticking member of the Montreal Victorias hockey team.

When he had established himself in Chicago, the elder Jim Norris went back to St. Catharines, Ontario, to marry Ethel Carlisle Dougan. Their son, James Dougan Norris, was born in Chicago in November, 1906. His mother was a beauty, and Jim inherited her good looks. By the time he was enrolled in public school, his mother was dead. Several years later his father remarried.

Years later, Jim Norris told how his stepmother trailed after him from one prep school to another. "I was in and out of more of them than a second-rate teacher," Norris said. The occasion for his confession was an attempt by Markson to purchase new curtains in Norris's private office in Madison Square Garden.

"I hate new curtains," Norris explained. "Every time my stepmother used to hang them in my room at prep school, it seemed I was expelled in a matter of weeks. You don't know how much my family spent on curtains."

In prep school, young Norris played football. He had grown to be more than six feet tall and was physically mature. One football season he grew a moustache to appear older. It may have helped him on the gridiron and with the girls but it did nothing for his academic status.

He did get as far as Hamilton, New York, where he attended Colgate University for one semester on a trial basis. He did not make it, although his father hired a team of tutors and a warder to keep him in tow.

Once, so a story goes, he was eager to see a girl in Chicago and left Hamilton without his dad knowing about the trip. When his train reached Chicago he called the elder Norris's office and talked to his father's secretary.

"Where are you?" she asked.

"Chicago," Norris said. "I just got in on the train."

"My gosh," the secretary said. "Your father is just going down to the station to take a train to see you."

Young Norris purchased a return ticket, got on the same train as his father, hid out until the train reached Utica, New York, the main-line station closest to Hamilton, and got off in time to greet his father at the station.

"How'd you know I was coming?" Norris's father asked.

"I called your office," Jim explained.

"It was awfully nice of you to come and meet me," the elder Norris said.

More than a dozen years ago *Life* magazine published an article on Jim Norris. It was written at a time when the International Boxing Club had been in existence for only two years and there had not yet developed the bitter antagonism that was to burgeon forth later. It said, in part:

> His apathy to book learning was heightened by the fact that, at nineteen, he had secretly bought a stable of race horses and was far too busy studying the *Daily Racing Form* to bother about Shakespeare. Before long he even had his keeper betting and making an occasional flying trip to Belmont Park.
>
> After college Norris made some passes at hard work—when it did not interfere with campaigning his racing stable.
>
> He went through the motions of being groomed to take over the grain business, but as a floor trader in the grain pit his mind was more occupied with buying oats for his racers than wheat for his father's elevators. At Hawthorne and Washington Park he called jockeys by their first names and could not walk a hundred yards through the stable area without being touched for a fin or a sawbuck. He was good-natured, free with his money, and he separated the human race into just two categories—right guys and wrong guys. He never refused a friend a loan. He would peel off a hundred or two from a big roll without asking any questions, although a month or two later he might inquire: "What did you want it for?"

The 1929 stock market crash and the resultant Depression brought a change in the direction of the Norris fortune. Real estate was depressed and was being offered at 10 per cent of its value at bankruptcy sales. Along came Arthur Wirtz to lead James Norris,

Jim's father, into the real estate business. Wirtz was an aggresive operator with unusual acumen in the real estate field. He was a big man, perhaps even bigger than the elder Norris, and he was possessed by a driving ambition to become wealthy. He showed the way to the Norrises.

The three went on a buying spree. They purchased thousands of acres of land in Indiana and acquired controlling interest in the Chicago Furniture Mart. In Detroit, the Olympia, the city's largest indoor arena, was in financial distress. The Norris interests began negotiations to buy it in 1931. By November, 1933, the deal was concluded. With the deal came the Detroit Red Wings of the National Hockey League. It was the brightest moment of the elder Norris's life. With all his wealth he had always been driven by an overweening ambition to own a major league hockey team.

Young Norris had also developed a driving interest in hockey. He had played the game with his dad on their outdoor rink at Lake Forest, Illinois, where the elder Norris owned an estate, and it was inevitable that he should take a hand in running the Red Wings. He was named vice-president of the team.

He was not as demonstrative as his dad at rinkside, but suffered inwardly when fate went against his team. When one of the Red Wings' players was treated roughly by the enemy or was penalized for rough play by the officials, old Jim would shout an angry protest; young Jim would sit by quietly, never once raising his voice. Introverted to a degree, he was overwhelmed by his father's insensitivity. It manifested itself later in his ability to lay about him with a strong hand.

In 1935 the Norris interests acquired the Chicago Stadium, which had been a $6.5 million "white elephant." Like the Olympia, it was purchased in a bankruptcy proceeding at ten cents on the dollar. Later, the Norrises and Wirtz were to acquire other arenas, including stock control of Madison Square Garden, but for the moment there was a marking of time and, for young Jim, an avenue to boxing.

He had been an ardent fan of the ring sport since 1919, when his father had taken him to the Bay View Park Arena on the shore of Maumee Bay in Toledo, Ohio, to see Jack Dempsey knock out Jess

Willard in three rounds and become the world heavyweight champion. There were only 19,650 persons in the wooden arena, but to a young boy it came to a great throng. Within him grew two wishes: to become a fight promoter and to manage a world heavyweight champion.

These dreams had lain latent until the purchase of the Chicago Stadium, which had a formidable history as a boxing venue. Fights were still being put on there, and young Norris came into contact with many fight managers. Within a short time he was a bankroll man for at least two managers, Nate Lewis and Jack Hurley. He staked Lewis to the contract on a fighter named Harry Thomas, a railroad worker from Eagle Bend, Minnesota, and Hurley put him in with Lem Franklin, a heavyweight from Mobile, Alabama. He would never forget them.

Part Two

Trial

ONE

THE INTERNATIONAL BOXING CLUB announced that its first promotion would be the heavyweight championship bout between Charles and Walcott at Comiskey Park, Chicago, on June 22, 1949. Selection of the date was not without coincidence. Louis had won the title from Braddock in the same baseball park on the same night a dozen years before.

When the bout between Cerdan and LaMotta came along, a revision of the schedule was in order. It was decided that the new combine's inaugural title promotion would be a middleweight championship bout at Briggs Stadium on June 15, a week before the heavyweight title event.

Michigan law insisted that only a local corporation could promote a bout in the state. Consequently, the Detroit Olympia, which was owned by the Norris interests, fronted for the International Boxing Club of New York, inasmuch as the International Boxing Club of Illinois was promoting the Charles-Walcott bout.

On May 23, Cerdan and LaMotta signed exclusive service contracts with Norris. The IBC now had control of the heavyweight and the middleweight divisions. In the years ahead it would gobble up all the other world championships except the flyweight and bantamweight divisions. This was not an oversight; interest in the two lightest classes was virtually nonexistent in America, and Norris could not waste his time on nonessentials. Tomorrow, the world.

The morning of the bout between Cerdan and LaMotta, June 15, 1949, unfolded a cloud-filled sky. In his suite at the Book-Cadillac Hotel, LaMotta was up early. A reporter who visited him in his suite remarked that he had come a long way from the fighter who, on his first visit to Detroit, had taken breakfast in a greasy spoon in Skid Row.

LaMotta was worried about his weight, and his trainer, Al Silvani, insisted that he sneak over to the offices of the State Athletic Commission to check his weight before the official weigh-in, which was set for noon. It was nine o'clock. Furtively, LaMotta left the hotel. He was being watched by gamblers, hoodlums, and fans for telltale signs.

Carbo was around, operating in full view, even taking a drink or two with Norris in the hotel. He had been seen with LaMotta several times, flamboyantly parading his interest in the outcome of the bout.

When LaMotta stepped on the scale at the Commission offices, he was stunned. He weighed 161½ pounds, a pound and a half over the middleweight class's limit. The official weigh-in was only two hours off.

Silvani reacted immediately. He rushed Jake out of the Commission offices and into a taxi. "Take me to a Turkish bath," he ordered the cab driver. They drove to one in Skid Row. Silvani registered LaMotta at the baths as "Vito Perez" in order to avoid suspicion. For more than an hour, LaMotta sweated in the steam room. Silvani rubbed him down several times.

Finally, after ninety minutes, Jake stepped on a scale. He was down below 160 pounds. "Okay," Silvani said, "let's get dressed."

When LaMotta weighed in at noon, he hit 159½ pounds. He had made the weight. Nobody knew of his visit to the Turkish bath.

LaMotta was extremely confident as he sat in his hotel suite awaiting the fight. Visitors who came to see him virtually ignored him. LaMotta's wife at the time was a beautiful blonde named Vickie. She wore an off-the-shoulder blouse and was much more attractive than her husband.

Later that afternoon it started to rain. At about five o'clock Norris postponed the bout until the next day. It was his first public decision as a fight promoter. Now the question was raised: Would LaMotta have to weigh in the next day? Nobody on the Michigan boxing board seemed to know the rules. First the Commission ordered that no weigh-in be held; then, in a fevered official meeting, the solons reversed themselves. LaMotta screamed. He insisted he would not step on the scale again because it would be a hardship on him.

Finally, at midnight, Norris came to LaMotta's hotel suite. He was accompanied by Nick Londes, who was the nominal promoter at the Detroit Olympia. Silvani was also present. Carbo was not, although he was the spiritual leader of the group.

"You've got to weigh in," Norris insisted. "We can't put off the show, and the Commission insists on a weigh-in."

LaMotta, who had been doing setting up exercises, sat on a bed. He was wearing several sweaters and the sweat rolled down his nose. He wiped the perspiration from his face. Then he smiled.

"Tell you what, Jim," he said. "I'll go for another weigh-in, but at ten o'clock in the morning. That'll give me more time to get my strength back. If it's at noon, I won't be there."

"It's a deal," Norris said.

Now Norris went into conference with Burston and Richman, Cerdan's American representatives. At first they balked at the ten o'clock weigh-in. Then Burston made a suggestion. "Let's compromise," he said. "Make it half-past ten."

Norris called LaMotta on the phone and told him of the compromise offer. "Okay," said Jake. "I'm going to bed." He picked up a thick book from the dresser in his bedroom. "Guess I'll read a while," he told a visitor.

The visitor took the book from the fighter's hand and read the title. It was the *Psychoanalysis of Leonardo da Vinci* by Sigmund Freud. "Do you always read things like this?" the visitor asked.

"Sure," he replied. "I even read *The Microbe Hunters*."

The next morning, at the weigh-in, LaMotta hit 158¾ pounds. It was less than he had weighed the day before.

That night LaMotta won the middleweight championship of the world. He won it by taking command of the fight from the opening gong. He rushed the favored Cerdan across the ring, beat him with a left hook, and then punched him around generally. The challenger was so strong that he tossed Cerdan to the ring floor when their arms locked. The knockout came in the tenth round, with Cerdan sitting on his stool unable to continue. LaMotta jumped around deliriously. Cerdan was a dejected, beaten figure. The elevator muscle in his left shoulder had been injured when LaMotta had tossed him to the floor. His left arm was useless throughout most of the fight.

The IBC was launched profitably. Not only had the gate of $127,810 after federal taxes left a profit, but LaMotta was one of the boys, a controlled fighter who was tied hook, line, and Carbo to the International Boxing Club.

The next week, on June 22 as scheduled, the Chicago store of the IBC ran the Charles-Walcott bout at Comiskey Park. The gate receipts came to $179,032.90, and there was additional revenue of $37,500 from the radio and television broadcasts. Charles won the title on a decision in fifteen rounds in a dull bout. The IBC was off the ground.

Within the next four years forty-four world championship boxing bouts were held in the United States. The International Boxing Club of Illinois promoted or participated in 80 per cent of them. Gross receipts from admissions and the sale of television, radio, and motion picture rights came to $7.5 million. Joe Louis should have become a rich man; he didn't.

The corporate setup of both the New York and Illinois clubs were identical insofar as Louis was concerned. In each instance, he was granted two hundred shares of Class A common stock and twenty shares of Class B stock. Louis's shares were held in trust by Gibson and Theodore B. Jones, an accountant who was associated with Gibson's law office in Chicago.

There was a stipulation that the ratio of dividends to be paid would be 100 to 1 in favor of Class B shares. It proved to be of academic consideration. Although Louis was nominally the owner of 20 per cent of the New York and Illinois corporations, he could put his income from his stock holdings, apart from his annual salary of $15,000, into his right ear.

The way the deal was arranged, much of the receipts of both the

IBC in Chicago and the IBC in New York went for arena rents, not to the boxing clubs. This was best illustrated by two contracts entered into in October, 1950, with Warwick & Legler, Inc., a New York advertising firm which represented its client, Pabst Beer, in the deal.

One contract "dated and executed October 17, 1950, as of October 4, 1950," called for a rental of $5,000 nightly on the Chicago Stadium, the Detroit Olympia, the St. Louis Arena, and the St. Nicholas Arena in New York City. The contract was between Warwick & Legler and the Stadium Corporation, a Delaware corporation owned and controlled by Norris and Wirtz. Under the contract, Warwick & Legler would pay the Stadium Corporation $170,000 over a period running from October 4, 1950 through May 23, 1951, for the weekly rental of arenas owned, leased, or controlled by the Stadium Corporation.

The fight shows would be promoted by the International Boxing Club of Illinois, which would receive only $4,000 per show from the television sponsor, for a total of $136,000. Thus, a larger sum flowed into Stadium Corporation than into the IBC of Illinois. Louis held no interest in Stadium Corporation.

The result was not surprising. In its first year of operation, when it was writing off huge organizational costs, the IBC of Illinois had a net loss of $339. In New York, in that same year, the IBC had a net profit of $927.92. The next year the IBC of Illinois showed a surprising net profit of $19,324. In New York, in the same year, there was a net loss of $45,142.60. In 1952, IBC of Illinois made $16,500 net, while the New York Corporation had a net loss of $75,405. The IBC of Illinois made $111.96 in 1953. In 1954, the Illinois corporation showed a profit of $34,834. New York also surprisingly showed a profit of $37,327.04. Louis did not collect a cent in dividends during the years he held stock in both corporations.

Indeed, when Weill was hired as matchmaker for the International Boxing Club, he asked for and was given a profit-sharing contract. At the end of the first year, when the IBC's profit in New York was only $927.92, he received a check for an infinitesimal sum. He charged around his office like a stabbed bull. The next year, 1951, there were no profits. Weill was shut out. He went storming to Norris, who listened to his wailing and agreed to a new deal. Instead of a profit-sharing base for income beyond his salary, Weill was promised a bonus. Thereafter, as long as he worked for Norris, he collected.

Gibson was not enriched either. On September 16, 1949, Wirtz, in Chicago, wrote a letter to Norris on the stationery of the International Boxing Club of Illinois. It was addressed to Norris in his role as president of the International Boxing Club of New York. It said:

I had a talk with Truman Gibson today concerning his compensation for work that he will be doing for both the New York and Chicago clubs.

Truman's value to our organization lies in handling certain contracts which benefit our respective organizations and I, therefore, feel that his compensation should be divided between the New York and Illinois Internationals.

In talking with Truman, he said it was practically an impossibility to arrive at a fair basis of compensation, not knowing what he would be called upon to do and how much time he would be expected to spend and he suggested that we work it out on a nominal salary basis of $7,200 and to review our arrangements at the end of the year based on the amount of time he has had to spend and the results accomplished.

I, personally, think this is a fair arrangement and this would mean that the New York International would pay him $3,600 a year at the rate of $300 per month and the Illinois International would do the same.

In addition to the salary, if you want Truman in New York, it is no more than fair that you pay his traveling expenses on any trips. I believe that Truman, being an attorney, would prefer to take his monthly payments on a retainer legal basis, rather than as compensation, in which event there would be no deductions from the gross amount.

I would recommend the acceptance of this proposition and if you concur, I think that you should write Truman a letter on behalf of New York International and the same letter on behalf of the Illinois International, confirming the arrangement.

I am sure that you can explain to both Ned [Irish] and the General [Kilpatrick] the value that Truman has been to our companies and I hope that they will concur.

In the years ahead, Truman Gibson would pay dearly for this pittance.

TWO

GIBSON quickly became Norris's right arm. In moments of relaxation, Norris would say, "Truman's my number-one man. He will do things I can't get Markson to do, so he's first." This was especially true in the sense that Gibson knew Carbo conversationally; Markson never did.

In New York, Herman ("Hymie") Wallman, a manufacturer of mink coats, was a manager of fighters. One night in January, 1950, he went to the St. Nicholas Arena in New York—one of the arenas on which the IBC had gained an exclusive lease—to see Johnny Bratton, a Chicago welterweight, fight Gene Hairston, a deaf-mute fighter from the Bronx. Bratton knocked Hairston out in the second round. Wallman was smitten with Bratton's ability as a fighter.

"Gee, I would love to own that boy," Wallman said. "So graceful, so beautiful, and a fine boxer."

At the time, Bratton was being handled by Izzy Kline, a Chicago trainer who assisted Gibson in the making of matches for the Chicago Stadium. Kline was, in a sense, only the nominal manager of Bratton, whose contract had been purchased some time earlier by Norris from Irving Schoenwald and Jack Begun. Norris knew Schoenwald and Begun because they had co-promoted boxing at the Chicago Stadium before the organization of the IBC.

Wallman told a friend in Chicago, one Manny Abrams, an insurance man, about his infatuation with Bratton. A few days later, Abrams called Wallman on the phone from Chicago.

"You know, I can get this Johnny Bratton for you from Izzy Kline, but it will cost you a lot of money," Abrams said.

"How much?"

"It will cost you $12,500," Abrams said.

"Well, I think I ought to be able to tackle that."

A few days later, Wallman was summoned to Chicago by Gibson. In Chicago, he attended a conference with Norris, Gibson and the omnipresent Carbo.

Wallman did not want to lay out the $12,500. "If you are going to trust me with the money," he told Norris, "I can buy the fighter; but I will not lay out any cash money for him. You can deduct it as the fights go on, from his purses."

Carbo's word was collateral. Later, by way of explaining Carbo's role in the deal, Wallman said, "Carbo played the part that he recommended me to those people, that I was honest and they would not lose no money with me."

Carbo had become the Rasputin of the Norris boxing empire. He would turn up again and again in one devious way after another, and when the empire tumbled he would be revealed in the naked light of truth as its arch manipulator.

His influence ran deep from the very moment the IBC was organized, though it was hidden from view by the imposing figure of Norris, who quickly found that the business of boxing was a vermiform appendix in the total body of sports.

For one thing, Ezzard Charles was less than a hero to the public. While mechanically an adept in boxing, Charles was less than magnetic at the gate. He boxed beautifully, but he could not punch powerfully. Some years before his coronation he had fought Sam Baroudi in a Chicago ring. Baroudi was mortally wounded in the bout, and Charles had never forgotten the starkness of his opponent's death. Its memory held him in thrall; somehow, he never again punched with the power he had possessed before Baroudi's death.

The fight public sensed this inadequacy. While the sporting folk of America frequently regard boxing in its pure form as senseless brutality, they are held in the clutches of ambivalence: they decry a fight devoid of terror as a pallid imitation of the real thing.

The IBC was stuck with Charles as the heavyweight champion.

On hand was contract for a bout between Charles and Gus Lesnevich, one of the four fighters who had been signed originally by Louis. On August 10, 1949, Charles fought Lesnevich at the Yankee Stadium. It was the IBC's first outdoor promotion in New York, and the financial result was less than warming. The gross receipts were a mere $62,061.24, even though the fight was not televised. The radio broadcast brought in only $17,500. Although Charles stopped Lesnevich in the seventh round, the New York State Athletic Commission persisted in its refusal to recognize him as world heavyweight champion. Only the National Boxing Association accorded him this honor. The public could not care less.

Meanwhile, Louis was in financial difficulty. His $15,000 salary from the IBC paid for peanuts. It had been intended that Louis would, in Norris's language, "be a great help to the IBC with his wide acquaintanceship with managers and boxers and the regard I thought the boxing public and the youth of America had for him. I think Joe had always thought that he would do what we expected him to do, and he just never quite got around to it."

What Louis did was to attempt futilely to rescue Ezzard Charles from the miasma of public disinterest into which the NBA heavyweight champion had drifted. In mid-1950, the federal government, through the Internal Revenue Service, slapped a tax lien of $246,-055.79 on Louis, going all the way back to his second bout with Billy Conn in 1946. The tax obligation stemmed from the government's refusal to accept as valid a payment of 25 per cent of the purse from the Conn bout to Marva Louis, Joe's first wife, who had been cut in as one of his managers by Louis in lieu of a cash alimony settlement.

Norris was pleased by Louis's decision to make a comeback and matched him with Charles. The television and radio rights to the fight, which was scheduled for the Yankee Stadium on September 27, 1950, were sold for $200,000. Louis looked forward to making enough money to help defray some of his tax debt. The way it turned out, he not only did not earn enough to put a dent into his obligation but he was badly beaten by Charles in fifteen rounds. The gross gate for the bout was most disappointing, only $165,878.76. Louis's share came to $36,919.01. For Charles, it was a night of achievement in one sense. The New York State Athletic Commission accorded him recognition as heavyweight champion.

Louis's small purse was not the dismaying aspect of the bout with Charles; his ineptness was. Louis took a lesson in boxing. Charles had him hurt and bleeding early, but somehow he relented in his attack, confessedly because he had too much regard for "the old fellow who did so much for the Negro in boxing."

In his dressing room after the fight, Louis was a shambling hulk. He was cut above both eyes, one which was shut tight by swelling. He could not see well enough to pull on his trousers. Friendly hands helped. Sugar Ray Robinson leaned down and pulled Louis's shoes on for him. The old champion was led out of the Stadium by friends.

He had been beaten and he had not earned much money, but there was within him a gnawing belief that he could somehow retrieve the timing that had made him a great fighter. He decided to continue his comeback.

In August, 1951, he went down to Baltimore to fight Bivins. The fight was important to the IBC because it marked the first time that a fight held outside of New York City would be televised on a theater TV basis. Theatre Network Television, Inc., was hired to transmit the television picture to several theaters and the occasion was so important that Norris, Gibson, Markson, and Weill went down to Baltimore. In Baltimore, Norris took a suite at the Lord Baltimore Hotel. Early in the evening, before going to dinner, Norris suddenly disappeared from the suite.

After a few minutes, Markson became curious and went in search of his boss. As he looked down a long corridor on his way to the elevators, he spotted Norris talking with Carbo. Markson ducked back into the suite. He did not want to see Carbo nor did he want to embarrass Norris.

Later, at the fight, Carbo calmly took a front-row seat. He was at home in Baltimore, where his pal, Benny Trotta, was the promoter. Norris's IBC hirelings were not as relaxed. When they spotted Carbo seated in the front row they moved swiftly. It would have been a most unhappy coincidence if the peering television cameras had picked out Carbo's picture for closed-circuit transmission to New York.

Carbo was shifted to a seat safely removed from the television cameras.

Louis won a ten-round decision over Bivins but was less than impressive in combat. Markson took Louis's relative ineptness as a text for a sermon. He approached Weill and said, "Al, after seeing Louis, how can you turn him down for Marciano?"

"I manage my own fighter," Weill said.

"Louis will be easy for Marciano," Markson insisted.

"I manage Marciano, not you," Weill said.

It was an assertion he would not make in public. Under New York State law, a matchmaker is not permitted to manage a fighter. Weill employed a subterfuge. His son, Marty Weill, was listed with the New York State Athletic Commission as Marciano's manager. Sports writers constantly japed at the Commission for permitting this duality in violation of the law. It was a source of real embarrassment to Norris, but nothing was done to change it. Carbo was in favor of the status quo. Subsequently, Carbo would use his influence in at least one instance to force Weill to accept an important match for Marciano, but he was not disposed toward upsetting Weill's role as matchmaker. The matchmaking position was much too critical a function, involving as it did the employment of fighters. With Weill, his friend, in office, Carbo could be assured of steady work for his fighters.

Some months later Norris finally persuaded Weill to permit Marciano to fight Louis. By this time it had become a most attractive match. Louis had won seven straight fights on the comeback trail, and there were persons foolhardy enough to believe that the old Brown Bomber had regained his timing and his power. At admission prices ranging from $3 to $25, the fight attracted net receipts of $125,256.19 at Madison Square Garden. In addition, the Gillette Safety Razor Company paid $82,500 for the radio and television rights.

Later, Marciano, in his own story in *The Saturday Evening Post,* described the bout with Louis:

> I remember standing in the ring and thinking how big Louis was. I had never remembered Louis being such a big guy. The top of my head seemed to just about reach the bottom of his chin.

I was prepared, though. In the first three rounds I was surprised I was doing so well. I remember even jabbing him a few times, which was unexpected because Louis had the best left-hand jab in the business. Then in the fourth, fifth, and sixth rounds he started hitting the mark, and he was hurting me with that jab. It was like getting hit in the face with a hammer. I was bobbing and weaving and getting in all kinds of positions, trying to get away from it. I was finally able to get underneath it and come up punching myself, which I did in the seventh and eighth rounds.

In the seventh I hurt him with a left hook. In the eighth I stepped in with my left hook. I knocked him down. He took an eight count and got up. I pinned him into the ropes and threw two left hooks that really hurt the man. I think they really knocked him out. The right hand I threw shoved him through the ropes out of the ring and onto the apron, and that's where he got counted out.

Sugar Ray Robinson was in a ringside seat. He came rushing toward the ring the moment Louis went down for the first time. By the time Marciano's final right had knocked Louis through the ropes, Robinson was almost in the ring. Louis lay on the apron with one leg inside the ring, under the lower rope. Robinson came into the ring and consoled Louis, who never fought again.

THREE

DURING THE formative years of the International Boxing Club Norris enjoyed widespread good relations with sports writers. His arrival on the boxing scene was greeted with journalistic applause. He was mild-mannered and seemingly frank in conversation. Columnists wrote that he was a welcome addition to boxing because he was, in their phrase, a millionaire sportsman who did not need the money to be gained from boxing.

Furthermore, they detected in him a surface enthusiasm for other people and their feelings. He was, for the most part, a thoughtful employer who remembered to utter pleasantries to his employees. His secretary at the IBC's office in Madison Square Garden was Mrs. Rose Cohen Bromberg. He treated her with great kindness. Mrs. Frances Hogan Romes was another employee in the office of IBC. She, too, found Norris "a charming man who never forgets to say 'good morning' when he comes in."

Perhaps his greatest charm was manifested at press conferences. Reporters on small newspapers were shown the same courtesies as writers for big-circulation newspapers. If a reporter arrived late at a press conference, Norris never failed to rise from his chair and reach across the large glass-covered desk in his office to shake the latecomer's hand. He even played "banker" to some.

Once, a New York sports writer on the verge of purchasing a house told Norris about the impending deal. "I'd take the place immediately," the writer said, "but I need $10,000 to swing it."

"I'll write a check for it," Norris said.

"Only if there's a mortgage," the writer said.

"We'll handle it any way you want it," Norris said.

Two days later a check for $10,000 was handed to the sports writer. For one reason or another the deal fell through. Perhaps the house the reporter was to purchase turned out to be too small for his needs. He returned the $10,000 check to Norris's office.

"Hell, you could have kept it until you found a house you liked," Norris said.

Norris would sit in his office in the Garden, and if a newspaperman came in and discussed the odds on an approaching bout he would ingenuously phone his bookmaker to obtain the current betting price.

"Might as well get it straight," he would say.

Frequently, he made bets on his own. And just as frequently he would say to Morris Krasnick, alias Mushky McGee, a supernumerary in the office, "Mush, you have a piece of my bet on the Yankees today."

"I can't afford it," McGee would say.

"You collect if I win, you don't pay if I lose," Norris would say.

"That I'll take," McGee would say.

Norris dressed carefully, in good taste and in good suitings. His suits were tailor-made in Chicago by a man name Pucci and cost $225 each. He had one apartment at 1420 Lake Shore Drive in Chicago and another at 710 Park Avenue in New York City. He had a beautifully appointed home at 5911 Granada Boulevard in Coral Gables, Florida, and a summer home at Mattituck, Long Island.

For the most part he was a temperate man, but when the grape was in him he was his own worst enemy. He would become insensitive to other people's feelings and flex his muscles.

One afternoon in 1951, just after Governor Thomas E. Dewey had appointed Robert K. Christenberry to replace Edward P. F. Eagan as chairman of the New York State Athletic Commission, Markson arranged a post-luncheon meeting between Norris and Christenberry.

"What'll you have?" Christenberry asked Norris.

"Beer."

"What'll you have, Harry?" Christenberry asked Markson.

"The same."

Christenberry also drank beer.

Christennberry, who had been a U. S. Marine during the First World War, had lost his right hand when a training grenade exploded prematurely. He was tall and handsome, with a graying pencil-thin moustache and an upright bearing. He was a Tennesseean and his tongue was edged with the soft drawl of his homeland. He was exceedingly polite and charming.

The afternoon wore on. Norris consumed five bottles of beer to every three washed down by Christenberry and every one taken by Markson. At first the conversation was polite, but when it turned on a personal note Norris rose from his chair and challenged Christenberry loudly.

"They say my family is worth three hundred million," Norris asserted. "Some say it's worth two hundred million. I know damn well it's worth one hundred million. As for you, Wingy, I'll tie one arm behind my back and beat the hell out of you."

Markson was alarmed. He went to a telephone and called the IBC's office in Madison Square Garden. Dominick Mordini, alias Billy Brown, was Weill's assistant in the matchmaking department. He rushed to the Astor with a special policeman on the Garden's staff. Together they virtually carried Norris out of the hotel and into a taxicab.

The next day, remorseful, he apologized to Christenberry.

For some years, Norris and Wirtz operated a restaurant called the Cameo on Chicago's Near North Side. It was a fastidiously turned out eating house, with plush banquettes along the walls. Delicate lighting gave the place a romantic air.

One night, at the Cameo, Norris encountered Tom Duggan, a Chicago television and radio announcer who had been taking verbal pokes at Norris and the International Boxing Club's conduct of boxing in Chicago and elsewhere. Duggan's acerbic attacks on Norris nettled the promoter. Words were exchanged. Norris lunged at the announcer, and there was an exchange of blows.

Duggan was in an untenable position. The television station for which he worked was an owned and operated affiliate of the National Broadcasting Company, which televised and broadcast the International Boxing Club's Friday night bouts. He was not long for his job. Sometime later he transferred to another station in Chicago.

One afternoon, Norris showed up at his office in the Garden with a bandage just below his left eye.

"Run into a door?" Markson asked.

"How'd you guess?" Norris replied, laughingly.

When the bandage was removed some days later, a small scar was visible. Norris was loathe to explain it. What happened was this: Friends of Norris ran into him one evening in the vicinity of the Copacabana nightclub in New York. He had been drinking, and he was urged to accompany them to a restaurant for some cake and coffee. He went along with them and in the restaurant, while taking their fare, they met a Broadway character named Matthew Santora, who was known to them as Matty Brown. He was dining at the next table.

Suddenly, there was an exchange of words between Norris and Santora. A coffee carafe went flying in Norris's direction. It smashed against his face, cutting him below his left eye.

The next day, Frank Carbo went looking for Matthew Santora in a spaghetti house off Broadway. "You shouldn't have done it," Carbo said.

Santora replied smirkingly, "Tell your friend to have some respect." That was all.

Some years later, in the waning days of Fulgencio Batista's presidency of the Republic of Cuba, a new sports arena was opened in Havana. Joe Brown, who was the world lightweight champion at the time, was matched to fight Orlando Echevarria, a Cuban, in the inaugural bout. A party of newspapermen and friends, including Julius Helfand, chairman of the New York State Athletic Commission, went to Havana for the opening of the arena as guests of the Cuban government. Norris was in the party, which stayed at the Capri Hotel.

Just off the scarlet-walled gambling casino at the Capri, in the hotel restaurant, Norris encountered Santora. Those who knew of Norris's earlier brief encounter with Santora ducked. Their fear was groundless. Norris and Santora shook hands, Americans together in a foreign capital, each conscious of his manners.

Indeed, Norris's manners for the most part were so broad and winning that they caused men who knew him to wonder just what made him tick and just what permitted him the company of persons like Frank Carbo and Blinky Palermo.

FOUR

TROUBLE EARLY piled on trouble for the International Boxing Club. While there was hidden prosperity, there was also overt difficulty. Norris gave the impression of devotion to principle in public while embracing expediency behind the scenes. In the beginning this was made necessary by circumstances developing from events that had happened before Norris ascended the boxing throne.

On November 13, 1944, five years before the birth of the International Boxing Club, the Boxing Managers' Guild of New York was incorporated under the laws of the State of New York. Its certificate of incorporation granted it the usual rights pertaining to a social club and, in addition, permitted it to accept voluntary contributions by gifts, devise, or otherwise, and to use such funds for the assistance of any of its needy members. In fact, however, the Boxing Managers' Guild was a trade organization.

By guile, Mike Jacobs had caused to be inserted in the official New York State boxing contract a clause which granted to the promoter all rights to radio and television revenues. It said:

> The club and its licensees have the exclusive right to broadcast said bout by means of radio broadcasting, on a commercial or sustaining basis, and the exclusive right to transmit by means of television, on a commercial or sustaining basis, pictures of said bout, the contestants and ring officials, and the right to use the names, photograph and likeness of said contestants in conjunction with any publicity campaign relating to any broadcast, sight and/or sound of said bout.

This clause was a bone in the collective throat of members of the Boxing Managers' Guild. In its early days, the organization was militant in behalf of their rights and proceeded to force Jacobs to agree to pay each main-event fighter, at Madison Square Garden or wherever the Friday night TV bouts took place, $186.60 from the radio and television proceeds. This was a pittance compared with the sums to be derived from the televising of boxing later, but it was at the time in fair ratio with Jacobs' proceeds from television.

The Guild quickly decided that the fee they had settled upon with the 20th Century Sporting Club was too small; the membership voted to "strike" and refused to permit fighters to work in Madison Square Garden. Strauss, the 20th Century's lawyer, went to the law, and the Attorney General of the State of New York expressed the opinion that the Guild was acting illegally:

> A membership corporation composed of licensed boxing managers may not be licensed as a manager . . . and has no authority to negotiate as to terms upon which boxers will appear or restrict right of licensed managers to do so.

Despite this ruling, the 20th Century Sporting Club agreed, as of June 4, 1948, to raise the television fee for each fighter to $212.05.

Of course, this sum was in addition to a fighter's purse based on his percentage of the net receipts from the sale of tickets at the box office.

Thus, when Norris came into the Garden with the International Boxing Club in September, 1949, he was presented with a new demand by the Boxing Managers' Guild. This time he settled for a fee of $1,000 for each main-event fighter, which was consistent with the $18,500 rights' fee paid by the television sponsor, the Gillette Safety Razor Company.

This agreement was in effect until July 12, 1950, and encompassed all bouts except championship matches, for which separate agreements were made on a richer basis.

In the spring of 1950 Al Weill signed Jake LaMotta to fight Rocky Graziano for the world's middleweight championship at the Polo Grounds on June 28. There were snickers all around. LaMotta and Graziano were old reform-school buddies. Graziano often visited LaMotta at the champion's home at 994 Neil Avenue in the Bronx. Furthermore, LaMotta was under the influence of Carbo, while Coco owned a "piece" of Graziano. It was a family affair.

Fight managers insisted the bout would not come off because the Guild was about to "strike" in support of its demands for more TV revenue from the International Boxing Club.

On May 12, 1950, Norris wrote a letter to General Kilpatrick. It said, in part:

> During the past year I have worked without salary as President of the International Boxing Club in an endeavor to get boxing back on a profitable basis. The March results are the first encouraging signs. The IBC made a profit of $52,000 in March and the Garden a direct profit from boxing of $43,000. [Three big money bouts: Charley Fusari vs. Jimmy Flood, Rocky Marciano vs. Roland LaStarza, and Graziano vs. Tony Janiro had taken place in the Garden in March.] Naturally my primary interest is in making boxing a profitable venture for the IBC, for our Chicago-Detroit and St. Louis interests, as well as for Madison Square Garden in which our interest is considerable. I am not in favor of giving up to the boxers or to the managers one more dollar than is absolutely essential. If we could keep all of the television and radio income I would favor it, but a care-

ful study of the facts and rather extensive experience in the boxing field convinces me that this is impossible.

Our agreement with the Boxing Managers' Guild with reference to the division of television revenue expires the 31st of this month, and I have been working with them for some time to arrive at an acceptable basis of agreement which would permit the Garden and the IBC to enter into commitments with Gillette and NBC for Friday night fights, and Pabst and CBS for the Tuesday or Wednesday night shows . . . A strike of the boxing managers with its resultant disruption of our relations with major sponsors would be most unfortunate.

While the television receipts for each Friday night bout at the Garden during the first year of the IBC's operation came to only $7,500, the Pabst Brewing Company, sponsor of the Wednesday night bouts of the IBC of Illinois on CBS, was paying $16,666.67 for each bout. Later, in 1950, there was a revision of the contract which called for payments by Pabst of only $4,000 for each fight, with an additional $5,000 going to the Stadium Corporation, which owned the leases on the Chicago Stadium and other stadiums in which the Wednesday night bouts were held.

At any rate, Norris was saguine about the outcome of his negotiations with the Boxing Managers Guild. Then, suddenly, he received word that Graziano had been injured in training; the bout with LaMotta was off. Norris, in trouble, summoned Carbo to a war council.

"It looks like a strike," Norris said.

"What'cha worrin' about? I'll take care of it."

"What'll you do?"

"Leave it to me."

Carbo was working both sides of the street.

FIVE

THE LEADERSHIP of the Boxing Managers' Guild was cabalistic. While seeming democracy prevailed under the presidency of Charles Brooks Johnston, a brother of Jimmy Johnston, who had been ousted as promoter of boxing in Madison Square Garden by the advent of the 20th Century Sporting Club, policy in the lodge actually was made in secret. Carbo's stooges were numerous, and the membership did his bidding.

Thus, Carbo ordered the Guild to hold out against Norris. At the same time, he made certain that the International Boxing Club should show its strength by promoting a nontelevised bout at Madison Square Garden. LaMotta, as usual, was Carbo's and Norris's ace in the hole. In apparent defiance of the Guild, the middleweight champion agreed to fight Tiberio Mitri, of Italy, in the Garden on July 12, 1950. Every seat in the Garden was filled, and the gross receipts came to $99,841. LaMotta retained his title by getting the decision after fifteen rounds.

A few weeks later, the Guild and Norris reached an agreement. Each main-event fighter at the Garden would receive $2,250 as his share of the television proceeds. Carbo sauntered up Broadway wearing a bifurcated smile.

The next year, the Guild was back for more swag from the television receipts. This time Norris granted them $3,000 for each Garden main-eventer on Friday nights. The fee for main-event fighters on the Wednesday night TV shows promoted by the IBC of Illinois on CBS came to $1,500. By now, the IBC of New York also had a Monday night TV series at the St. Nicholas Arena in New York City. Each main-event boxer in this series was paid $570 from the television revenue.

Norris was not satisfied with the situation. His memorandum to General Kilpatrick had stated his position clearly. "If we could keep all of the television and radio income, I would favor it," he had written, "but a careful study of the facts and a rather extensive experience in the boxing field convinces me that this is impossible."

A new approach was needed. Norris was quite willing to do business with Carbo. Obviously, Carbo could control the Guild, but was it worth the trouble and the cost? Norris decided to take another tack. This time he did not go to Carbo, but went instead to Jack ("Doc") Kearns, a legendary figure in the prize-fight business who had, according to John Lardner, a great "ability to make money in large, bold scoops without recourse to day labor."

Kearns managed Jack Dempsey when the "Manassa Mauler" was the world's heavyweight champion and, later, he also handled Mickey Walker, a middleweight champion; Joey Maxim, a light-heavyweight champion who was noted for his punchless devotion to peace; and Archie Moore, who won the light-heavyweight title from Maxim and then, quaintly, turned up in Kearns' stable.

Kearns was a dapper figure who earned perhaps $10 million in boxing and cleansed himself of the gold dust almost as quickly as it came in by an almost religious addiction to pleasure. By the time Norris came to know Kearns intimately, Kearns was almost seventy and virtually broke. He was still rich in charm and cunning, and Norris put this to work. Eventually, the International Boxing Club would pay Kearns $137,000 for his work, but in 1951 Norris was desperate and in need of a cushion against Carbo's strangling power. Kearns was hired to break the Guild. He did it by a simple device— subversion by charm. One of his allies was "Honest Bill" Daly, the same man who had been present in the Park Arena in the Bronx the night Carbo and Palermo had talked to LaMotta about the fight with Billy Fox.

Charley Johnston was another ally in Kearns's campaign, a most important crony because of his leadership in the Boxing Managers' Guild. With Kearns making the bullets and Daly firing them, the Guild was soon torn by dissension. There were 135 members in the Guild. Most of them were hard pressed to make a living because the main-event fighters usually were in the hands of just a few members. It was a simple task to set the "rich" managers against the "broke" managers.

The Guild headquarters was located in an old loft building a few doors from Stillman's gym on Eighth Avenue in New York City.

Meetings were conducted most informally, without recourse to parliamentary procedure, and it was easy for Johnston and his claque to control the routine of business.

In the spring of 1952, dissension broke out in the ranks. A member named Jimmy DeAngelo stood up at a meeting and proposed that the $30,000 in the treasury be split up in equal shares for distribution among the membership. Unthinking and avid at once, the members quickly accepted the suggestion. By the time each member received a "bonus" of $200, only $3,000 remained in the Guild's defense fund. Weakened and at the mercy of the plotters, the Guild was storm-tossed. There was talk of defections.

On April 13, 1952, a meeting of the Guild was held. Johnston was in the chair. Without warning he lay down his gavel and left the meeting room. A few days later, in Chicago, boxing managers from all over the country assembled to organize a new national organization. It was called the International Boxing Guild; Charley Johnston was elected president. Its New York arm was called the New York Boxing Guild, to distinguish it from the old Boxing Managers' Guild.

For a time, the Boxing Managers' Guild struggled to stay in business. It was hopeless. There was an exodus from the first organization to the new group. Those diehards who chose to stay with the original group found themselves unable to get work for their fighters in Madison Square Garden or elsewhere. Widespread boycotting was practiced.

Finally, Christenberry ordered an investigation. A series of hearings were held by the New York State Athletic Commission. Lies were commonplace. Christenberry did not know whether to laugh in public or cry in despair. George Gainford, the discoverer of Sugar Ray Robinson, testified concerning a "peace" meeting arranged by Norris between the original guild and the new guild.

He told how Johnston, in a moment of anger, shouted that there could not be peace between the two guilds because members of the original group had been writing letters to the District Attorney concerning the activities of the newly-organized guild.

"If I opened up," Johnston was quoted as saying, "all you guys would be in jail."

Christenberry threw up his hands. The investigation, he said, was "temporarily postponed because of confusing testimony."

The old guild struggled on, but its fate was inevitable. Resignations were a daily routine. Within a few months it was gone from the boxing scene. Norris had accomplished his purpose; he now had a "friendly" union with which to deal. The pattern of monopoly was abundantly clear.

SIX

THE INTERNATIONAL BOXING CLUB's monopolistic practices had not gone unnoticed. By 1951, it offered televised bouts on three nights each week, a minor network show Monday nights from the St. Nicholas Arena in New York City, a Wednesday night bout on CBS under the promotion of the IBC of Illinois, and a Friday night bout on NBC under the promotion of the IBC of New York.

Small clubs were being driven out of business. New York City had once had a boxing show on each night of the week. In time only one club, the Eastern Parkway Arena, survived Norris's steamroller. Monopoly foredoomed competition.

In Seattle, a lean, dyspeptic fight manager named Jack Hurley watched and waited. Once, years before, he had been associated with Norris, first in the management of Lem Franklin, a hard-hitting heavyweight, and later in the promotion of boxing at the Chicago Stadium in partnership with Irving Schoenwald and Jack Begun, the pair of entrepreneurs who had promoted Graziano's bout with Zale in Chicago.

By now, Hurley was in the possession of a new, chalk-skinned fighter called Harry ("Kid") Matthews, an Idaho-born light-heavyweight who was living in Seattle. Matthews had been around for years before serving in the U.S. Army during 1944 and 1945 and had failed to distinguish himself as a premier ring athlete.

Soon after his discharge from the service Matthews came under the wing of Hurley, who was regarded as a peerless teacher of ring craft. Hurley called Matthews "my athlete" and insisted his boy could become the world light-heavyweight champion if the title holder, Joey Maxim, would give him the opportunity.

"We will never get the chance," Hurley told Royal Brougham, sports editor of the Seattle *Post-Intelligencer,* "because Jim Norris and those people run a nice little store and monopolize everything."

Norris scoffed at Hurley as a sour ball who had provoked trouble wherever he had gone. Norris did say that he was curious about Matthews' ability as a fighter and would like to find out whether Hurley's "athlete" really was as good as his impressive record indicated.

In Seattle, Hurley kept up a steady stream of invective against Norris and the International Boxing Club. He chided Norris for hiring Weill as his matchmaker and pointed out that Weill was breaking boxing law by managing Marciano while serving as the IBC's matchmaker.

In August, 1951, Senator Harry P. Cain, a Republican from the State of Washington, arose in Congress and demanded that the Senate launch an investigation of the IBC. He was joined by another Republican, Senator Herman Welker of Idaho, the state of Matthews' nativity.

The IBC, Senator Welker asserted, "is a closed corporation which governs and controls the professional boxing business in most every major city of the United States. It has nearly a wide-open field in the handling of championship bouts. And as a result of the monopoly it exercises over contestants, promoters, and managers, the boxing profession has reached a new low, to a point where it is ruined in the eyes of most of the American people."

The outcry reached the ears of Attorney General Howard McGrath, who ordered a special assistant, Melville C. Williams, to launch a grand jury investigation in New York City. By October, the grand jury was hearing testimony on the monopoly aspects of the IBC. Nothing came of it, apart from a sudden outbreak of sensitivity in the IBC, which asked Kearns whether he would permit Maxim to defend his light-heavyweight title against Matthews.

Kearns jumped into the breach. Without disclosing that his "undercover" partner in the management of Maxim was a Chicago bookmaker named Salvatore Morelli, Kearns sent a telegram to

Senator Cain offering to match his tiger with Hurley's "athlete" for the world light-heavyweight championship.

"It is rare in boxing," Kearns telegraphed the Senator, "for the champion to appear in the role of a virtual challenger, and I go back to the days of the incomparable Jack Dempsey, whom I had the delightful pleasure to manage."

Kearns said the telegram was authorization for a public announcement of Maxim's willingness to meet Matthews for the championship.

When word of Kearns' offer was relayed to Hurley by Senator Cain, Matthews' manager rejected the match. Senator Cain was outraged and announced publicly that he had changed his mind about asking the Senate to investigate the IBC.

"Last August," the Senator said, "Senator Welker and I and others urged the Senate to investigate the International Boxing Club's being a monopoly and refusing legitimate challengers an opportunity to fight for the light-heavyweight crown.

"We were serious in believing that Kid Matthews was being discriminated against. We sought to establish this contention as being fact.

"Our intention became effective and the International Boxing Club, through Al Weill, its matchmaker, offered recently to have Matthews fight the champion on Washington's Birthday. The IBC offered 20 per cent, or a higher figure than challengers usually get.

"This offer was turned down by Hurley, but I have never read his stated reasons for rejection. . . . In a word, Senator Welker and I sought a title fight and opportunity for Kid Matthews. Unless he agrees to terms, Welker and I must withdraw our resolution, which has already served one of its major purposes, and advise the Senate publicly that the IBC has offered a title bout which Hurley has turned down."

Now, Hurley was on a spot. So were Norris and the International Boxing Club. Senator Cain's outcry against the IBC had set in motion a federal grand jury investigation. The effects of this inquiry were pinpointed in the reaction of the sponsors of the IBC's televised bouts. They didn't like it, and nobody knew this better than Norris.

In such situations, Norris always reacted like a boy caught with his hand in the jam pot. He sought an easy way out and hit upon a simple plan: why couldn't Matthews be matched to fight Marciano? The winner would then be sent into the ring with Jersey Joe Walcott, who had surprisingly won the world heavyweight championship by knocking out Ezzard Charles in July, 1951.

Norris asked Weill to permit Marciano to fight Matthews. Marciano was unbeaten and untied, and a meeting with Matthews gave every promise of being profitable.

"Let's put Marciano in with Matthews," Norris suggested to Weill.

"Not me. I don't want it."

"We need the match, Al, because it's one way to get Hurley out of our hair. He's causing us all kinds of congressional pressure. Let's put the guy on the spot and find out if Matthews can fight."

"Get somebody else," Weill said sneeringly.

Norris persisted in his request. He talked to Weill many times, but each conversation produced the same reaction. Norris expressed the opinion that Matthews wasn't much of a fighter and that his record was meaningless because it was the result of a mere build-up.

Finally, Norris took a course he had taken before and would take frequently in the future; he appealed to Carbo for help.

"Talk to Al," he told Carbo, "and see what you can do."

Carbo exercised his sway over Weill. A few days later, Norris's matchmaker came into the promoter's office and said, "I'll take the match. If I hadn't talked to certain people, I would never have taken that match for you."

"Certain people" meant Carbo.

Norris expected a bonanza from the bout. It was, at the time, a "hot" match, as much because Marciano was unbeaten as because of the build-up of Matthews by Hurley.

"We can get a lot of money for the TV rights," Norris told Hurley.

"No television," Hurley said. "You've ruined the game with TV, now you want to ruin my fighter with it. We'll draw half a million dollars without it."

"I don't agree with you," Norris said.

"I tell you if we don't have TV we'll draw 5,000 people from Seattle alone."

There was no television.

The weigh-in for the bout was held at noon on July 28, 1952, in the lobby of Madison Square Garden. Marciano arrived early and was quickly ready to step on the scales. Matthews was late.

"Where's Matthews?" Christenberry asked Weill.

"How should I know. All I know is my fighter's here."

It was a slip of the lip. Weill had openly confessed to the Chairman of the New York State Athletic Commission that he was the *de facto* if not the *de jure* manager of Marciano.

Some minutes later, Matthews arrived at the Garden for the weigh-in, which went off without further hitch.

That afternoon Harry Markson was summoned to Christenberry's office.

"Harry, I'm telling you this straight. I'm giving Norris twenty-four hours to get a new matchmaker. Weill must go. The masquerade is over. If you don't have his resignation by tomorrow at this time I will lift the IBC's license."

Markson rushed back to the Garden and informed Norris of the ultimatum.

"He's got to go," Norris said, not without a measure of pleasure. By now he was tired of Weill, who had too much cheek for him. "Call him in."

Weill got the word and handed in his resignation. That night, before a rather small crowd of 31,189 fans at Yankee Stadium, Marciano toyed with Matthews and knocked him out in the second round. Hurley's "athlete" was a cipher.

The next day Weill was through as Norris's matchmaker.

SEVEN

DOMINICK MORDINI, alias Billy Brown, was tapped as the new matchmaker of the International Boxing Club. This was a triumph for Carbo, who, according to Norris, would "have considerable influence on Billy Brown." For the next six years, Carbo exerted this influence to a degree unsuspected by even the most cynical observer of the boxing scene.

Brown had considerable experience in boxing. He had been the matchmaker and promoter at the Star Casino, an arena in Spanish Harlem, and had run fights at the New York Coliseum in the Bronx. In between his stints as a matchmaker and promoter, he had been "connected" with Marty Krompier, a member of the Dutch Schultz gang, in the management of Nathan Mann, a heavyweight from Connecticut who had fought Louis for the world's title in 1938.

Obviously, Brown did not hold conferences with Carbo in the International Boxing Club's offices in the Garden. The telephone was his ally. He would make calls to Carbo from public telephone booths in various shops in and around the Garden. In time, all these phones would be tapped by the police, but in the beginning Brown used them with impunity.

Managers allied with Carbo would telephone Brown at the IBC and relay messages. Their deviousness did not run deep. They began referring to Carbo as "Mr. Gray," "Uncle," "Ambassador," "Southern Salesman," "Traveling Salesman," "The Cousin," "Our Friend," "The Man." The wire tappers quickly saw through this shallow device.

Weill had been a "strong man" in his role as Norris's matchmaker; Norris described Brown as "a much smaller person than Weill." Weill also owned and operated Marciano, who was to become the world heavyweight champion; Brown had never managed a top-notch fighter. The new matchmaker fitted Carbo's purposes exactly, although he had not been hard-pressed to exert his influence over Weill. After all, Carbo was a friend of the boss.

The year before Billy Brown's appointment as matchmaker, Carbo had exerted enough influence to get a title match for Jimmy Carter, a lightweight from the Bronx, with Ike Williams, the world champion. This did not take much doing: Williams was managed by Blinky Palermo.

At the time, Carter was less than the leading challenger. Two months before going into the Garden ring with Williams, he had been beaten by Percy Bassett, a Philadelphian managed by Mike ("Bananas") Sokoloff. He had also lost a decision in ten rounds to Calvin Smith earlier in the year.

Bassett's case makes a point. Sokoloff was not one of the boys. He regarded Palermo with contempt and did not hold hands with Carbo. His fighter suffered. Bassett should have been matched for the world featherweight championship—he could make the 126-pound limit in that class—but he was forestalled by Carbo's trickery, which forced him into a bout with Teddy ("Red Top") Davis, a wily competitor. When he lost the decision, Bassett was denied a chance to fight for Sandy Saddler's featherweight crown.

Carter suffered no such dismay. He was managed by Willie ("Ketchum") Friedland, a disciple of Carbo, and despite defeat he moved right into a bout with Williams for the 135-pound, or lightweight, championship. Williams was the favorite to rebuff Carter's challenge when they met at Madison Square Garden, May 25, 1951.

Williams had been subjected to bribe offers before the two bouts preceding the one with Carter. On December 5, 1949, he met and defeated Freddie Dawson in a title bout in Philadelphia. Some days before the match, Palermo came to Williams and told him of a $30,000 offer to throw the fight.

"If it was me, I wouldn't take it," Williams quoted Palermo as saying.

Williams didn't.

The night of the bout with Dawson, Williams was visited in his dressing room by a friend and neighbor of his from Trenton, New Jersey, a man named Bill Keller.

"Ike," Keller said, "they are going to take the fight from you."

Williams did not consult with Palermo, who was his manager. Instead, he summoned his seconds, Jesse Goss and Calvin Taylor.

"I called a quick symposium," Williams said later. "I told Calvin Taylor, 'Go down and get the sports writers.' "

Two prominent reporters came to his room. They were Red Smith, now regarded as America's finest sports columnist but then locally respected for his daily contribution to the *Record*, and John Webster, of the *Philadelphia Inquirer*.

Williams told Smith and Webster, "After the fight tonight, come back, I have a story for you."

The way it turned out, there was nothing to tell Smith and Webster. Williams won the bout and received the decision.

Some days later, Williams was fined $500 by the Pennsylvania State Athletic Commission on a charge of casting doubt on the honesty of the ringside officials. It was not his first experience with bribe offers.

Earlier in 1949, before Williams' bout with Kid Gavilan in Madison Square Garden, Williams was told by Palermo that he could make $100,000 simply by throwing the fight to Gavilan. He rejected the offer. Gavilan won the decision after ten rounds.

"I'm sorry I didn't take it," Williams said later. "I lost the fight anyway, although I thought I won it. Most of the New York papers gave me the fight.

By the time Williams returned to the Garden, against Carter two years later, the price had gone down. Instead of being offered $100,-000, as was the case in the Gavilan bout, only $50,000 was dangled before his eyes. The offer was delivered by Palermo.

"I'd pass it up," Palermo told him, according to Williams. "I wouldn't take it."

Carter knocked out Williams in the fourteenth round, and the loser blamed his defeat on a shoulder injury. "I should have taken the money," he said.

Carter was less than a stalwart as champion, and Carbo, who shared in the management of the new champion, had difficulty maintaining control of the lightweight title. Within a year Carter lost the title to Lauro Salas, a Mexican, and then regained it. Carbo was determined to get rid of him.

One afternoon, Norris summoned Markson to his inner office in the Garden.

"Ever hear of Joe Brown?" Norris said.

"Sure, Jim, he's just an ordinary fighter."

"Well, he's going to be the next world lightweight champ."

"No, Jim. He can't be; he's not good enough."

"He will."

"Listen, there's a kid up in Providence called George Araujo who deserves a shot faster than Brown."

"Don't want him," Norris said. "Brown'll be the next champ."

At the time, Brown had just come under the sway of Lou Viscusi, a large, saturnine man who took his orders from Carbo.

Markson pressed this point regarding Araujo vs. Brown. Finally, the two were matched, at the St. Nicholas Arena on October 10, 1952. Araujo knocked Brown out in the seventh round. Carbo's plot, and Norris's cooperation, had failed.

Not long afterward, Norris again summoned Markson.

"How do you get along with Sammy Richman?"

"Okay if I have to," Markson said, "though he was difficult when he was in with Burston on Cerdan."

"You'll have to get along with him now," Norris said. "He's just become co-manager of Araujo."

Richman was Carbo-controlled, to put it nicely, and had been put in as the partner of Frank Travis, Araujo's manager, as protector of "Mr. Gray's" interest.

Six months later Araujo fought Carter for the lightweight championship in Madison Square Garden. By the end of the twelfth round, Carter had established a considerable lead. Araujo needed a knockout to win.

He came out slugging in the thirteenth round and scored effectively to the head. Carter withstood the assault and came back with a right to the jaw over a left lead. Araujo went down. The fight ended at two minutes and sixteen seconds of the thirteenth round. It didn't matter. Carbo was still the winner. He couldn't lose.

EIGHT

NORRIS HAD GRAVE DOUBTS about his conduct in boxing. He was an ambivalent creature torn between a zealous devotion to money and a creeping crypto-ethic that forced him to hate inwardly his association with Carbo and Palermo. In 1951 he suffered a coronary thrombosis and spent seven weeks at the Eastern Long Island Hospital. As a result of the attack he was subject to severe chest pains, or angina pectoris. He also had high blood pressure. Upon his release from the hospital he went to his home in Florida to convalesce. While Norris was recuperating, his father, James Norris, suffered a heart attack and was taken to Passavant Hospital in Chicago. On December 4, 1952, Jim Norris's father died. He would have been seventy-five in six more days.

The father-son relationship had been warm and meaningful, and Norris was shaken by his father's death. His nerves were shot. He broke out in a skin rash and sought relief by man's age-old remedy —scratching. He tore into the top layer of his skin and left blotches on his torso. In public he was charming, as always, and polite, as always, but the cup came to mean more to him by way of solace.

One night, in Miami, he went to Joe's, a restaurant famous for the delicacy of the stone crabs served in abundance. While Norris was dining there with his wife, Walter Winchell came into the restaurant and sat down to talk with Norris.

"I am getting an awful lot of criticism in boxing," Norris told Winchell. "We are doing the best we could. We put our money, our integrity, whatever we had into this. I don't know what to do about it. I have an idea. I don't imagine it will work, but what do you think of it?"

"What is it?" Winchell asked.

"Well, I would be willing to pay Mr. Hoover (J. Edgar Hoover, director of the Federal Bureau of Investigation) $100,000 a year for ten years or a minimum of a million dollars to take over and run the IBC. He's the only man in the world that would regain the confidence of the public, the newspapermen, and the integrity of boxing."

"Aw, I don't think so," Winchell said.

"Well, would you do me a favor? Would you ask him? Would you see if he's interested?"

"I will do that for you," Winchell said.

Joe Weiss, the owner of the restaurant, was summoned.

"Can we make a phone call?" Norris asked.

In Weiss's office, Winchell put in a call to J. Edgar Hoover in Washington. Winchell said, "I'm here with Jim Norris. He had some ideas. I told him I didn't think you would be interested in it, but he has said that he knows you are a dedicated man, and he would like to give it a try."

Mr. Hoover prodded Winchell for an explanation.

"Mr. Norris would like to pay you $100,000 a year for a minimum of ten years to run the International Boxing Club," Winchell said.

"I would not be interested," Mr. Hoover said.

"That was what I thought would be your answer," Winchell said, "but I wanted to give Jim the satisfaction of having made the attempt."

Winchell said good-bye and hung up. He turned to Norris and said, "Just as I thought. It is a lot more money than he makes with the government, but he has got a job to do and he is a very dedicated man. Mr. Hoover asked me to tell you that the next time you are in Washington give him a ring and come and have luncheon with him."

Some time later, when Norris had returned to New York, he discussed the episode with Gibson and Markson. It was decided that a formal offer should be put into a telegram to Mr. Hoover. The reply was the same; Mr. Hoover rejected the offer.

In one way or another, the offer to Mr. Hoover and his rejection of it reached the ears of newspaper reporters. They printed stories about it.

"I was not very popular with Mr. Carbo or anybody else for quite a period of time after the newspapermen printed that story," Norris said years later.

NINE

ROCKY MARCIANO won the heavyweight championship from Jersey Joe Walcott at Municipal Stadium, Philadelphia, on September 23, 1952. It was, as A. J. Liebling had described it, "one of the stubbornest matches ever fought by heavyweights." Marciano weighed 184 pounds, twelve pounds less than Walcott.

Walcott surprised everybody, especially Marciano, by moving forward to attack, instead of circling, and within one minute of the start of the bout he hit the challenger so hard with a left hook to the jaw that Marciano went down. The count went to three, and when Marciano once again faced the champion he was hard-pressed to last out the round.

The second round brought more travail for Marciano, but in the third round he began pressing Walcott back with blows that hurt wherever they landed—the top of the head, the body, and the jaw. By the sixth round a strong tide was running for Marciano. There was blood all over the gladiators: Walcott's from a cut over his left eye, Marciano's from an improbable scalp wound.

Now Marciano changed tactics. He pressed in and fought at close quarters. Suddenly, he seemed to be in trouble, groping for a rope for support. He hadn't been hit, and the precipitate change in his condition was unaccountable until later, when Weill, who worked in Marciano's corner, charged that Walcott's seconds had used a liniment laced with a solution of pepper on the champion's torso. Apparently, some of the liniment had been rubbed into Marciano's eyes when he had pressed his head against Walcott's chest in the sixth round.

Walcott was in command throughout the eighth round, but in the ninth Marciano took over and belabored the old champion. It had been expected that Walcott, who was at least thirty-eight years of age, would collapse under a pressing assault by Marciano, who was nine years younger, but it didn't happen. Walcott was still fresh, still fighting formfully, still giving as well as taking.

In the next two rounds, Walcott added to his lead, and the 40,379 persons huddled in the closed end of the horseshoe-shaped arena were at the edges of their seats. Coming out for the thirteenth round, Walcott appeared fresher than the challenger, but instead of moving forward Walcott went back toward the ropes for a moment. Marciano started a smashing right to the jaw. It caught Walcott squarely, and as the old champion started to fall Marciano came through with a grazing left to the side of the head that was vivid but not nearly as contributory to Walcott's downfall as the short right which had preceded it. The fight was over after forty-three seconds of the thirteenth round.

Now Marciano was the champion, apparently the master of his fate. In fact, he was not. Walcott had a contract for a return bout, and Norris was eager to put it on because the first fight had been so exciting that there was anticipation of great profit from the second meeting.

Unexpectedly, Norris encountered difficulty. Felix Bocchicchio of Camden, New Jersey, Walcott's manager, was, according to Norris, "dragging his feet." Bocchicchio was a former convict whose police record was formidable. He could be both stubborn and irascible, and in this instance he was manifesting the worst side of his personality.

Bocchicchio attended a series of conferences with Norris at Madison Square Garden, but each meeting was fruitless. "He was just making it difficult," Norris said.

Finally, Bocchicchio came storming into Norris's office one day, accompanied by a lawyer. He was, according to Norris, "quite surly."

Bocchicchio said quickly, "Well, they put a lot of pressure on me. I guess I have to go through with the match."

Norris was pleased, and he made what he later described as a "very foolish deal" with Bocchicchio, who extracted from Norris a guaranty of $250,000 for Walcott, who had received only $188,070 the night he lost the title to Marciano.

Norris pledged Bocchicchio to secrecy because he did not want Weill to know of the enormous guaranty. Marciano, after all, was working for a percentage of the gate and radio and TV receipts.

Then Norris went out and sold the television and radio rights to the bout to the Gillette Safety Razor Company for $300,000.

The fight was held at the Chicago Stadium on May 15, 1953. It was a travesty. Walcott came out and flicked a jab or two at Marciano as he backed away. The champion chased the former champion and threw a few tentative rights which did not reach their mark. They wrestled around for a time, then Marciano threw a left hook, followed by a rather ineffective right, and Walcott was on the floor. There were 16,034 persons in the hall and not one of them dared believe that Walcott would stay down for the count. He did, taking it with his right arm dangling over the middle rope, half-smiling. The moment Referee Frank Sikora reached the count of ten, Walcott arose and took a walk to the other side of the ring. The customers let out a roar of derision. Walcott was suddenly outraged. He stamped around the ring and charged that he had been given a fast count. It was all over. Walcott took his $250,000 and went back to New Jersey; Marciano's purse came to $166,030.60. The champion had been shortchanged.

"Norris did that to me," Weill charged. "He took advantage of me."

The old professionals in boxing laughed. They had often seen Weill get the better of promoters when he was a manager and of managers when he was a matchmaker. Carbo laughed loudest of all. It was he who had set up the deal for Bocchicchio.

TEN

B Y NOW, Norris's control of boxing was towering and total, and though it would take half a dozen more years to tear it down, the destructive processes had already begun.

On March 17, 1952, the Department of Justice filed a suit in the United States District Court in New York City charging the IBC of New York, the IBC of Illinois, and Madison Square Garden with "conspiring to restrain and monopolize the promotion and broad-casting of professional championship boxing in the United States."

Undaunted by the shadow of federal law, Norris went right on with his business. He held all the weapons and appeared impregnable to assault by writ or competition. He controlled the activities of every champion. Those fighters that he did not control by contract he held in financial bondage, because the IBC alone was in a position to promote important matches. And, through the International Boxing Guild, he controlled the managers.

Just one year after the federal government filed its suit against Norris, the International Boxing Guild held a convention at the Hotel Edison in New York City. Delegates from all over the country attended the meeting and spoke out against the horrors of Norris's control of boxing. They were, for the most part, innocent of the deviousness of their leadership and believed each spoken word as they would the truth of the Gospels.

At the time, Norris was paying each main-event fighter $3,600 from the television proceeds, in accordance with an agreement in effect since September 1, 1952.

At the convention, Bill Daly rose and assailed Norris as an enemy of managers and fighters. He demanded an increase in the fees to be paid main-event fighters and shouted, "Any member who lets his boxer fight for less than a $5,000 television minimum should be kicked out of the Guild and boycotted."

George Parnassus was a delegate from California. He had been the manager of Ceferino Garcia, who had once held the world middleweight championship, and he naïvely was concerned with the welfare of fighters.

He was an "outsider" with whom the IBC did little business, although in later years he would become the Los Angeles matchmaker of bouts televised by Norris's organizations. In 1953, however, he was militantly anti-Norris and was not afraid to say so. "The IBC with its television Monday night, Wednesday night, Friday night," he shouted, "has hurt us more than anything. Take a fighter, he used to fight twenty times a year; now he is lucky to fight half a dozen times a year. They're ruining us, so make them pay."

Daly was the secretary-treasurer of the Guild, but Jack Kearns, who had been a leader in its foundation, held no office. He did not need a portfolio to control the organization. His influence was implied but effective, devious but rewarding, silent but heard. He had Daly and Johnston, the president, under his thumb.

Despite all the threats of strike heard at the Guild meeting, the IBC was not required to pay $5,000 to each main-eventer from the TV proceeds. Norris settled for a payment of $4,000, starting on September 1, 1953, an increase of only $400 from the previous scale.

In New York, Norris's IBC was watched over carefully by the Madison Square Garden which was a public corporation. Television fees paid by the Gillette Safety Razor Company went directly to the IBC of New York, which in turn paid Madison Square Garden. Although Norris and Wirtz held a considerable number of shares in the Garden, neither was yet in full control of the arena; both had to submit to the thinking of a board of directors. In Chicago, it was another story. The Chicago Stadium, which owned the IBC of Illinois, was wholly owned by Norris and Wirtz. They were their own bosses. They could regulate the flow of money from television receipts in any way they wanted to, in accord with their own interests.

Wirtz, according to Norris, was an arch conceiver of multiple corporations in a pattern so bewildering that not even Norris knew the "myriad of companies" used to control the flow of television money into the IBC of Illinois.

One of the companies organized by Wirtz was Telradio Promotions, Inc., which was used to funnel television money to the Nevill Advertising Agency, a wholly-owned subsidary of the Wirnor Corporation, of which Wirtz and Norris were the sole owners.

On September 24, 1953, just three weeks after the start of the agreement between the Guild and the IBC for the payment of $4,000 to main-event fighters appearing on television, a check for $5,833 was drawn in the name of William P. Daly by Telradio Productions, Inc., still another company owned by Norris and Wirtz.

Apparently there was a change of signals. The check made out to Daly was voided, and another check, dated the same day and in the same amount, $5,833, was drawn on Telradio Productions, Inc., in Kearns' name. Thereafter, Telradio Promotions, Inc. was to issue checks amounting to some $142,000 to Kearns. The money was paid to Kearns, Norris said later, to "ease certain problems with managers" and to smooth the way for an accommodation with the Guild.

A year after the first check was drawn to Daly's credit and canceled, a check for $6,000 was drawn on the account of Telradio Promotions, Inc. in the name of Tex Pelte. Pelte was one of Daly's hired hands and later would be involved as a go-between in the payment of $5,000 to Carbo by a Denver promoter who needed Carbo's approval before he could promote a world lightweight championship bout in the "Mile High" City.

Kearns and Daly were obviously prosperous. Others sought to lay velvet in *their* wallets. In Brooklyn, a dress manufacturer named Emil Lence owned a converted garage called the Eastern Parkway Arena. While it was devoted largely to roller-skating, the arena was a likely place for the presentation of boxing bouts. Lence was a diminutive figure, but he knew his way around. He had, as they say in the underworld, enough "muscle" to withstand subversion by Norris's cohorts and proceeded to get a contract with the old Dumont Broadcasting Company for the televising of bouts on Monday nights.

Although Lence's bouts were televised on a smaller network, with a consequent smaller fee of $8,000 weekly, he was ordered by the Guild to pay $2,900 to each main-eventer appearing on television. At the same time, Norris was paying only $4,000 to main-eventers at Madison Square Garden, although the sponsor was paying about $22,500 each week. When Lence moved his fights to another network, his television receipts rose from $8,000 to $12,000 weekly. By this time, the Guild was operating a series of its own TV bouts at the St. Nicholas Arena on Monday nights. These fights were telecast by Dumont, which had been forced out of Lence's arena. Opportunistically, the Guild became concerned with decency. An anonymous letter to the New York State Athletic Commission informed Chairman Christenberry that Lence's fee had been raised and that New York State had been done out of taxes. Christenberry ordered a hearing. Lence was fined $1,400, but was permitted to stay in business under another license.

Steve ("Tex") Sullivan, who had been a matchmaker at Madison Square Garden under Mike Jacobs, served as a promotional "front" for the Guild at the St. Nicholas Arena. Main-event fighters there were paid only $2,100 each, according to the Guild's self-protective dictum.

The Guild itself was growing rich by demanding and receiving a tribute of $100 from the manager of each fighter appearing on television, whether or not the manager was a Guild member. "Collectors" were assigned to each arena to make sure the Guild's "fee" was forthcoming. One of the collectors was Constantine ("Cus") D'Amato, the manager of Floyd Patterson. Once, Truman Gibson was in Cleveland at a Wednesday night boxing show. He was given an envelope to bring back to the Guild in New York. He was not aware of its contents. The envelope contained a tribute check in the sum of $100 made out to the Guild.

In the midst of all this, a group of managers who were being kicked around by the Guild organized the Metropolitan Boxing Alliance. These were mostly impoverished managers who could not get work for their fighters in Madison Square Garden or the other arenas controlled by the Guild. They began writing a series of letters to District Attorney Hogan of New York County. His office began a fruitless investigation.

The New York State Athletic Commission also moved into action. Some of the managers submitted affidavits to Chairman Christenberry alleging discrimination and shakedown. Had Sullivan collected tribute of $100 each from nineteen fighters who had appeared in main bouts at the St. Nicholas Arena? He had. The State Athletic Commission fined him $1,000 and ordered the repayment of the money he had collected from each fighter.

Sullivan's corporate name was the London Sporting Club, Inc. The Commission checked the corporation's telephone number against the telephone number of the Boxing Guild of New York. They were the same.

One of those summoned to the hearing was Ray Arcel, a sharp-faced former trainer of fighters. Arcel had worked with outstanding boxers going back to the days of Benny Leonard. He was soft-

spoken and gentle, although the vagaries of the sport had forced
him from time to time to train boxers owned and operated by mobsters.

In 1952 he had organized with two other fight men, Sol Gold and
Dewey Fragetta, a promotional firm that somehow obtained a contract for the televising of bouts Saturday nights. With total unorigi-
nality, these were called the Saturday Night Fights.

The televised bouts were to commence in January, 1953, but just
before each show one of the principals would suddenly ask for a
postponement because of injury or illness. Finally, on February 7,
1953, Arcel's troika was able to present its first Saturday night fight
—Norman Hayes vs. Bobo Olson, in Boston. The dark hand of the
Guild had been removed from Arcel's throat.

It was not until Arcel testified before the New York State Athletic
Commission that the true story was told. Arcel had agreed, under
what form of persuasion he did not say, to contribute $500 weekly
to the Guild. The money was to be delivered to Daly, but when it was
offered by check it was rejected. Finally, $17,000 was laid aside
for the Guild.

Three years later, while testifying in another investigation conducted by the New York State Athletic Commission, Arcel admitted
the $17,000 had finally been passed to the Guild in the form of pay-
ment for advertising in a minimum-circulation magazine started by
the Guild and printed in New Jersey. The magazine's bank account had been opened in the name of Bill Daly.

Ordinary advertisers paid $100 a page for space in the magazine.
Arcel agreed to take three pages per issue at $1,500 per page. By
this method, the $17,000 was collected by the Guild.

One Saturday in September, 1953, Arcel was in Boston for one
of his televised boxing shows. He was standing in the street in front
of the Manger Hotel with Willie ("Ketchum") Friedland, manager
of Jimmy Carter and disciple of Carbo.

In a flash, a thug reached over Ketchum's shoulder and hit Arcel
on the head with a piece of lead pipe wrapped in a brown paper bag.
Arcel slumped to the ground. Ketchum leaned down to help Arcel
up and was joined a moment later by Hal James, an executive of

the Ellington Agency, which represented the advertisers on the Saturday Night Fights' telecasts.

"Let's get him to a hospital," James cried.

"Take me to my room," Arcel insisted.

James and Ketchum helped Arcel to his room. He was semiconscious. He was obviously seriously injured. James finally had his way; Arcel was removed to a hospital where he was questioned by police. He could not identify his assailant. Neither could Ketchum. Some time later, the Saturday night fights went off the air.

ELEVEN

FROM THE INCEPTION of the IBC in 1949 through May of 1953, thirteen heavyweight championship bouts were fought. All were promoted by Norris and his organizations. Three of the four light-heavyweight championship bouts in the same period were put on by Norris and his affiliates. A total of eight middleweight title bouts were fought during the same time, all promoted by Norris. It was the same story of control in the welterweight, lightweight, and featherweight classes. Despite the antitrust action filed by the Department of Justice, the IBC went along blithely extending its monopoly.

The wagging of journalistic tongues did not deter Norris and Wirtz from their course. Gibson, as their secretary of state, went all over the country lining up matches and signing up fighters. Carbo operated almost openly and was frequently seen in Norris's company. Whenever Norris was involved in the promotion of a big bout in Philadelphia, he would set up headquarters at the Essex Hotel, off Broad Street. His suite would be near Carbo's suite, and the occasion was marked almost always by a seeming convention of gangsters from all over the country. Carbo and Palermo were the hosts.

Wherever one went in the vicinity of Norris's headquarters, he came upon a known gangster. One evening in Philadelphia, Norris invited Markson to have dinner with him. Markson went to Norris's suite at the appointed time and found Carbo seated on a bed talking to his boss. Markson turned and left. Norris came running after him.

"Aw, Harry, where are you going?" Norris asked abashedly, like a boy caught in an apple orchard.

"I wish you hadn't asked me here while he's in there."

"He'll be gone soon."

"I'll wait downstairs."

A few minutes later Norris came into the lobby.

"Harry," he said, "you are the most sensitive man I know."

"Jim, I don't want to be in his company."

"I don't like it any better than you do. What am I going to do about it?"

Norris knew he was hooked.

Quickly, however, he learned he was "off the hook" in one sense. In New York, Federal Judge Gregory F. Noonan dismissed the federal government's suit against Norris and Wirtz, the IBC of Illinois, the IBC of New York, and Madison Square Garden. His judgment was based on the opinion that the United States Supreme Court had intended to place all sports outside the Sherman Antitrust Act when it had ruled baseball was not in interstate commerce in the spring of 1953.

Immediately, the Department of Justice entered an appeal, but for the moment Norris was relieved of anxiety. He could go about the business of devouring the boxing business with impunity, at least insofar as the courts were concerned. There was dismay elsewhere for him, and it came from a most unexpected source and in connection with his activities of years ago.

In New York, Henry R. Luce, the proprietary giant of *Time, Life,* and *Fortune* magazines—collectively, Time, Inc.—decided at this time to venture into sports journalism. Putting his hired hands to work, he evolved a format for a magazine to be called *Sports Illustrated*. The first issue was dated August 16, 1954, and its publisher, H. H. S. Phillips, Jr., pledged in a public memorandum that *Sports Illustrated* would, in lower-case type, be accepted as the "essential weekly reporter of the Wonderful World of Sports."

The first issue of the magazine was mindful of boxing. It in-

cluded coverage of Marciano's heavyweight championship defense
against Ezzard Charles at Yankee Stadium and noted in a picture
caption:

> Never before had a challenger remained so pridefully erect to take
> so heavy a pounding; never had the moment of the kill seemed so in-
> cessantly near and yet so elusive; never in modern times had a fifteen-
> round fight for the heavyweight championship of the world been more
> dramatic. That was the first meeting of Ezzard Charles, a superb boxer,
> and Rocky Marciano, the champion whose style is to absorb all the
> power his opponent can produce and then return it double. For five
> rounds Charles maneuvered and boxed and was winning. Then the
> champion shook his head and began to shoulder forward. Although
> he missed his mark more often than he hit it, the results of Marciano's
> blows on the perfectly conditioned body of ex-champion Charles
> amply proved the power of Marciano's rights and lefts. When it was
> over, a battered Ezzard Charles whispered: "I thought I won . . . I
> want him again."

Norris welcomed *Sports Illustrated* as an addition to the ballyhoo
brigade. Some months later he had cause to believe that the new
magazine was not going to cuddle to him in journalistic surrender of
its rights to keep the public informed and entertained in the "Wonderful World of Sports."

On December 13, 1937, Max Schmeling had fought Harry
Thomas, a rugged railroad worker from Eagle Bend, Minnesota, at
Madison Square Garden. At the time, Schmeling was matched to
fight Joe Louis in June, 1938, and the bout with Thomas was regarded as a tune-up.

Two years later, Arch Ward, sports editor of the Chicago *Tribune,*
wrote a story in which he charged that the bout between Schmeling
and Thomas had been "one of the biggest swindles in the history of
boxing."

The Illinois State Athletic Commission conducted an inquiry and
found no evidence to support Ward's allegation. Indeed, along the
way, Attorney General Edwin T. Breen of Illinois, in rejecting the
charge of a "fix," indicated he believed that Thomas was "punch
drunk."

The investigation by the Illinois State Athletic Commission was apparently cursory, and perhaps necessarily so. While Thomas made his confession to Ward in Chicago, the bout with Schmeling had taken place in New York. Illinois had no jurisdiction over the fight. Still, the chairman of the Illinois commission, Joseph Triner, did go to the trouble of asking Mike Jacobs, who had promoted the Schmeling-Thomas bout, for his opinion. On January 4, 1939, thirteen months after the fight had taken place, Promoter Jacobs wrote to Triner:

> Pursuant to contracts duly signed by all the parties, Max Schmeling and Harry Thomas were matched during the month of October, 1937, for a professional boxing contest to a decision at Madison Square Garden in the City of New York on the 13th day of December, 1937, under the auspices of the 20th Century Sporting Club.
>
> The said bout took place on the said 13th day of December, 1937, at Madison Square Garden. According to our records there were 16,857 persons who attended this bout, among which were members of the State Athletic Commission and their staff and representatives of the metropolitan press, as well as many other newspaper reporters representing the various services and out-of-town papers. All the press reports on this bout were highly favorable.
>
> It was the unanimous opinion of every newspaper representative present as well as the opinion of the spectators at said bout that they witnessed a great bout.
>
> Each of the contestants fought honestly. Harry Thomas made a courageous and heroic effort to win. In the eighth round his mouth was bleeding profusely, and the referee stopped the bout while Thomas was still on his feet fighting.
>
> The club paid Thomas precisely the amount of money it was required to pay, pursuant to the State Athletic Commission form of agreement.
>
> There was no irregularity.

On December 13, 1954, on the seventeenth anniversary of the fight between Schmeling and Thomas, *Sports Illustrated* printed Thomas's first person account of the fight.

In the article, Thomas told how he had come under the management of Norris and had signed a contract with him, although Nate Lewis had "fronted" as manager. Thomas continued:

In October of 1937, Nate received a wire from Joe Jacobs (Schmeling's manager) in New York. It said to meet him at a certain room in the Drake Hotel here in Chicago at a certain time. Nate phoned me. I met him at the Clover bar on Clark Street. We took a cab to the Drake.

Nate said, "You wait here, Norris will be here after awhile." I was there quite awhile, then somebody came down to the lobby and said, "Go to such and such a room." When I came in the room, there was Lewis, Norris, and Joe Jacobs, Schmeling's manager. I tossed my hat on the bed. Jacobs grabbed it and yelled, "What's the matter with you, don't you know it's bad luck?"

To me it was a joke. He was really serious.

Norris started talking. He said Jacobs was here to sign me for a fight with Max Schmeling. Jacobs said, "You got that farm up there in Minnesota. You can make more money on this one fight than you could make on that farm the rest of your life."

He said, "You do business with us and you'll be taken care of." I said, "What do you mean, 'do business'?" Then Norris said to me, "You'll have to take a dive, lose the fight by a knockout." I told him, "Jim, I've never been knocked off my feet in my life." He said, "All you got to do is keep going down. You don't have to take counts. Keep getting up and they'll stop it." He said, "I want you to be in good shape, I don't want you to get hurt."

Jacobs said I'd make at least $65,000. He said I and Schmeling could split the gate. They figured they'd fill the Garden. Norris and I were splitting 50-50, so he'd get half of that. We signed the contract there. Part of the deal was that I also was to fight Jimmy Adamick in the Garden in February, and was to carry him for ten rounds. The deal was that I was to lose to Schmeling, carry Adamick, and was to get a shot at Louis, and the Louis fight was to be on the up and up. If I beat Louis I got another shot at Schmeling.

Thomas went on to tell how the contracts for all three bouts were signed and then notarized by Wirtz's secretary at a North Side hotel in Chicago. In the ring with Schmeling, Thomas played rough through the first three rounds. Nate Lewis, who was in his corner, told him, "Take it easy, Harry, you're too rough."

Thomas took a knockdown in the seventh round and then went down several times in the eighth round. The fight was stopped; he wasn't hurt. The next day, according to Thomas's story, the fighter and Lewis went to Norris's hotel in New York:

> They told me to wait in an outer room in a suite. They were in a huddle in an inner room. Joe Jacobs, Nate Lewis, Jim Norris were in there.
> Then Jim Norris came out to me and handed me a bunch of money. Some one-thousand-dollar bills, some hundreds. That was the first thousand-dollar bill I ever saw. I was sitting on the davenport, and he tossed it down to me. I looked at him and said, "Jim, where's all that money we talked about for the fight?" It looked like about one-third.
> Norris said, "That's the pay-off, Harry. What can we do about it?" I took one of those thousand-dollar bills, I want to show it to my folks, they'd never seen one. I think I took six-one-hundred-dollar bills. I told Norris I wanted the rest by check. He gave me a check, I'm not sure how much it was, maybe thirty-two hundred, around there. I think we got a total of $15,000. Expenses were about one-third, and Norris and I split the rest.

Later, Thomas fought Adamick in Madison Square Garden. Arthur Donovan, who had refereed his bout with Schmeling, penalized Thomas with the loss of two rounds because of low punches. Adamick received the decision. Thomas had indeed "carried" his rival. Two months later, Louis knocked out Thomas in five rounds.

Thomas's "confession" in *Sports Illustrated* was confirmed by Sig Hart, a former bantamweight fighter who was eighty-two years old. Hart told *Sports Illustrated*: "Norris admitted to me that they were arranging for Thomas to lose the fight. I refused to go up (to the room at the Drake Hotel in which the 'fix' was arranged) because I'd been in the boxing game fifty years and nobody could point his finger at me."

When the story was printed, Norris said, "I've been a friend of that old man for twenty years. I've given him money and I've paid his rent. He's an ingrate."

Norris also threatened to sue *Sports Illustrated* for $5 million. The libel action was never filed.

TWELVE

CARMEN BASILIO, the son of an onion farmer in Chittenango, New York, near Syracuse, took up boxing in high school. By 1948, he was fighting as a professional in upstate New York rings. He was an aggressive little fellow possessed of a deep sense of decency and determination. He was soft-spoken and articulate, and a vigorous and sharp competitor in the ring.

When Arcel's Saturday night bouts were being televised, Basilio was one of his star performers. The bustling welterweight twice fought Billy Graham in Syracuse in bouts promoted by Norman Rothschild, an upstart in the promotorial business who was not yet ensnared in Norris's orbit. Suddenly, Basilio's vital services were no longer available to Arcel.

Basilio's managers were John DeJohn, a handsome, olive-skinned, dark-haired native of Syracuse, and Joe Netro, an obese resident of Ithaca, New York. One afternoon during the summer of 1953, DeJohn was invited to take lunch with Carbo in the Warwick Hotel in New York City. He was flattered by the invitation and accepted. When he arrived at the Raleigh Room in the hotel, he found two others lunching with Carbo. One was Wallman, the other was Angel Lopez, owner of the Chateau Madrid night club in New York and the manager of Kid Gavilan, the welterweight champion.

Lopez' presence, in terms of developments, was anomalous. Later he would testify before the New York State Athletic Commission that he had received $50,000 as his share in the Arcel's Saturday night promotions, but on this occasion he was being used as a tool in Carbo's plot to "steal" Basilio away from Arcel and present him on a platter to Norris's International Boxing Club.

Carbo's method was simple. He offered Basilio, through DeJohn, an opportunity to fight Gavilan for the world welterweight championship in Syracuse on Friday night, September 18, 1953. DeJohn demurred. He did not want the match because he believed Basilio was not ready to cope with a fighter of Gavilan's ability.

"You'll make a lot of money," Carbo insisted.

"What do you mean, I'll make a lot of money?" DeJohn demanded.

"Well, look, if you are going to fight for the championship, you are going to get 20 per cent, and the champion gets 40 per cent, and they will draw a lot of money, which means that you will earn more money than you ever earned."

Carbo took a pencil and began writing numbers on the tablecloth in an attempt to prove that Basilio would earn a considerable sum by fighting Gavilan.

"If you win the championship," Carbo continued, "you are going to make a lot more money with him."

"It looks all right to me," DeJohn said.

When word of the match was brought to Basilio, he did not believe it. In all honesty, he knew he was not one of the IBC's boys. A year before, he had fought Chuck Davey, one of Jim Norris's darlings, in the Chicago Stadium. He had opened cuts on Davey's left cheek and over his right eye. When the fight was over, the decision went to Davey. Basilio rushed to his dressing room and proceeded to assail verbally the officials, his opponent, and the International Boxing Club.

"It was a lousy house decision," Basilio insisted, "and if it had been somewhere else they'd have stopped it. It's nice to be on the 'right' side—the IBC's side."

But now, unexpectedly he had himself became one of the Norris's "house" fighters. In the ring with Gavilan, he won many more friends; he knocked Gavilan down in the second round. This was an astounding achievement, because Gavilan had been floored only once before in his career. It was a close fight and when it was over, one of the judges voted for Basilio. The referee and the other judge cast their ballots for Gavilan. Basilio had lost officially, but he was certainly the leading challenger for Gavilan's championship.

In the ordinary course of sportsmanship, Basilio should have been given a return bout with Gavilan immediately, but Carbo had many allies to satisfy. Gavilan's next bout was against Bratton, Wallman's fighter. He beat Bratton mercilessly and moved on to make still another of Carbo's clients, Blinky Palermo himself, happy.

Palermo's fighter was Johnny Saxton, a bug-eyed kid out of Harlem. Even then Saxton was a nervous lad who was psychically unfit for the ring; in the years ahead he would break down mentally and turn to burglary and petty thievery to keep alive.

Gavilan met Saxton in Philadelphia on October 20, 1954. The bout was a travesty. Neither fighter landed a vital blow. Saxton was inept, indifferent, and a failure. Gavilan was only slightly better. The fight was malodorous, but the decision was even worse. The decision went to Saxton.

The entire country had seen the bout on television. The outcry was widespread. Dan Parker, writing in the New York *Mirror,* said:

> Jack Kearns told some friends before the fight to send in all they had on Saxton who, he said, couldn't lose. In New York many fans who tried to put money on Saxton were told that they could bet only on Gavilan. After the fight (?), Palermo said there would be no return match for Gavilan. And before and after it, Goombar Carbo lavishly entertained fight mobsters from all over America at a hotel suite. He had good reason to celebrate.

A few days after Saxton's unwarranted coronation, Carbo ran a party at the St. Moritz Hotel in New York. Gavilan was present. He walked up to Carbo and in Cuban-accented English, said, "Mr. Blinky Palermo told me that they do whatever you want. That's what he told me. And if that what you told him, for what they do to me I want my return match."

"Right," Carbo said.

Gavilan was never given a chance to regain the championship. There were mob obligations elsewhere.

In Boston, Tony DeMarco was managed by Anthony ("Rip") Valenti, a friend of Carbo's. He got first crack at Saxton and, as expected, knocked out Saxton. In Syracuse, DeJohn and Netro were determined to get Basilio another opportunity to fight for the world's welterweight championship. In pursuit of the match, they hit upon an upstate link to Carbo—Gabe Genovese, a barber by profession who, years before, had shared with Carbo in the management of Babe Risko, a world middleweight champion.

Genovese established a rate of exchange. He would exert his influence on Carbo and, in return, would be cut in on Basilio's purses. During 1955 he received $5,000 from DeJohn and Netro. Basilio was matched to meet DeMarco for the welterweight title in Syracuse's War Memorial Auditorium on June 10, 1955. Basilio won on a knockout in twelve rounds. Five months later he repeated the knockout in the Boston Garden.

Carbo still had to take care of Palermo, his colleague. Saxton had been sidetracked in the process of Carbo's maneuvering, and now Palermo was insisting that Carbo prove his affection by getting Saxton back into the picture. Norris went right along with the program. He signed Basilio to defend his title against Saxton in the Chicago Stadium, March 14, 1956. The bout went the full fifteen rounds, and Saxton somehow received the decision, although Basilio was the obvious winner.

Dismayed, Basilio returned to New York. He went before the New York State Athletic Commission and asked Julius Helfand, who had succeeded Christenberry as chairman, to permit Saxton to fight in New York. Helfand had been adamant in this regard. He had turned down Palermo's application for a license and Palermo, in rebuttal, had insisted that Saxton would never box in New York State.

"Let Saxton sign his own contract," Basilio pleaded. "New York is the only place I can get a fair shake."

Helfand granted Basilio's request. Rothschild, the Syracuse promoter, was determined to promote, as Norris's partner, the return bout between Basilio in Syracuse. Like all others in boxing, he knew that Carbo was the boss, although Norris had the monopoly. He, too, appealed to Genovese.

"It'll cost $10,000," Genovese said.

"It's a deal," Rothschild said.

Basilio knocked out Saxton in nine rounds on September 12, 1956, in a bout promoted by Rothschild in Syracuse. Carbo laughed. His man Genovese had delivered on both sides of the street, from Basilio and Rothschild. It was a pattern that was to be repeated again and again, and it eventually would result in bitter consequences for Genovese, Palermo, and Carbo.

THIRTEEN

BY THE LAWS of order and logic, the fate of boxing in the United States should have been decided in the arena and not in the highest court in the land. A bloody-nosed sport existing on the frontiers of civilization, boxing has survived ordeal by chicanery and plunder because it is inherently no less moral than other sports. It is, as Red Smith once wrote, "a rough, dangerous, and thrilling sport, the most basic and natural and uncomplicated of athletic competitions and—at its best—one of the purest of art forms."

The Supreme Court of the United States was not concerned with the morality of boxing when it delivered a momentous decision on Monday, January 31, 1955; nor was it determined to drive it out of existence. The Court simply was concerned with a fact of law: was boxing in interstate commerce and therefore susceptible of restraint by the federal government?

In 1954 Justice Noonan had expressed the juridical opinion that the Supreme Court had granted boxing immunity from antitrust attack when it ruled, in 1953, that major league baseball was not in interstate commerce. The Department of Justice had asked the Supreme Court to reverse Justice Noonan's decision in its suit against Norris and Wirtz and their various boxing organizations.

Six justices of the United States, including Chief Justice Earl Warren, decided in favor of the federal government. "We hold," the decision stated, "that the complaint states a cause of action and that the government is entitled to an opportunity to prove its allegation. The judgment of the court below is reversed."

There was a dissent by Justices Felix Frankfurter and Sherman Minton.

Justice Frankfurter asserted, "It would baffle the subtlest ingenuity to find a single differentiating factor between other sporting exhibitions, whether boxing or football or tennis, and baseball insofar as the conduct of the sport is relevant to the criteria or considerations by which the Sherman Law becomes applicable to 'trade or commerce.' Indeed, the interstate aspects of baseball and the extent of exploitation of baseball through mass media are far more extensive than is true of boxing."

Beyond this, Justice Frankfurter stated, "Whatever unsavory elements there be in boxing contests is quite beside the mark. The states to which these exhibitions are distasteful are possessed of the honorable and effective remedy of self-help. They need not sanction pugilistic exhibitions, or may sanction them only under conditions that safeguard their notions of the public welfare."

Frank Carbo could not have cared less about the Supreme Court's decision, which opened the way to the destruction of the International Boxing Club. The year before, his girl friend, Viola Masters, had been placed on the payroll of the Nevill Advertising Agency, the device used by Norris to move television receipts into and out of the IBC's coffers. She had been hired, Norris was to say later, to "influence" fight managers, though he acknowledged that she had not contributed to the welfare of the IBC, despite payments of some $40,000 over a span of three years.

Norris was in Florida the day the Supreme Court handed down its decision. In Chicago, the IBC issued a statement in his behalf which was aimed largely at allaying the fears of the sponsors of the Wednesday night and Friday night television bouts.

"These are unaffected by the decision," the statement asserted.

Privately, however, Norris suggested flippantly, "So the Court voted six to two. Well, at least it was a split decision."

In Washington, the Department of Justice was not concerned with the juridical difference of opinion. It had won its fight to drag Norris and Wirtz and others before a bar of federal justice, and it proceeded to gather ammunition. Fifteen months later, there would be a confrontation in the United States District Court, Southern District of New York, but in the meantime Norris went about his boxing business. The year 1955 was to be a difficult one for him.

FOURTEEN

EDDIE COCO had been Rocky Graziano's co-manager, but while his fighter used gloved fists in combat, Coco was disposed toward the pistol as a weapon. On the morning of February 21, 1951, Coco became involved in an argument with one John Smith, a parking attendant and car washer, in front of his Miami Beach home. Hastily, Coco dashed into his house, emerged with a pistol, and shot Smith to death. Four years and three months later, on May 5, 1955, Coco began serving a life sentence for the murder.

It was at about the same time that it was disclosed that Norris, in a moment of sympathy, had written a character reference for Coco to the judge who had sentenced the murderer.

"I have known Eddie Coco for a period of ten years," Norris wrote. "In my association with him, I have always found him to be a man of his word, well liked and highly respected by his friends."

Acknowledgment of this association was made freely by Norris, obviously in an attempt to persuade the court to mitigate the murderer's punishment.

Of itself, Norris's letter was of little moment; it was written, no doubt, in a spirit of easy indulgence, perhaps at the behest of Carbo, who was Coco's friend.

It served, however, as a frame of reference later, when Norris was asked point-blank, while under oath, whether he was associated closely with Carbo. His answer became a millstone he was to carry thereafter, like the character reference indited in Coco's behalf.

The day after Coco began serving his sentence, the New York State Athletic Commission opened an investigation in New York City "into alleged irregularities in the conduct of boxing in New York State and violations of the rules and regulations of the New York State Athletic Commission."

Julius Helfand was the chairman of the Commission. He was a short, sharp-nosed, sharp-eyed, sharp-tongued lawyer who had been an assistant district attorney in Brooklyn during the prosecution of Murder, Inc., and had, as a result, gained a reputation as a foremost expert on crime in the United States.

A familiar name was involved in the investigation, that of William Phillip Daly, whose striking personality had colored every major inquiry or trial of boxing in the United States. Indeed, Daly's activities had touched off the inquiry.

For some years, he had been the manager of a welterweight contender named Vince Martinez. In July, 1954, Martinez went to Los Angeles to fight Art Aragon, a magnetic California brawler, and won a decision in ten rounds. The fight took place on July 1. Six days later, Daly came to the fighter's home in New Jersey to split up a purse of some $27,000. There was an argument: the fighter accused Daly of adding $3,000 to the managerial expense account. According to Martinez, Daly insisted the $3,000 had been spent wisely. He quoted Daly as saying, "Well, $1,000 of it was for plane trips. The rest, we had to take care of the referee and the judges."

In the ensuing argument, Daly dashed out of the house and refused to meet again with the fighter. Martinez appealed to the International Boxing Club, which offered to sign him to an exclusive service contract, but even after he had signed the contract the IBC went back on its corporate word. It developed that the International Boxing Guild, in which Daly was a high poobah, had imposed sanctions against Martinez. He was unemployed.

The investigation disclosed an amazing arrogance among fight managers individually and as members of the Guild. It also indicated a willingness on the part of Norris to hold hands with the Guild and to sustain the embargo on Martinez.

Helfand called Markson, who was managing director of the International Boxing Club of New York, as a witness. Markson testified that the contract with Martinez had not been consummated because it soon became evident to him that the Guild's boycott on Martinez was effective.

"Mr. Markson," Helfand asked, "can you tell me whether or not it was common knowledge, common talk at least around the boxing fraternity, that Vincent Martinez was grounded because of his difficulties with Mr. Daly?"

Markson drew himself up to his full cultural height. "Well, it seemed to assume, sir, the form of an exalted sympathy on the part of other managers, if I may use the expression," he replied. "The other managers would not permit their fighters to fight Martinez in sympathy for Mr. Daly."

Some days later, Markson received a telephone call from Helfand.

"I want Jim Norris to come in and testify," the chairman said.

"Well, all I can do is talk to him," Markson said.

"Make it firm. Either he comes in and talks or I'll take up the license of the IBC," Helfand said angrily.

Norris was in Florida. Markson called him.

"Aw, Harry, do I have to?" Norris asked petulantly when he had learned of Helfand's demand that he testify.

"I think you'd better."

"Okay," Norris said.

That night, Markson obtained the number of Helfand's private telephone. He called the Commissioner at his home.

"Mr. Norris will testify," he reported, "but can we know the line of questioning?"

"You may," Helfand said. "It'll cover the scope of the investigation, or at least any points on which Mr. Norris can offer pertinent testimony. How about making it this Thursday?"

"No good," Markson said. "That's five days before Marciano fights Cockell. Mr. Norris will be in San Francisco."

"All right. Then let's make it the nineteenth. That's three days after the fight."

"That'll be all right," Markson said.

Norris spent the next weekend in San Francisco, where Rocky Marciano fought Don Cockell, a blubbery, inoffensive Englishman, at Kezar Stadium on Monday night, May 16, 1955. The bout was a joint promotion of Jimmy Murray, a San Francisco promoter, and the International Boxing Club. Marciano knocked out Cockell in the ninth round in a one-sided, dull battle. Four days later, Norris entered the hearing room of the New York State Athletic Commission at 226 West 47th Street, just off New York's Great White Way.

The inquisitorial session drew a larger audience that day than many movie houses on Broadway. Newspaper reporters occupied several rows of chairs and newsreel and television cameras were on hand. Truman Gibson showed up as Norris's counsel.

Norris testified at length that he was not totally familiar with the Martinez case and denied ever discussing the boycott of Martinez with Daly. Then, as necks craned and ears moved closer, Helfand moved to the question of Norris's association with Carbo.

"Mr. Norris, did you have anything to do, or did your club, the International Boxing Club, have anything to do with the promotion of the Saxton-Gavilan fight in Philadelphia last year?"

"Yes, we co-promoted it."

"You what?"

"Co-promoted it."

"With whom did you co-promote the fight?"

"Herman Taylor."

"Of Philadelphia?"

"Yes."

Carbo's name was invoked at last.

"How long do you know him?"

"Twenty years."

"Have you ever discussed the promotion of any fights with Mr. Carbo?"

"No, I haven't."

Newspapermen snickered. Helfand went right along.

"What is Mr. Carbo's business, to your knowledge."

"I couldn't answer that."

"You don't know?"

"No."

"In twenty years you haven't been able to find out what his business is?"

"I am not a social friend of Mr. Carbo's, Mr. Chairman. I know Mr. Carbo. I talk to him. I have a cup of coffee with him occasionally."

"Would you say that it is a normal and natural thing during an association of friendship of twenty years to find out a man's business, what he does for a living?"

"I think you misconstrued something. You asked me how long I had known Frankie Carbo, not how long I had been friends with him."

"You said you knew him twenty years?"

"Yes, I would say that I have seen him around and have said hello to him for twenty years."

Norris's answers developed the information that Carbo had been at the Saxton-Gavilan bout, but that he had not talked with him at the fight.

"Other than at fights, where have you seen Mr. Carbo?" Helfand asked.

"I don't recall seeing him at fights, Mr. Chairman. I have seen him occasionally at the race track, at a ball game, possibly at a restaurant around town, something like that."

"Have you ever heard it said that Mr. Carbo had a financial interest, or a piece of fighters?"

"I have read that for many years."

"Have you ever heard it in the trade other than having read it?"

"No."

"Have you ever discussed with Mr. Carbo fights or fighters?"

"No."

Mr. Norris was excused.

In all, the New York State Athletic Commission took 500,000 words of testimony, covering 1,500 pages, before a judgment was made.

The Commission had heard testimony about the payment of tribute by managers enrolled in the Boxing Guild of New York, an arm of the International Boxing Guild. Each member was required to pay $100 each time one of his boxers engaged in a main event anywhere in the United States.

Ray Arcel, the man who had been forced to pay the Guild $17,000 in the form of "advertising" fees in order to obtain the services of Guild-managed fighters for his Saturday night television series, gave testimony as to his difficulties with the Guild.

Furthermore, Tex Sullivan, promoter of boxing at the St. Nicholas Arena in New York City, was unveiled as a mere "front man" for the Guild, which kept all its records in a safe in Sullivan's office at 2 Columbus Circle, New York City.

Finally, on December 12, 1955, the State Athletic Commission, through Chairman Helfand, announced its decision. It was decreed that any member who did not resign from the Guild by January 16, 1956, would have his license revoked.

Three weeks after the decision was announced, Helfand received word that Sullivan and his partner, Willie Gilzenberg, an old-line fight promoter, were going to move their bouts to the Baltimore Coliseum in order to safeguard their television contract with the Dumont Network, which had been broadcasting the bouts from the St. Nicholas Arena each Monday night.

Helfand went to work. He communicated with James M. Hepborn, Baltimore's police commissioner, who promised to investigate the background of the switch of the St. Nicholas Arena bouts to Baltimore.

Sullivan and Gilzenberg, it developed, would be associated in the Baltimore promotion with Benny Trotta and Trotta's son-in-law, Angelo Munafo. Trotta, the Baltimore police informed Helfand, was an alias for Benjamin Magliano, a convicted bookmaker and draft dodger.

Nine days after Chairman Helfand's decision on the Guild had been announced, Trotta went to the Pennsylvania Railroad Station in Baltimore, where he greeted three men who had just arrived from New York. Two of the three men were identified as Gilzenberg, Sullivan's partner, and the ubiquitous Daly. Trotta drove the visitors to the Trocadero, a night club licensed in his name. A week earlier, Trotta had greeted another visitor from New York—Frankie Carbo.

Helfand, although pleased with the report from Baltimore, knew that there was a need for haste. It occurred to him that if the St. Nicholas Arena boys were shifting their fights to Baltimore, why couldn't Norris also move his bouts out of Madison Square Garden?

Hurriedly, he communicated with Markson. "I want to see Mr. Norris tomorrow morning in my office," the Chairman declared vigorously.

"He's in Florida," Markson said.

"Get him back here," Helfand insisted.

That night the Boxing Guild of New York held a meeting in its drab quarters around the corner from Stillman's gym on Eighth Avenue. The sixty-eight members in attendance decided unanimously "that under no circumstances will the Guild be dissolved on January 16, 1956, or any other date, as ordered by Chairman Julius Helfand of the New York State Athletic Commission."

The next morning, Friday, January 6, Norris appeared at the Commission's offices. He was accompanied by Markson and Truman Gibson.

"I want to talk with Mr. Norris alone," Helfand said.

The country's most powerful promoter, a man of great wealth and background who had been denounced in some quarters as a bad influence on boxing, walked into the Chairman's office.

No record was made of the confrontation, but some time later Helfand described it in his own words in an article in *The Saturday Evening Post*:

> I did most of the talking. I told him frankly that our clean-up drive probably would fail if he gave up the Friday night Madison Square Garden shows to line up with the Guild boycott. I asked him to announce within the next few hours that he would continue to operate in New York. "You must make a decision to stand on the side of law and order," I said, "or stand convicted of the charges made by some people that you are on the side of the Guild and the kind of people who run it."
>
> Norris replied that he wanted to keep the Garden fights going. But he said he was afraid that if he went against the Guild in New York, then its national organization would keep him from getting fighters for his IBC promotions in other cities. He told me that it would be much easier for him to comply with my request if he could hold out hope that I would permit a new managers' organization to be set up in New York.
>
> I was reminded of a statement he had made when I questioned him about the Guild during our hearings last summer. "I need the Guild and the Guild needs boxing," he had said. Now he was still trying to save the Guild. I heatedly told him that I would not compromise the Commission's decision by discussing the possibility of a new Guild with him or anyone else.

Finally, he said, "Well, I'm willing to make a statement to the effect that I will support the Commission and continue to run boxing in New York, but I would still like to be able to say something in such a statement about a new organization."

As I remember, I almost came out of my chair at this point. I told him that was out. I insisted that he issue a public announcement that very afternoon supporting the Commission without any ifs or buts. I further demanded that, as concrete evidence of his compliance, he announce the main event for a television show in Syracuse on January 20—the IBC's first promotion in New York State after the January 16 deadline for Guild resignations. No contract had been presented to us yet for this Syracuse show, and there had been talk that it would never come off.

At first Norris protested that he couldn't arrange a feature match on such short notice, but in the end he agreed to this demand, too. As he left, I could sense that he was feeling better. I told him I wasn't going to discuss the attacks that had been made on him in some newspapers and magazines, but that he could be an important part of the fight for decent boxing.

"I want to be part of that fight," he said.

Before the day was over, our struggle against the Guild was as good as won. Jim Norris came through as pledged, first with a statement that he would continue to stage fights in New York in compliance with state laws and regulations, and then with an announcement that Gil Turner and Gene Fullmer had been signed for the wind-up at Syracuse on January 20. Then in late afternoon came word from Maryland that Governor McKeldin had decided that "the new fight program scheduled to begin on January 23 at the Coliseum in Baltimore should be cancelled."

By January 16, the Commissions' deadline for resignations from the Guild, all but a few diehards had defected from the organization. The Guild was destroyed. The licenses of Sullivan and Gilzenberg were revoked, along with that of the London Sporting Club, Inc., their promotional corporation.

There were plaudits for Helfand on all sides. He had encountered a dragon and had slain it. The ghost of the dragon was to haunt Norris.

FIFTEEN

PRIVATELY, Arthur Wirtz had long been worried by Norris's covert alliance with Carbo. He stood silent publicly about it, but in private he expressed concern over his partner's headlong association with the tough guys. He was a businessman solely interested in profit, and although he drove a hard bargain he preferred to deal with businessmen, not with gangsters.

Soon after Norris's testimony before the State Athletic Commission, Wirtz set about trying to "rehabilitate" Norris, whom he called "Jimmy" and regarded almost as a blood relative. His plan was simple in concept and rather easy in achievement; he wanted to make Norris president of the Madison Square Garden Corporation.

He informed Gibson of his plan. "I think Jimmy will settle down if he's president of the Garden," he said. "He'll feel the responsibility and maybe he'll chase all those fellows around him."

For several years Wirtz had been involved in a disagreement with Edward S. ("Ned") Irish, who was vice-president of Madison Square Garden. Irish had become an officer in the Garden as a result of the introduction by him of college basketball games as a regular attraction in the arena.

For many years, he had shared in the proceeds of these college games and had, by a display of business acumen and administrative skill, worked his way up to the position of executive vice-president. For the most part straight-laced, he clashed repeatedly with Wirtz over Garden policy.

Perhaps Wirtz was dismayed because Irish seemed to represent the viewpoint of those members on the Garden's board of directors who were not allied with the Norris-Wirtz interests. Furthermore, Wirtz believed that Irish's income from the Garden was exorbitant. From 1945 through 1951, Irish received these sums from the Garden: 1945, $65,308.74; 1946, $72,086.75; 1947, $72,666.75; 1948, $101,665.90; 1949, $86,003.50; 1950, $89,784.59; 1951, $80,109.77.

Wirtz's proposal to make Norris president of the Madison Square Garden Corporation would surmount Irish's powers. It also included the "elevation" of General Kilpatrick to the chairmanship of the board of directors, a position of honor rather than authority.

In June, 1955, there were rumors that many long-time members of the Garden's board of directors were displeased by the way Norris had testified before the State Athletic Commission. One director, speaking anonymously, said, "Norris stated at the hearings that he had known Carbo for twenty years, but had never had any financial transactions with him and that he was unaware of Carbo's underworld background. Norris could have just as easily taken a definite stand. He could have told the hearing, 'Yes, we've got to deal with people like Carbo, who are inextricably mixed up in the fight game.' "

At the same time, Bernard F. Gimbel, the department store man who had served for many years as chairman of the board of the Madison Square Garden Corporation, disclosed that he was resigning. Five other Directors followed him—Walter P. Chrysler, Jr., the auto man; Stanton Griffis, former ambassador to Spain; Sidney J. Weinberg, a Wall Street broker; and Jansen Noyes and William M. Greve, financiers.

A special meeting of the board of directors was held on June 9, 1955. The meeting lasted ninety minutes, during which time Norris was elected president and the resignations of the six directors were accepted. Norris, as the new president, made a report on the federal government's antitrust suit against the International Boxing Club of New York, the International Boxing Club of Illinois, the Madison Square Garden Corporation, and both Norris and Wirtz. Irish, who was now a member of the new nine-man board of directors, did not attend the meeting. No explanation was made to justify his absence.

When the meeting was over, Norris spoke to newspaper reporters. General Kilpatrick attempted to explain away the mass resignations. For many years, he said, "the board has operated as a harmonious unit but it was felt that many decisions of policy on important pending matters could be effectively resolved by a smaller board."

Norris, being a millionaire, put his three-cents worth in. He explained that it would be easier to get a quorum of five with a newer, smaller board. He said a quorum of the old board comprised nine members.

"It was five, too," General Kilpatrick corrected the new president.

SIXTEEN

THE MIAMI SOCIAL SEASON was in full swing in the fall of 1955. If a roster of visiting gentry had been available, it would have included socialites Frankie Carbo, Jack Kearns, Bill Daly, Charley Johnston, and two other fight men, Harry Curley and Andy Niederreiter. Norris was also in the area, at his home in Coral Gables, where he was taking his ease after being named president of Madison Square Garden.

One morning, Kearns played host at a levee in his Miami home. The guests included Carbo, Daly, Johnston, Niederreiter, and Curley, although the latter had come only in his role as Carbo's chauffeur. History does not record the fare served by the host.

The way it happened, Kearns was to explain later, was that Daly frequently visited at Kearns' home, accompanied by Mrs. Daly and their children. "I mean," Kearns would say, "that Mr. Daly and his wife and children know my children and visit me very often down in Florida and stay at my home, and one afternoon, Carbo, or morning or noon, I don't know which it was, around noontime I think, Carbo and his wife and a fellow called Harry Curley pulled up in a car."

Kearns' memory was faulty. Carbo had not yet married Viola Masters, who was then on Norris's payroll as a person of "influence" in boxing. That bond was to be sealed in holy matrimony some eight months later.

In any case, Carbo was at Kearns' home with the others when Norris arrived.

"Jim Norris comes by my house a lot," Kearns later told the Kefauver Committee. "He goes to the race track and drives out and I take a ride out with him now and then. He came into the house and went out in the yard and in the patio there and Carbo and Daly and Norris was all sitting down there talking in the patio."

When Kearns was asked whether he knew the nature of the conversation among Carbo, Daly, and Norris he said, "I wasn't interested in anything Carbo had to do with anything."

From Kearns' viewpoint, it was a perfectly reasonable reply. In the strange ways of boxing, it was logical for Carbo to be at Kearns' home, despite Kearns' known disregard of Carbo. Obviously, the house had been chosen as a "safe" meeting place, away from the eyes and ears of quidnuncs, both official and unofficial, who might let the world know that Norris, who had testified to a passing acquaintanceship with Carbo only a short while before, was, in fact, a colleague of the underworld's overlord of boxing.

SEVENTEEN

IN CLEVELAND, a local television station began the broadcasting of bouts from its studio and the International Boxing Guild, which had been undermined and wiped out in New York State, took it upon itself to impose a boycott. Guild members were warned by the leadership to turn a cold shoulder on the studio-boxing program.

When a complaint reached the federal government, evidence purportedly involving the Guild in a conspiracy was presented to a grand jury. The leaders of the Guild, including Johnston, as president, and Daly, as secretary-treasurer, were indicted on charges of organizing a criminal conspiracy in restraint of trade and plotting to fix television fees for fights.

The indictment, in a sense, was quite fashionable in that year of 1956. Norris and Wirtz were on the verge of going before a federal judge in the United States District Court, Southern District of New York, on charges of conspiring to monopolize the promotion of championship bouts in the United States from June, 1949, through May, 1953.

"This case," the government would contend in its trial brief, "presents classic instances of violations of the antitrust laws. A group of men have banded together to seek domination of a field. In this, they have succeeded.

"It is submitted that the equity powers of this Court should be invoked to dissolve that amalgamation of powers and enjoin the illegal practices through which it was achieved."

The news of boxing's difficulties spread across the country, and there seemed to be a frantic race among officials to be the first to bestir the muddy waters of the business. In California, Governor Goodwin J. Knight ordered a special committee to investigate the nature of the game in his state.

Babe McCoy, *né* Harry Rudolph, had been a matchmaker in Los Angeles for years. He was an obese, porcine man with a criminal record and a measure of arrogance in direct ratio to his two hundred and fifty pounds. He was a bosom pal of Mickey Cohen, the West Coast mobster, and consorted with Carbo whenever the boxing racketeer was in California.

The investigation disclosed that McCoy was a dictator who controlled the destiny of almost every boxer on the West Coast. It was established, through testimony, that McCoy had fixed seven fights not only in California but also in other states.

Tommy Campbell, a former lightweight contender, testified concerning a bout with Art Aragon at the Olympic Auditorium in Los Angeles on May 16, 1950. He said that McCoy had told him he would get a good payday for the bout but that he would have to "take one" and go down in the fourth round.

"I see," the inquisitor said. "In this discussion about your losing it, were any instructions given you, Tommy, as to how you were to do it? Will you just tell us to the best of your memory on that, please."

"Well, I was to fight him until the fourth round and then I was to get hit and that was to be all."

"Did anyone say anything to you about Aragon being a good puncher or a hard puncher?"

"Well, it was all based on the theory that he is known to be a hard puncher and that would be excuse enough."

"Did you fight him in the first round or two?"

"Yes, I did."

"Did you knock him down in the second round?"

"Yes, I had him down."

"Did you go down in the third round, Tommy?"

"Yes."

When the investigation moved to San Francisco, the names of Weill, Norris, and Gibson were on the lips of witnesses. Norris, it will be remembered, had been in San Francisco the night Marciano knocked out Cockell, the Englishman, in a bout promoted jointly by the International Boxing Club and Jimmy Murray.

Now, in the course of the California investigation, a letter written by Gibson to Murray on the stationery of the International Boxing Club of Illinois was introduced into the record. It was dated May 9, 1955, and was addressed to Murray at 415 Fourteenth Street, Oakland, California.

Dear Jimmy: Jim will arrived in San Francisco Wednesday evening on Flight No. 723 United Air Lines from Chicago. Benny made reservations for him at the St. Francis. I expect to arrive on the same flight on Thursday.

In the meantime my understanding of the deal with you on the fight is—$10,000 off the top of the promoters' percentage which will be charged to you for services and then a 50-50 division of profits and the same percentage share in losses, if any. Usual expense items will be mutually agreed on. The purpose of this note is to merely confirm the arrangements previously made with you by Jim. I am enclosing a copy of this letter which you can okay for our audit files. I'll pick it up in San Francisco.

Regards.

    Sincerely,

               TRUMAN K. GIBSON, JR.
               Secretary, International Boxing Club.

The amount of $10,000 mentioned in the letter above should be borne in mind; it was the sum the Governor Knight's special consultant on boxing, James E. Cox, would stress again and again by way of proving it went into Weill's pocket from the promotional profits without Marciano knowing a thing about it.

Cox showed Murray, on the stand, a list of promotional expenses. It included an item of $10,000 credited to Al Weill.

"What is that $10,000 item called on this one, Mr. Murray?"

"It says Al Weill."

"Does it refresh your memory?"

"No, sir, it doesn't."

"You have no explanation to give us about it?"

"No, sir."

"And you instructed the bookkeeper to make the check out?"

"No, sir."

"Do you think it is likely, Mr. Murray, that she would make up sheets and those marks on that check stub all on her own?"

"She has made many mistakes before, so she can make another one."

In the committee's report to Governor Knight, three inferences were drawn from Murray's testimony:

From the documentary evidence alone it appears that Al Weill either got the $10,000 or his friend Murray was "framing him." Consider further the following:

1. Murray told three different stories on three different occasions as to the whereabouts of the canceled checks representing the disbursements of these moneys. They were never produced. His conduct in this regard was extremely evasive and suspicious. Although he produced some checks, pursuant to subpoena, going back as much as seven or eight years, the $10,000 check and the balance of the checks with it were never really accounted for. Investigation disproved all three Murray stories.

2. This check for $10,000 cleared the bank the day after the fight, whereas all other checks to boxers for any purpose did not clear until much later. (As the check did not go through a clearing house in San Francisco, it was never microfilmed.) Murray never gave an explanation for his need for $10,000 cash at this time. The check was cashed and ten one-thousand-dollar bills received. (Unfortunately, the person cashing it could not remember to whom it was made payable or what persons were present at the bank.)

3. Murray lied under oath as to what he had done with the money. First he said he had taken it to Golden Gate Fields, a local race track, and gambled it away. Later, when he was advised that Golden Gate Fields had been closed at the time in question and it was impossible

for him to have disposed of the money as he had testified, he then could give no explanation or accounting as to what he had done with these funds.

On April 27, 1956, only brief days after the Case of the Missing $10,000 came to light, Marciano announced his retirement from the ring.

"What about Al Weill and those charges in California that he took $10,000 off your purse?" Mariano was asked.

"I believe Al is an honest guy," the retiring champion said. "We've been together nine years and Al wouldn't do that to me."

Former fighter and former manager haven't been friends ever since.

Marciano's retirement left Norris in a lurch. The IBC, which was involved in a fight for its life in the federal court, had lost control of the heavyweight championship at a moment when its entire empire seemed to be crumbling.

The California investigation not only had disclosed the strange disappearance of $10,000, but it revealed that Norris and Gibson were actually partners of Sid Flaherty, the manager of Carl ("Bobo") Olson, world middleweight champion at the time, in California Boxing Enterprises, Inc., a promotional firm.

Under California law, it was illegal for a manager to promote bouts. Flaherty had managed to circumvent the law in association with Norris and Gibson, who had used $15,000 in International Boxing Club funds to buy into Flaherty's corporation.

EIGHTEEN

WEDNESDAY, APRIL 25, 1956, was mild and sunny. Sylvester J. Ryan of the United States District Court, Southern District of New York, came early to his courtroom in Foley Square. He had shaved and breakfasted, and he was ready for the physical strain of a long trial. All antitrust trials, he probably thought, drag on and on.

142   JAMES NORRIS AND THE DECLINE OF BOXING

Judge Ryan was accustomed to long days in court. His manner
on the bench gave the impression that he enjoyed his work. His face,
round, clear-skinned, and bespectacled, wore expressions running
from judicial serenity to amused concern. He had been on the federal bench for some years, after a long career as an assistant district
attorney in Bronx County, and had gained a reputation for a lucidity
of juridical thought. He also had a sense of humor.

The courtroom was only partly filled when the United States of
America, plaintiff, faced the International Boxing Club of New
York, Inc., a corporation of New York; the International Boxing
Club, Inc., a corporation of Illinois; the Madison Square Garden
Corporation, a corporation of New York; James D. Norris; and
Arthur M. Wirtz—defendants.

The defendants and their employees were present in array. Norris,
well-dressed as always, was accompanied by Wirtz, General Kilpatrick, Irish, Gibson, and Markson. None appeared dismayed,
though Irish seldom smiled; his record for impassivity remained in-
tact.

William J. Elkins, for the Department of Justice, conducted the
trial of the United States of America. A slender man of medium
height, he was dwarfed by Whitney North Seymour, chief defense
counsel, whose wide midriff stretched a dark blue vest and whose
neck rested on a high, white collar.

The Government's brief had contended, "This case presents classic instances of violations of antitrust laws. A group of men have
banded together to seek domination of a field. In this, they have succeeded. It is submitted that the equity powers of this Court should be
invoked to dissolve that amalgamation of powers and to enjoin the
illegal practices through which it was achieved."

For the most part, the case against the IBC was presented in documents, but those witnesses who did appear in behalf of the government presented evidence of Norris's ruthless use of power to control
boxing.

The IBC, the government contended, had promoted 80 per cent
of all world championship bouts from June, 1949, through May,
1953. It had cost the Norris combine $165,000 to gain control of
boxing; its promotions had accounted for many millions of dollars
in gate receipts.

Samuel Becker, a Cincinnati promoter, was an early witness for the government. He identified himself as a clothing manufacturer and testified that he had promoted most of Ezzard Charles' early fights.

"Did you have any discussion with Mr. Norris in relation to the promotion of the first Charles-Walcott championship contest?" Elkins asked him.

"Yes, sir."

"Will you tell us what those discussions were, Mr. Becker."

"After my big boxing show in Cincinnati with Charles and Maxim, during the advertising we made an offer to Mr. Joe Louis to fight the winner for the championship. In the meantime, the headlines come out and said Louis is retiring. So I find out that Walcott is next and the winner of Charles-Maxim, and a couple of days later I find out that if I want to get Joe Walcott to fight the winner, I have to go to Florida to talk with Mr. Jim Norris. So I didn't waste no time and I went to Florida."

"Had you had a discussion with Mr. Walcott and Mr. Charles with relation to the possibility of a bout?"

"When I heard that Mr. Louis is quitting boxing and Walcott is coming up next, I called Joe Walcott, his manager, and they came to Cincinnati and they were my guests at the fight between Charles and Maxim."

"You say eventually you were referred to Mr. Norris?"

"Yes, sir."

"You had a discussion with Mr. Norris?"

"That's right."

"Where was that discussion, by the way?"

"At Miami Beach, Florida."

"Will you tell us what the discussion was?"

"The discussion was when I got there I met Mr. Jim Norris and Mr. Art Wirtz, and they told me Louis just stepped out, Joe Louis, and Mr. Norris—here is the information he gave me. He says, 'If you want to promote Walcott and Charles fighting,' he says, 'you have to give me $150,000. Then I can turn this fight over to you.' I says, 'Why all that money? After all, I promoted Charles ever since he was fourteen years old. What happened?' He says, 'Well, Charles belongs to me now. Mr. Walcott belongs to me.' He says, 'I just paid

Louis $100,000 to retire, and that is what I want. I want to get the $100,000.' That was the conversation. He says he paid Joe Louis $100,000."

At one point, Becker told Judge Ryan that he had just celebrated his fifty-first year in the clothing business.

"*Mazel tov*," Judge Ryan said.

Everybody laughed except Norris.

Dewey Michaels, a boxing promoter in Buffalo, New York, was another witness for the government.

"Did you, sir, have any association with the Ezzard Charles-Freddie Beshore championship contest in August 15, 1950?" Elkins asked Michaels.

"I promoted the show."

"With relationship to that, sir, did you execute a contract providing that the IBC of New York would receive 5 per cent of all moneys received by you?"

"Yes, I did."

"With whom did you have the negotiations that ultimately resulted in that contract?"

"I had negotiations with Al, the manager of Marciano, Al Weill, and Harry Markson and Sol Strauss, the attorney."

"Were they all associated with the IBC at the time?"

"Yes, they were."

Elkins wanted to know the "substance of the negotiations."

"I wanted to make the match," Michaels said confidently, "so they told me to come to New York to make it, and he said they have the exclusive service contract with Charles, and if I wanted to get Charles I would have to pay them part of the profits, I mean part of the receipts, to obtain him."

"That was of the gross, not just of the profits?"

"Off the top with the exception of state and federal taxes."

It was developed that the fight had taken place after a series of postponements asked by Charles because of an illness diagnosed as a heart condition.

"And as a result of that did you have unusual expenditures?" Elkins asked.

"I had an awful lot of expenses."

"As a result of the postponement. The fight was eventually held on August 15, 1950, and thereafter did the International Boxing Club make any effort to collect the 5 per cent?"

"The night of the fight, Al Weill said he came to collect the money for the IBC."

"What discussion did you have with him?"

"I told him I wasn't going to pay it."

Elkins asked for a description of the full discussion.

"Well, I said I wasn't going to pay it on account of they didn't deliver their fighter," Michaels said boldly. "Their fighter was sick once and then the New York State Boxing Commission said his heart was bad, and I incurred all the expenses. Then, when we finally put the fight on it was dead, so I lost a lot of money. I lost about $20,000 on the fight with all the expenses ahead of it."

"Will you tell us what Mr. Weill had to say in response to that?"

Weill says, 'You ought to pay it, you should pay it. If you don't you will be in wrong with the IBC and you won't get any more fights.' "

Later, Michaels explained, he attempted to make a match between Charles and Lee Oma, a clever boxer from Detroit.

"Were you successful in getting any rights to that Charles-Oma fight?"

"No."

"Was it subsequently held, Mr. Michaels?"

"In New York, yes," Michaels said with a great deal of satisfaction.

In all, the government presented only eight witnesses in two sessions, the first on April 25, the second on April 27. When the last government witness had been presented, Elkins addressed the Court: "That is our last witness, your Honor, and the government rests at this time."

Seymour rose to his full and awesome height. He faced the bench as Norris and Wirtz peered at him from a row of seats just inside a guard rail.

"I will want to make, for the record, if your Honor please, a motion to dismiss because I think the government has wholly failed to make out a case within the antitrust laws, but obviously any disposition of that motion would require extended argument, and I would be glad to suggest that if it meets Your Honor's notions, you might reserve decision on that, and we will go ahead with our case on Monday."

Judge Ryan thanked the defense counsel for the suggestion. "The motion now is on the record," he said, "and I reserve decision."

NINETEEN

GENERAL JOHN REED KILPATRICK, tall and seemingly corseted, strode toward the witness chair in Judge Ryan's courtroom in Foley Square on the morning of April 30, 1956. He was the defense's first witness and he was an imposing figure in a dark blue suit as he sat down in the witness chair flanking the right side of Judge Ryan's bench.

Truman Gibson sat in the front row of spectators, his chin resting on hands held together in prayerful attitude. He watched carefully and listened attentively as Seymour took General Kilpatrick through a catechism aimed at proving that Madison Square Garden was a busy arena which derived most of its income not from boxing, but from the rodeo, hockey, professional basketball, college basketball, the circus, ice shows, a dog show, a horse show, track meets, and professional tennis.

Then, after defense counsel had finished with the General, the government's Mr. Elkins proceeded to draw from Kilpatrick a series of dates that helped cook the defense's bird.

"Referring now to your diary entries, General," Elkins said, "what was the first occasion on which you had any discussion with Messrs. Wirtz or Norris about a possible venture for the promotion of boxing at the Garden?"

"April 4," the General replied, "but I would like to qualify that or elaborate it very slightly. I had discussed over the past year or so—that is, the year proceeding that date—boxing with Messrs.

Wirtz and Norris, but I never would let the discussion get into detail."

"What I am asking you about," Elkins asked vigorously, "is not a discussion of the general problem created by Jacobs' illness or anything of that kind, but any venture in which the Garden might participate with Messrs. Wirtz and Norris in the boxing field. When was that first discussion?"

"April 4, 5, 6, 1949," the General said.

Two months before this testimony was given, a government attorney had found a back issue of *The New Yorker* magazine in which there appeared a profile of the General. The General, according to the profile, was an habitual diarist.

Put on the trail, the government found General Kilpatrick's diary a valuable source of information. Tipped off by the diary, the Department of Justice's lawyers found in General Kilpatrick's file the letter written by Wirtz to him on March 13, 1949, a letter in which Wirtz expressed his concern about the future of boxing in the Garden. The letter said:

> Early last summer, I spoke to you about the boxing situation when I had information that the Tournament of Champions, which is owned jointly by CBS, Music Corp., and Allied Artists, were going to make a strong bid to tie up the various boxing champions so they could control the television of major boxing events with the long range view of controlling boxing in the Garden.
>
> I mentioned to you at this time [that] it looked as if Mike Jacobs was losing his hold on boxing and suggested a program of getting together on an agreement of our respective buildings and try to work out mutual protective agreements that might save this situation.

The letter sealed the government's case against Norris's boxing monopoly.

TWENTY

WHEN NORRIS himself came to the witness stand, his cohorts sat straight up in their chairs. He was dressed, like the General, in a dark blue suit and a thin veil of embarrassment. His chief counsel's questions seemed to burden his memory, but he answered with becoming modesty.

At one point, after Norris had pointed out that the prices of fight tickets at the Garden were lower than they had been during Mike Jacobs' promotional days, Judge Ryan asked, "Do you remember when we used to go up to the Fairmount as boys and get in for twenty-five cents? The Bronx, Mr. Seymour, was the home of boxing."

"And of many other good things," Norris's counsel replied.

Norris wasn't having as much fun. He testified that his organizations had promoted only two championships bouts outdoors that had been financially profitable.

He was asked about Sam Becker.

"I wish you would tell us now about your discussion with Mr. Becker," Seymour suggested.

"I can't tell you the exact date, but it would be—I'd place it somewhere around the 20th of February. I was in Miami. Mr. Wirtz was there. We were vacationing."

"Let me stop you for a moment. Was it the 20th of February or was it in March?"

"March, I'm sorry, around the 20th of March. I did not know Mr. Becker, but I received a message, a telephone call or wire, or someone said, 'Mr. Becker would like to come over and see you.' I had no knowledge of what Mr. Becker had in mind. The message went back, would he meet me at the Roney Plaza on that particular day, whatever day it was.

"Mr. Becker came over to the Roney Plaza and introduced himself and we shook hands and so forth and to the best of my recollection I said to Mr. Becker, 'What's on your mind?' and he said, 'We'

148

or 'I would like to promote the Charles-Walcott fight in Cincinnati,' and I recall saying to Mr. Becker at the time, 'Well, I have no interest in discussing it with you. We are only thinking of Chicago for this match.' "

Seymour pointed out for Norris's benefit that Becker had testified that he had offered $100,000 for the match, but that Norris had demanded $150,000.

"Is that in accordance with your recollection?" Seymour asked.

"That is not," Norris insisted.

Norris described in detail the circumstances surrounding Louis's resignation as world's heavyweight champion and the birth of the International Boxing Club, Inc. of Illinois.

Under cross-examination by Elkins, Norris's memory failed him when he was asked whether the first Charles-Walcott bout, the initial offering of the IBC in Chicago, June 22, 1949, had been included in the package deal with Madison Square Garden.

"I don't know," Norris replied.

Once again General Kilpatrick's skill as a diarist helped the government.

"To refresh your memory, sir," Elkins said to Norris, "I would like to read from Government's Exhibit 265, which is a memorandum written by Mr. Kilpatrick and dated April 5, 1949, entitled 'Memorandum Regarding Boxing Setup.' I would like to direct your attention to the last paragraph which reads:

'When this arrangement is to go into effect is subject to study and whether or not the Walcott-Charles bout scheduled for Chicago is to fall within the scope of this agreement to be dependent upon whether or not joint groups divide expenses heretofore incurred by International.' "

Norris demanded, "Whose memorandum is that?"

"That," Elkins replied, "is a memorandum of Mr. Kilpatrick."

Judge Ryan moved in to end the colloquy. "The question is," he demanded, "does that refresh your recollection as to matters concerning which you have already testified?"

"Have you any idea what the date of this is?" Norris asked.

"April 5, 1949."

"This is a memorandum from General Patrick [sic] to his board of directors, is it, or what is it?" Norris asked, not without a note of nervousness in his voice.

Elkins explained that the memorandum simply bore the title of "Memorandum Regarding Boxing Setup." He said, "The question is merely does that refresh your recollection as to whether or not the Charles-Walcott bout would be made part of it or to fall within the scope of the agreement?"

"Well, I would say yes."

Judge Ryan was not satisfied. "You say that it does refresh your recollection?"

"No, sir, I can't say that, but I am going to disagree with this gentleman about it. I will say yes."

"We are not concerned with whether you disagree or do not disagree with another individual," Elkins said. "What we want to know is your honest recollection, your own independent recollection, whether it agrees with other testimony or it doesn't. Now, what is your independent recollection of these facts, or the facts concerning this Walcott bout?"

"I will say yes."

"You say yes to what?"

"That is the agreement the way it was. I don't really remember it."

"Thank you," Elkins said gallantly. "You are saying yes, then, to be agreeable; is that what you mean?"

"No."

"Is that what you mean?"

"No, sir."

"I do not mean to be funny about it," Elkins said.

There were other "funny" moments. When, on direction examination, Seymour asked Norris why the IBC lent large sums of money to fighters, the witness replied, "Oh, to help boxers, to help their managers when they are in trouble, when they need a little money, and rather than have them go to a loan shark or possibly sell part of the contract of their fighter to someone who might not be acceptable in boxing, I have advanced money at different times to fighters."

Judge Ryan asked, "To help them stay out of the clutches of those who might influence them, perhaps in throwing their fights, you give them money?"

"I wouldn't say that, Your Honor," Norris said, "but I think it helps them."

TWENTY-ONE

THERE WERE ONLY nine days of testimony in Judge Ryan's courtroom. During the last session, on May 3, both Gibson and General Kilpatrick were subjected to cross-examination by the government. Gibson strove to correct an impression conveyed by earlier testimony that Madison Square Garden had, in fact, contributed part of the $150,000 given to Louis by Norris and Wirtz.

"The deal," Gibson testified, "was one that was presented to Wirtz and Norris and to Wirtz and Norris alone, and everything that developed with respect to Madison Square Garden was a subsequent development. However, the negotiations did continue over a period of some time, but the later events had nothing to do with the first meeting and with the first offer to Norris and Wirtz."

The intent was obvious: Gibson wanted to convince Judge Ryan that Norris and Wirtz had acted unilaterally in the organization of the IBC, apart from the subsequent amalgamation with the Garden.

General Kilpatrick's diary was the subject of his cross-examination. "Did you keep a record book in which you recorded various events relating to Madison Square Garden and its operations?" Elkins asked the General.

"Yes," General Kilpatrick said.

"I show you this Government's Exhibit 269 for identification and ask you if these are accurate excerpts from that record book?"

"No dispute about that," Seymour said.

"It appears to be," General Kilpatrick said.

When Seymour objected to the introduction of the excerpts as evidence, Judge Ryan snapped, "The objection is overruled; received in evidence."

General Kilpatrick's diary was Norris's burden. In a real sense it established the point that Norris and Wirtz had been conspiring with the Garden even before the formal organization of the various boxing clubs through which the conspiracy operated in restraint of trade.

When both the defendants and the government had rested, Seymour asked Judge Ryan to dismiss the government's case.

"I am going to reserve decision on your motion to dismiss," Judge Ryan said, "as I did at the very close of the government's case. I feel a very serious question of law is presented here. I feel that very few factual issues, if any, are presented. I think this case might almost have been tried upon a stipulated set of facts. Perhaps there may be some dispute as to the inferences to be drawn from the facts which are undisputed and whether or not these inferences find sufficient support in the evidence, but I don't find many factual issues here."

Norris and Wirtz were not in court on the last day. When Robert Boyle of *Sports Illustrated* asked General Kilpatrick how he evaluated his diary's effect on the outcome of the case, the General rose to his full and awesome height. "Why, when the rest of them foundered on dates, I knew *every one* of them," he said.

Part Three

Divestiture, Dissolution, Divorcement

ONE

I N THE MIDST of the International Boxing Club's trial, Marciano announced his retirement from the ring. The heavyweight championship, which, the federal government contended, was a decisive factor in the IBC's conspiratorial control of boxing, was up for grabs.

In September, 1955, Marciano had fought Archie Moore at Yankee Stadium. It had been a hard fight. Marciano was knocked down but got up to knock Moore out in the ninth round. Weill looked forward to a continual flow of gold into his coffers; Marciano began pondering the sacrifices a fighter makes to retain his championship.

A fighter, Marciano had come to know, had little time for his family. He was neither father nor husband totally. Later, he was to cause his literary ghosts—he had them in tandem—to write, "I've hung up my gloves and I'm not getting into a ring again, except maybe to take a bow. I've got a lot of wonderful memories and I'm not going to spoil them."

On April 27, 1956, reporters were summoned hastily to the Hotel Shelton in New York, where Weill had his office. In a private meeting room, Weill sat on a dais flanked by Marciano and Charley Goldman, the heavyweight champion's trainer. Norris was at Marciano's left.

The champ wore a blue suit, a white shirt, a white brocaded tie, black shoes, and a rather glum countenance. He was saying good-bye and it was not easy. He declined to say he was retiring from boxing because of an old back injury that had caused him considerable pain throughout his ring career. Nor was he leaving because he could no longer face the physical ordeal of training.

"It's being away from the folks, being away from home, not being together," he said.

Skeptics whispered that Marciano was retiring because he did not want to continue under Weill's management. "He's mad," a fellow said, "because of the $10,000 somebody got under the table from his bout with Cockell." There was no comment by the champion.

So Marciano turned and went away, and it was a distant cry from the way Louis had gone out of the game. Marciano did not presume he had the right to "sell" the championship, as Louis had done, nor did he emphatically impose his cachet on those best qualified to fight for the title he had abandoned.

"Archie Moore, I happen to know about him," he said quietly, "and he has a good chance. From what I've been reading, Floyd Patterson seems to be everybody's favorite. I think Hurricane Jackson has a good chance."

Norris said little. Downtown, in a federal court, he was on civil trial for attempting to monopolize world championship boxing; he could not make an overt move in the direction of Marciano's successor.

"Rocky's named the best—Moore, Patterson, Jackson," the promoter said.

The inclusion of Hurricane Jackson in the triad was important. Jackson was managed by a furrier named Lippy Breidtbart, who had purchased the fighter's contract from several partners for $10,000, which he had "borrowed" from Norris. Jackson, in a phrase, was Norris's fighter.

TWO

FOR SOME TIME, Norris had been engaged in a running verbal battle with Cus D'Amato, Patterson's manager, who accused the promoter and Weill, as the IBC's matchmaker, of trying to get Patterson "knocked off."

D'Amato proclaimed his "independence" of Norris's gang, which he accused repeatedly of being dominated by Carbo, but he conceded that he would permit Patterson to fight Jackson under Norris's auspices "if the price is right."

"I do not especially want to fight for the IBC," D'Amato asserted, "but such is the power of the IBC, independent promoters can't compete with it."

When it was suggested that D'Amato would have to join forces with Norris, who reportedly was worth $200 million, to assure Patterson a bout for the championship, D'Amato declaimed: "I say Floyd Patterson has to be beaten in the ring and nobody's going to do that, nobody around right now. I'll defeat $200 million with Patterson. The public wants to see him fight and knows he is the best around. When Marciano retires, if he does, nobody will be recognized as the champion until he fights Patterson."

D'Amato's point was historically accurate. Though he was given to hyperbole and rhetoric, D'Amato was, in boxing, unique. An eclectic reader, he had a smattering of Freud and Adler to guide him through the psychological half-world in which he lived alone.

He spent hours orating against the villany of the IBC and invoked a jumble of pseudo-scientific terms to bulwark his arguments. It was a waste of time; Patterson, with his fists, could say more in seconds than D'Amato could, verbally, in days. This did not stop the manager from setting records for speechifying from standing, sitting, walking, and prone starts. Nor did it deter Norris from doing business with D'Amato.

About a month after Marciano's retirement, a reconciliation was

157

effected between Norris and D'Amato. Word of it was brought to Markson by Norris himself.

"It's all set," Norris told Markson one afternoon.

"Have you got D'Amato's word that he'll fight for us if he beats Jackson?"

"I've got that, Harry," Norris insisted.

Markson was worried. He was aware that neither Norris nor the IBC could sign either Patterson or Jackson to an exclusive service contract at the time; Judge Ryan was then in the process of determining his judgment in the antitrust action, and only the most brazen would have flown in his face by negotiating an exclusive service contract with a heavyweight contender.

Patterson and Jackson met in Madison Square Garden on June 8, 1956. Patterson was the favorite, although some among the self-anointed experts in boxing expressed the opinion that Jackson's unorthodox manner in the ring would cause Patterson a certain measure of discomfort. Jackson was an improbable, preposterous young man of low intellect and considerable stamina. He fought in fits and starts and threw punches from all angles, mostly purposelessly. He was hard to hit, seemingly impervious to pain, and woefully unfit both by temperament and background for the role of a heavyweight contender.

The bout was scheduled for twelve rounds. Patterson won easily, despite a broken bone in his right hand, and now only Archie Moore stood between D'Amato and control of the heavyweight championship. Norris would not worry. He somehow believed that all would work out to his advantage: Judge Ryan would rule in favor of the IBC against the federal government, and Moore would dispose of Patterson and, collaterally, D'Amato.

Markson prodded Norris. "Jim are you sure we can have Patterson's services if he beats Moore?" he asked repeatedly.

"Don't worry," Norris said.

The bout between Moore and Patterson was set for the Chicago Stadium, November 30, 1956. Moore was the favorite at odds of 8 to 5, although he was thirty-nine years old, eighteen years Patterson's senior. At twenty-one, Patterson would become the youngest man ever to hold the heavyweight championship.

The fight lasted six rounds. Patterson knocked Moore down with a short left hook to the jaw. When he arose at the count of nine, Moore was put down for the count of ten by another left hook followed by a right to the jaw.

Norris would never again promote a world heavyweight championship bout.

THREE

IN JANUARY, 1957, there was in boxing a feeling of impending doom. Norris was still awaiting word from Judge Ryan; D'Amato was making it clear that he alone would choose the promoter of the next world heavyweight championship match and that Norris would not be considered for the assignment; the International Boxing Guild was on trial before a federal court in Cleveland on a charge of conspiring to restrain trade by boycotting televised studio bouts and by fixing TV fees for fighters.

Inevitably, Daly was one of the defendants in his capacity as treasurer of the Guild. Johnston, the Guild's president, also faced the court.

Abruptly, Judge James C. Connell granted a directed verdict of guilty. "As has been said," Judge Connell said, "boxing may be a dying industry. It's a sociological problem. As people move to the suburbs, they want to go to college, and when guys think enough about their nose to put it in a book they also think enough of it not to put it in the ring."

Later, in retrospect, Judge Connell added, "TV studio bouts are bad psychologically. Men in boxing matches or in any sport will do their best when they are cheered. TV eliminates the human element of encouragement."

He was speaking, of course, about bouts put on in studios and not about bouts televised from an arena in which a live audience has assembled to cheer the boxers.

Johnston and Daly, among others, accepted the directed verdict with all good cheer. They both agreed that boxing was in decline because fewer young men were turning to boxing.

In his office in Madison Square Garden, Norris heard the news and said he was pleased to know that the Guild had been exonerated of creating a monopoly. Somehow he drew the conclusion that he, too, would be cleared of the same charge. In any event, business as usual was the theme at the International Boxing Club. Carbo was doing business at the same old stand.

FOUR

O N FEBRUARY 13, 1957, in Miami Beach, Joe Brown retained the world lightweight championship by knocking out Wallace ("Bud") Smith in the eleventh round. Lou Viscusi, his manager, strutted around the dressing room taking bows when Hymie Wallman walked in. Wallman was the manager of Orlando Zulueta, a lightweight contender from Cuba. He was also Carbo's friend.

"How about a shot at Brown with Zulueta?" Wallman asked Viscusi.

"If you can get a promoter with plenty of money," Viscusi said, "I will give you the chance."

Wallman went right to work. In Denver, Joe Dupler, a manufacturer of mink coats, was promoting fights. He was Wallman's friend.

"Wanna promote Brown-Zulueta?" Wallman asked Dupler.

The Denver furrier jumped to the bait. "Yes, I will take the match, I like it," he said.

"Get in touch with Lou Viscusi," Wallman said.

Thereafter, Wallman went to see another old friend.

"Frank, it is possible to get Joe Brown to fight Zulueta," Wallman told Carbo, whose response was both swift and financial. "If he wants the fight, let the furrier pay for it," Carbo said.

"How much do you want?" Wallman asked.

"Five thousand."

Wallman took the demand to Dupler, who agreed to pay the $5,000 from funds he had on deposit at the New York office of the Hudson Bay Company, with which he did considerable business.

"Go up there and get the $5,000," he told Wallman.

When the money was obtained, Wallman handed the $5,000 in cash to Tex Pelte, the same man to whom a $6,000 check had been mysteriously drawn in 1954 by the IBC's Telradio Promotions, Inc. Later, Carbo told Wallman he had received the $5,000. On June 19, 1957, Zulueta got his chance to win the world's lightweight championship from Brown in Denver. He was knocked out in the fifteenth round. Carbo suffered no pain.

FIVE

MARCH 8, 1957, was a Friday fight night at Madison Square Garden, and in the ring Sugar Hart and Walter Byars, welterweights, fought a ten-rounder without distinction. Byars was the winner, although Hart had been the betting favorite, but among the regular fans, talk was concerned with an opinion handed down by Judge Ryan.

Judge Ryan ruled that Norris, Wirtz, Madison Square Garden, and the various International Boxing clubs had indeed engaged in a conspiracy in restraint of trade and had monopolized the promotion of world's championship bouts in the United States in violation of the Sherman Act. He asked both sides to propose decrees to him to end violation of the Sherman Act.

Harry Markson remembers the day clearly. "Mr. Norris was in Florida," he recalls, "and when we called him to tell him of the decision, he said, 'Well, now it's a job for the lawyers.' That's all."

It was a job for the lawyers. A series of hearings followed. The defendants produced a line of witnesses whose testimony was aimed at mitigating the punishment. Finally, on June 24, 1957, the court was ready to pronounce its decision.

Norris, Wirtz, Gibson, Markson, and General Kilpatrick turned up in court. Judge Ryan took twenty minutes to read a thirteen-page outline of his decree. Categorized, the decision came to "divestiture, dissolution, and divorcement."

> We heretofore have found from the evidence presented at the trial and concluded that the defendants engaged in a combination and conspiracy in unreasonable restraint of trade the promotion of professional championship boxing contests in violation of Section L of the Sherman Act. We further have found that the defendants have conspired to monopolize trade and commerce in the same field, thus violating Section II of the Act. Defendants also were found to have actually monopolized commerce in the professional championship boxing field which was a further violation of Section II.
>
> We now, after full hearing of all parties and upon consideration of the evidence submitted, turn to the formulation of an appropriate decree to remedy the wrongs which were committed. The decree in a monopolization case should have three objectives:
>
> One, it puts an end to the combination or conspiracy when that is itself the violation.
>
> Two, it deprives the antitrust defendants of the benefit of their conspiracy.
>
> Three, it is designed to break up or render impotent a monopoly power which violates the act.
>
> The conspiracy which we found to have existed was made effective by the concert of action of the defendants. Thus, by stock ownership and control of stock voting power, defendants dictated the election and functioning of interlocking directors and officers and of management between the Chicago and Midwestern boxing interests—defendants Norris and Wirtz—and the New York interests—Madison Square Garden.
>
> The illegal conspiracy and monopolization was a direct and immediate purpose of this combination. There must be a dissolution of the combination which will permit the reestablishment of the competitive positions of the defendants and the entry of others into the market.
>
> The combination still exists and continues to function in only slightly altered form. Its purpose and objectives remain unchanged. The stock ownership of IBC-NY has been transferred to Madison Square Garden Corporation. IBC-Illinois has now Chicago Stadium Corporation as its sole stockholder. Wirtz and Norris and interests al-

lied to them still have controlling interest in Madison Square Garden and it stands undisputed that Wirtz and Norris control and direct the management of Madison Square Garden and dictate its policies and boxing activities. Wirtz and Norris are the sole stockholders of Chicago Stadium Corporation. Norris is the president and a director of IBC-New York, of IBC-Illinois, of Madison Square Garden Corporation, and of Chicago Stadium Corporation.

Wirtz is a director of all four corporations, and, in addition, vice-president of the board and treasurer of Madison Square Garden Corporation. Although the stock ownership of IBC-New York and IBC-Illinois has been changed, they still share the profits of championship contests as of old.

With respect to the control of television and radio rights a mere corporate structure change has taken place. A new corporation has been formed, Telradio Promotions, Inc., and its entire issued capital stock is owned by Chicago Stadium Corporation. To Telradio has been given the right to sell television and radio rights in connection with the Wednesday night television series. Thus, Wirtz and Norris control Telradio and IBC-Illinois through Chicago Stadium Corporation, and with it the Wednesday night television series, and through IBC-New York and Madison Square Garden these same combinations control the Friday night series. Truman Gibson is still found as one of the liaison between New York and Chicago. He is still an employee and secretary of IBC-NY and IBC-Illinois, and is now, in addition, an employee and secretary of Telradio Promotions, Inc.

The unlawful combination of the defendants still possesses and exercises its monopolistic control in the field of championship contests. It appears that since May 15, 1953, there have been held in the United States 37 championship contests, excluding one bantamweight contest. The defendants admit that they had promotional control over 24 of the 37 championship contests which were held, or of 65 per cent of the market, but we find that the defendants were not financial strangers to the other 13 championship contests which were held in cities other than New York and Chicago. Because the defendants are licensed by state authorities to promote only in New York and Illinois, they could not be the persons actually designated as the promoter of the 13 championship contests, but all five of the championship contests which originated in cities other than Chicago or New York on Friday nights were televised on IBC-New York's Friday night television series.

We find, too, that all of the 37 championship contests in this period from May 15, 1953, save only the five outdoor contests were televised on either the defendants' Wednesday or Friday night television series, and that the profits of the same of the telecasting rights inured to the benefit of the defendants.

The combination of the defendants is still in operation in violation of the law as we have heretofore found. The dissolution of the combination can only be accomplished by an immediate and complete severance of the interlocking ownership of Norris and Wirtz in Madison Square Garden. This means there must be a complete divestiture of the stockholdings of Norris and Wirtz in the Garden. The government has established Norris and Wirtz control the Garden Corporation.

The decree will direct Norris and Wirtz to divest themselves of all their stockholdings in the Garden. This includes all stock which they own individually or actually control through other entities.

In order not to unduly affect the market for stock or innocent stockholders the divestiture will be accomplished in the following manner:

One, Norris and Wirtz within thirty days after the entry of final judgment will resign as officers and directors of the Garden Corporation.

Two, Norris and Wirtz will be enjoined thereafter from holding any office or directorship in the Garden Corporation.

Three, Norris and Wirtz will be enjoined from voting by proxy or otherwise any stock at any meeting of the Garden Corporation stockholders, either for the election of officers or directors or for determination of any business policy of the corporation.

Four, Norris and Wirtz will be ordered to transfer all of their Garden stockholdings direct and indirect to a trustee to be named by the court, who will be empowered and authorized to vote the stock and exercise all other incidence of ownership.

Five, Norris and Wirtz are to effect a sale or other divestiture of their ownership of Garden stock within five years from the date of the decree, which divestiture shall be subject to the approval of this Court. Upon their failure to effect such sale or divestiture within the fixed time limit, the trustee will be authorized and empowered to effect a suitable sale of the stock within the next two years after expiration of Norris's and Wirtz's time limit.

The court's purpose here is to bring about the complete divestiture within seven years of the date of the final judgment and decree and in the meanwhile the defendants may receive and collect any dividends declared and paid on this stock.

The foregoing will effect a major step toward undoing the illegal combination found by the court to exist. Competition for championship contests will then be possible between Madison Square Garden in New York, on the one hand, and the Chicago Stadium, Detroit Olympia, and St. Louis Arena, all still owned or controlled by Wirtz or Norris or by interests allied to or associated with them on the other hand.

This, however, will not afford the full measure of relief required in this suit. The illegal monopoly of championship boxing contests was made possible by defendants because of their control of the promotion of championship fights together with their control of the principal stadia for the staging of the fights. In other words, combination between promotion and arena operation was a means by which the objects of the illegal conspiracy were accomplished.

Accordingly, there must be a limitation placed on the promotional activities of these defendants with respect to championship contests. The decree will enjoin the Garden for a period of five years from promoting more than two championship boxing contests in each calendar year. Likewise, the decree will enjoin for a period of five years Wirtz and Norris from promoting more than two championship contests in each calendar year. . . .

Divorcement is found to be a necessary remedy in this suit because defendants through ownership and control of the principal stadia for staging championship bouts are in a position to exclude other promoters from using these stadia to promote a championship fight.

The court determines that it is necessary to separate and limit promotions of championship boxing contests from the operation of areas where these contests are staged.

In connection with this limited divorcement which we have directed, the court will direct the compulsory leasing of Madison Square Garden and of Chicago Stadium as long as they are owned or controlled by the defendants.

The divorcement to be effected must be complete and irrevocable. Defendants brought the International Boxing Club of New York, Inc., and the International Boxing Club–Illinois into existence at the instrumentalities by which the illegal conspiracy was carried out. The stock of IBC-New York is wholly-owned by Madison Square Garden

Corporation. The stock of IBC Illinois is owned by the Chicago Stadium Corporation. These corporations are the promotional arms of the defendants, conceived and used to enable defendants to restrain and monopolize promotion of championship boxing contests. Their assets are of but nominal value except for the good will attaching to their names by virtue of the conspiracy.

Both IBC corporations must be dissolved. The decrees will enjoin both corporations until dissolved from functioning in the promotion of boxing contests, will declare illegal and void all existing and unexecuted contracts of either corporation for the exclusive services of any boxer and for the promotion of more than two contests in any calendar year within the period of five years and will require dissolution of each.

The final major provision of the decree must declare illegal and void all exclusive service contracts for championship boxers or contenders as well as all exclusive leases with stadia for the staging of boxing contests. By these exclusive contracts defendants preempted the championship field by requiring all championship contenders to sign up with defendants for future bouts. Likewise, the exclusive leases with arenas and stadia other than those owned or controlled by the defendants permitted them to preempt the field of places for the staging of championship contests.

Outside the courthouse, Norris posed with Wirtz, Gibson, Markson, and General Kilpatrick for the newspaper photographers.

"I am waiting for what my lawyers have to say," Norris said. "I would like to remain in boxing."

"There will be an appeal," Gibson said.

Norris went back to his office in Madison Square Garden. Carmen Basilio, the welterweight champion, was waiting for him to discuss terms for a bout in September with Sugar Ray Robinson for the middleweight championship. The match was made, thereby opening up another package of trouble for Norris.

SIX

ONE AFTERNOON in August, 1957, Norris was at work in his office in the Garden. Ray Robinson, who was scheduled to fight Basilio in defense of the middleweight title at Yankee Stadium on September 23, was making life miserable for the beleaguered promoter. One of the points of friction between Robinson and Norris was the designation of the company that would produce the pay-TV of the bout with Basilio.

Norris had assigned the rights to Theatre Network Television, Inc. while Robinson was insistent that TelePrompTer, Inc., handle the package. Furthermore, he was asking for a higher percentage of the gate, the right to handle a large number of tickets, and control over other areas of enterprise generally within the promoter's province. Robinson was aware that Norris's empire was crumbling and he was exerting pressure on an exposed flank.

In his office, Norris was in conference with Sidney Friedman, one of his lawyers, and Irish, Markson and Gibson. Long after his customary time for lunch, he asked one of his hired hands to bring in some sandwiches from a Broadway delicatessen. The others with Norris also ordered food. Half an hour after it was eaten, Norris complained of pains in his stomach and chest. He was carried across the street to Polyclinic Hospital, where his ailment was diagnosed as a coronary attack. He spent seven weeks in the hospital.

Norris's hospital room was a meeting place for his pals. Carbo came there regularly. The floral display was huge. One bouquet bore a card. It exhorted Norris to get well quickly. It was signed "Albert." The one who had sent the bouquet was Albert Anastasia, a leader in the *Cosa Nostra*. There were flowers from many newspaper reporters who knew Norris well and liked him despite his affinity for tough guys. When Norris left the hospital, he went to his home in Coral Gables to recuperate.

SEVEN

THE BOUT BETWEEN Robinson and Basilio at Yankee Stadium, September 23, 1957, was a financial success. A "live" audience of 38,072 persons paid $556,467. The pay-TV grossed $305,000. Basilio beat Robinson to become the world middleweight champion. He had to resign as the welterweight champion.

As a result of Basilio's abdication of the 147-pound throne, the New York State Athletic Commission ordered that a tournament be held to determine a successor as welterweight champion. Helfand, as chairman of the Commission, was determined to have a title holder crowned as quickly as possible to fill the royal vacancy. He named Isaac Logart, a Cuban; Virgil Akins of St. Louis; and Vince Martinez, of Paterson, New Jersey, as the outstanding contenders.

Now there was a jockeying for position. One of the three contenders would be fortunate enough to fight only once. Helfand decided that the luck of the draw would prevail.

One afternoon, he came to the office of *Ring* magazine in Madison Square Garden and conferred with Nat Fleischer, editor and publisher of the boxing publication.

"What we'll do," Helfand said, "is to toss the three names in a hat. The ones whose names are drawn first will fight. The one whose name is not drawn will get a bye."

"That's all right," Fleischer said. "Let's get some newspapermen in here to witness the drawing."

The three names were written on a single sheet of paper, which was then torn into three pieces, each piece bearing a name. These were placed in a hat and Fleischer, in the presence of the newspapermen, pulled out two slips of paper. Akins' name was written on one, Logart's on the other. Martinez had drawn a bye.

Akins was managed by Bernard Glickman and Eddie Yawitz. Glickman was a wealthy Chicagoan who owned the Kool Vent Awning Company, while Yawitz was a prosperous druggist in St. Louis.

Glickman was to admit later that he was a crony of both Carbo and Palermo, and had in fact received money from the purses of Johnny Saxton, who was nominally managed by Palermo.

Logart, the Cuban fighter, was managed by Eddie Mafuz, a newcomer to boxing who depended for guidance on Sam Crossner, a Bronx neighbor who was also known as Jimmy White. White had been a manager of boxers for many years, but he was without a license in New York and confined his activities for the most part to the promotion of bouts in Denver.

"We can draw real money there," he said. "What'll they give you at the Garden? A few bucks."

"Anything they do is all right with me," Mafuz said.

The Garden wanted the match, and word to this effect was passed to Carbo, who hastily called a war council. The meeting place was Wallman's apartment at 225 West 86th Street, New York City. Billy Brown, Norris's matchmaker, and White were summoned.

Carbo, according to Wallman's later testimony before a New York County grand jury, had come to New York from Florida to settle things for the return bout between Basilio and Robinson, which was to take place in Chicago on March 25, 1958. Indeed, Carbo had been present in Norris's Coral Gables' home some time earlier, when Basilio and his co-manager, John DeJohn, had conferred with the promoter regarding the second bout with Robinson.

Alfred J. Scotti, chief of the rackets bureau in District Attorney Hogan's office, questioned Wallman before the grand jury.

"Do you remember," Scotti asked, "the meeting of February 6 of 1958, which was at your home, attended by Frank Carbo, Jimmy White, Freddie Fierro, and yourself and a few others. Do you recall that?"

"I don't know the date. I do not recall the date but I know that . . . "

"Do you recall that it was February 10 of 1958 when Mr. Norris and Carbo met at your apartment?"

"Right."

"Was it shortly before that that you and Carbo and White . . . "

"And Brown," Wallman interjected.

"And Fierro and some others had a conversation?"

"And Brown."

"And Billy Brown had a conference at your residence?"

"Well, I wouldn't call it a conference."

"Well, if it was a meeting?"

"I will explain."

Wallman did, at a subsequent session of the grand jury.

"At that meeting on February 6, Mr. Wallman, isn't it a fact that White and Brown and Carbo were discussing where the Logart-Akins match should be held?"

"Yes, that's what I'm trying for, that; yes."

"Tell us about the discussion between White, Carbo, and Billy Brown."

"White wanted to fight in Denver, Colorado," Wallman said. "Because he claimed that the Commission—the Colorado State Commission—would sanction a championship fight, and they were interested in making it a championship fight and keep Martinez out of the picture. And Brown insisted that it be held in New York. Carbo, on the other hand, said, 'Look, wherever there is a championship fight, we better take the fight in there.' I mean, and that's what they were hemming and hawing."

"Where?"

"In Denver," Wallman replied. "Wherever they could get a championship fight out of it instead of just an elimination. To go whatever place they can."

"Did Carbo at that meeting also tell Billy Brown if the match were held in Denver it would draw good money? In other words, wasn't Carbo—Carbo was pushing Denver, wasn't he?"

"That's right; yes."

"And White was pushing Denver and Brown wanted it in New York; is that right."

"That's right?"

"Didn't Carbo say, 'You could draw more money out in Denver. Why hold it in New York?' "

"Well, I got to give you a specific answer."

"Do you recall any discussion by Carbo concerning the gate?"

"Yes."

"What did he say?"

"He said it quite a few times. He said, 'You can draw more money over there,' and kept repeating it."

"Meaning Denver, Colorado."

"Yes."

"Did he mention any specific figure?"

"No; figures weren't mentioned. I don't think they were mentioned at that time. Because Jimmy White said they can probably do $60,000, $70,000 over there, and with the television from the IBC they could have a lot of money in there. I mean I don't recall anything else there."

"When was the first time that Carbo mentioned any figure with regard to the fight?"

"I think that was that particular night."

"Any figures like $60,000, $70,000 or how much the match could draw?"

"Jimmy White said that."

"When was the first time that Carbo mentioned any figures?"

"Between themselves. It went back and forth."

"Did you overhear any conversation in which Carbo spoke about the amount of the gate?"

"No; he said we can draw all that more money. I remember that distinctly but I don't remember——"

"Carbo said, 'We can draw more money?' "

"Yes."

"When he said 'we,' whom did he mean?"

"The fight."

"On behalf of whom?"

"I don't know his mind."

"He has to represent somebody."

"Akins. He wasn't representing me nor you. He was representing Akins. Yes."

"What was your part in this discussion?"

"None whatsoever. It didn't concern me at all."

"They held the meeting in your house?"

"The reason they held the meeting in my house is because he was afraid, you know, to run around in different—in the restaurants or this or that, because he was afraid to be seen."

"Who was afraid to be seen?"

"Carbo."

Later, at the meeting, it was arranged for Norris and Carbo to meet at Wallman's apartment February 10, four nights later. When he appeared before the grand jury on May 1, 1958, Wallman testified about the second meeting in his apartment.

"What did Mr. Carbo have to say which you overheard and which concerned fights or fighters on February 10 of 1958?" Scotti asked Wallman.

"Well, I'll start from the very beginning."

"That's it. Start from the beginning."

"Yes. After Jim Norris and Billy Brown arrived at my house, there was Carbo up there, Jimmy White was there, Freddie Fierro, and myself. Now, we all walked into the back room. And I took out a bottle and I offered everybody a drink. Now, we sat down and we had one or two drinks and they started in first. The way they started in was the Zora Folley fight with [Eddie] Machen. Just started off first. There was a fight scheduled in California between two nationally known heavyweights, Number One and Number Two. And they said, 'Now, what are we going to do with the winner of this particular fight? If we could only get Patterson to fight him.'"

"Who said this again?"

"Norris to Carbo."

"To Carbo?"

"In effect to everybody in there. But mostly directed at Carbo."

"Go ahead."

"After this we filled up another drink, and they started talking about Logart. With that Jimmy White opened up his mouth and he says, 'Look, under no circumstance,' he says, 'I being a good friend of Eddie Mafuz, that is a manager of Logart,' he says, 'he promised me to take the fight in Denver.' Norris on the other hand said, 'No, we need the match.' But I do not recall. I mean, I am going back now to what went before, about this Helfand business."

"Go ahead."

"Then Jimmy got sore and walked out."

"You mean Jim Norris?"

"No, Jimmy White. Walked out and got sore and he walked out into the living room. Then I remained there with Billy Brown and Norris and Carbo. The four of us remained there, and they started talking. Now, they jumped off the subject of Logart and Akins. They jumped off the subject and well, 'We don't know what to do.' "

"Yes; go ahead."

"So I went in and I filled up a drink for them and with that Carbo says to me, 'Hey, you are a lousy bartender; you are a better furrier.' Which gave me an idea that they didn't want me in the room, see? So I went out and Jimmy White started to talk to me. He said, 'What the hell are they doing, running boxing? What is this here? I can't get a fight? Are they going to run my life, too?' "

"Meaning who?"

"Meaning Carbo, Brown, and Norris."

"Yes."

"So I said, 'Now, wait a minute. Go back and yell.' "

"You told that to White?"

"Yes, 'Go back and yell. You got the right to fight for your own livelihood.' Well, I heard so much commotion that I came back into the room. And Jimmy White started giving them the same thing again. He said, 'I want the match.' And Norris right back, 'We need the match in New York.' And hemming and hawing, Jimmy White says, 'Well, if that's the way you want it, go ahead, keep it,' and he walked out of the room. They sat down. Well, and Jim Norris says, 'Who the hell is he?' this way."

"Meaning Jimmy White?"

"Jimmy White. 'Oh, forget him.' "

"What did Carbo say?"

"Well, about the same thing. Once the boss said, 'The hell with him,' the other fellow didn't say any more."

"Who is 'the boss?' "

"Well, Norris, Jim Norris."

"He is the sole boss?"

"Well, I mean he is the big shot, the big promoter."

"How about Carbo?"

"Well, Carbo is in a different sense."

"A different kind of boss?"

"You asked me about the main boss last night and I says as far as I am concerned I don't know him as no boss."

"Let me ask you, as man to man, let us call a spade a spade."

"Yes, yes."

"You refer to Norris as the boss, but isn't also Carbo referred unofficially as 'a boss' too?"

"Yes. Yes."

"Unofficially as a boss, too."

"Yes."

"Would you say he is a boss almost with equal rights as Norris?"

"Well, one has got the money and the other one hasn't got no money."

"He has what, he has the contacts, the influence, though; is that right?"

"Yes."

"Right?"

"Yes."

"That is Carbo has the contacts and influence; is that right?"

"That's right."

"Go ahead, proceed with your statement."

"The minute he shirked him aside, he said, 'The hell with White,' they started to talk about back again to Folley, about what they were going to do in case there was a good fight and Machen won it and not Folley. In fact, Folley was thrown aside, also like Jimmy White. But they were more interested in Machen than they were in Folley. If they could only get Patterson to fight him, that would be a feather in their cap. And Frank said to Jim—incidentally, this is as I recall —he says, 'You will never get the crazy man [Cus D'Amato] to fight you.' With that, Mr. Scotti, and gentlemen, and lady, a phone call came in from Benny Trotta, in Baltimore. A phone came in. I'm not sure—I think I answered the phone. I says, 'Frank, your friend Benny Trotta wants you.' And then he got on the phone and while he got on the phone I went back into the living room, stayed there maybe another five minutes, ten minutes, and he was still talking when I entered back again into the barroom."

"When you say 'he,' whom do you mean?"

"Carbo."

"With whom?"

"With Benny Trotta."

"Go ahead."

"I overheard him talking about a [Holley] Mims fight; that he must get Mims a fight. And I don't know what transpired over the phone or what he said to him in the end, he says, 'All right, don't worry about Mims. Don't worry about Mims.' "

"You mean Carbo said this?"

"Yes, Carbo telling Trotta. He put me on the phone to say hello, or was it the first time when I answered the phone, 'Hello, Benny,' or was it the last time? But that's all for that conversation that he was going to; 'OK, don't worry about it, I'll get you a fight.' Well, after that I think they were hitting the bottle pretty good and they started off kidding me about [Alex] Miteff. 'What are you going to do with him?' Well I said, 'He is not ready for any big fights. He is just a starter and a youngster. I got plenty of time with him.' And we were all back again in what we were going to do with the fight with Logart."

"Who is talking to you at this time, Carbo?"

"Well, Jim is talking with Carbo for everybody to hear it already. A little big shot already."

"In other words, you are relating a conversation between Norris and Carbo?"

"Yes, I am relating everything that I can remember transpired up there that evening."

"This is Norris and Carbo talking now?"

"Yes, most of the time the only two that talked over there was Norris and Carbo, because the little sheep had nothing to say there."

"The little who?"

"The little sheep."

"Sheep?"

"Yes, Jimmy White and myself was the little sheep. I don't think Billy Brown had too much to say up there because the two big men were up there. The two big men, I expressed myself again, was Carbo and Norris. And they kept on and then they started in general with this fight and that fight, that I don't recall offhand exactly what fights they were referring to, for future, and with that my wife kept nagging, 'When do you eat? When do you eat?' I said, 'If I get rid of them, then I'll eat. What do you want me to do?' So then Norris forgot that he had an appointment for dinner. He makes an appointment with me for dinner. Then he forgot all of a sudden when he had too many drinks that he forgot that he had another dinner. He said, 'I must go.' So Billy Brown and Norris went away. They left. He took them downstairs, in fact. And then Billy Brown came back again and Frank, Jimmy White, Billy Brown, we remained, and we were having dinner when Jimmy White started the discussion again about, 'Who the hell is he running boxing and we can't get nothing? Does he want nobody to make a living?' Jimmy White was telling that to Carbo. 'Nobody is going to make a living. He's got everything. He got to own everything.' "

"Who is 'he'?"

"Norris."

EIGHT

IN ACCORDANCE WITH Fleischer's drawing from a hat, Akins and Logart were matched in a welterweight championship elimination bout at Madison Square Garden on Friday, March 21, 1958. The survivor would meet Martinez later for the world's championship.

All week long, betting on the fight had been heavy. Logart was the favorite all the way, first at 8 to 6, then to 9 to 7, and on the afternoon of the fight, 11 to 5. For five rounds, the Cuban boxer moved around his opponent and scored with smashing left hooks. Those who had bet on the favorite were pleased.

Suddenly, in the sixth round, Logart lost speed of foot and hand. He was battered by a long left hook and went down on his side. Referee Harry Kessler counted to four. Logart rose and moved unsteadily toward the ropes, where Akins caught up with him and hit him with both hands. Although Logart was not on the floor, the referee started to count. Logart, helpless, was unhearing. The count reached eight, and Kessler stopped the fight. The time was 2:53; only seven seconds remained before the bell would have saved Logart.

Strangely, Logart's corner did not protest the outcome. All was quiet until District Attorney Hogan's men started passing among the crowd. Subpoenas to appear before a New York County grand jury were being handed to an odd assortment of characters.

Mafuz and White received invitations. So did Mushky McGee, Norris's office boy. So did Willie ("Ketchum") Friedland, who managed Jimmy Carter, an ex-lightweight champion. Brown also received a subpoena, as did Glickman, Akins' co-manager. Eventually, Wallman was to receive one. He made several appearances before the grand jury, which indicted Wallman's house guest, Carbo, on several counts as an undercover manager of fighters.

Two days after the knockout of Logart by Akins, the Chicago Boxing Writers and Broadcasters Association held its 1958 Ring Dinner in the Walnut Room of the Bismarck Hotel in Chicago. Choice of the venue was fortuitous; Norris and Wirtz owned the hotel.

As was the custom of the writers' and broadcasters' association, annual awards were made at the dinner. Norris was given the Packey McFarland Award "for contributing most to boxing," while Glickman received the "manager of the year award," courtesy of Truman Gibson.

When Glickman was asked to speak, he told the two hundred diners he was overjoyed by the honor the association had bestowed on him. Then, referring to the subpoena he had received at Madison Square Garden, he said, "I do not know why the Honorable Mr. Hogan wants me. If he had called me up, I would be only too happy to talk to him." He also identified himself as the only man on the dais who had received a subpoena from Hogan.

Glickman's humor was not lost on Detective Anthony Bernhard of the New York City Police Department, who had been dispatched by District Attorney Hogan's office to Chicago to keep under surveillance those fight mobsters who had gathered there for the return bout, on March 25, 1958, between Basilio and Robinson. He was accompanied by Detective Frank Nostramo and Detective Frank Marrone.

Bernhard and Nostramo obtained tickets to the dinner and were seated at a table with several Chicagoans, one of whom was called "George." During the course of the evening, George left the table. When he returned, he said to the others at the table, "Frank just got in town and was dropped off at the hotel."

Bernhard left the table to communicate with Marrone. In the lobby he saw Palermo in a phone booth. Bernhard entered the next booth and heard Palermo say, "When did you get in? I have been trying to call you all day. I called all over."

The detective left his listening post and informed Marrone he had heard Palermo mention the Palmer House, another Chicago hotel. Marrone learned that Carbo had registered at the Palmer House and was occupying Rooms 1149 West and 1150 West. He had registered as "Mr. and Mrs. Frank Palermo." Carbo, it developed, was in constant touch with Room 1149 in the hotel. Room 1149 was registered in the name of Gilbert Lee, a bookmaker of widespread reputation.

On the night of the Basilio-Robinson bout, Carbo was trailed by the two detectives to the Ambassador East Hotel. Al Weill, Norris's former matchmaker and Marciano's former manager, was a guest at the hotel. At the time, Weill was being mentioned as the promoter of Floyd Patterson's impending title defense against Roy Harris in Los Angeles. He was Carbo's pal.

NINE

B Y MID-APRIL, 1958, the heat was really on. Whispering was heard concerning the testimony adduced before the New York County grand jury. It stressed the meeting of Norris and Carbo at Wallman's apartment. On April 18, the International Boxing Club of New York announced Norris's resignation as president.

"I hereby tender my resignation as President and Director of

International Boxing Club of New York, Inc.," Norris wrote, "and request that it be made effective immediately."

Norris said he was taking the action because "my doctors advised me last Fall following a severe heart attack to restrict my activities by resigning as head of this Company."

He went on, "Mr. Truman Gibson was elected Executive Vice-President of the Company last Fall and has been very helpful in relieving me of many of my executive duties, and I am sure that he and the organization can effectively carry on."

It was announced furthermore that Gibson had been elected Norris's successor at the meeting of the board of directors of the IBC. Markson was also elected a director of the company.

TEN

AKINS GAVE Vince Martinez a chance to win the world's welterweight title in St. Louis on June 6, 1958. The bout took place in the St. Louis Arena, one of the sports stadiums owned by Norris and Wirtz. St. Louis police were especially busy during the week of the bout.

The St. Louis Police Department Intelligence Division kept a covey of mobsters, including Palermo, under surveillance in the hotels where the fight crowd gathered. They harried Palermo because, at the time, they had information that Palermo shared with John Vitale, a leading St. Louis racketeer, in the management of Charles ("Sonny") Liston, a heavy-handed St. Louis heavyweight.

On the night of the fight they picked up Palermo on suspicion and questioned him about gambling and narcotics. He was released.

Akins won the fight with Martinez by knockout in the fourth round. His enfranchised managers, Glickman and Yawitz, were beside themselves with joy. Their hero now owned the 147-pound championship. Carbo and Palermo, in turn, were "pieced in" on Akins' contract.

Within a few months, Carbo would be indicted, but his clutches reached everywhere in boxing. In California, Al Weill was preparing to promote Floyd Patterson's third defense of the world's heavyweight championship, this one against Roy Harris, a quaint schoolmaster from Cut 'N Shoot, Texas.

D'Amato had been braying for years against gangster influence in boxing, yet he had chosen Weill as the promoter of the Patterson-Harris bout while knowing that Weill had been closely allied with Carbo. Furthermore, Harris was managed by Lou Viscusi, who had been known to be on talking terms with Carbo.

The California Athletic Commission rejected Weill as a co-promoter with the Hollywood Legion Stadium. D'Amato looked around him for a promoter.

In New York, William P. Rosensohn, thirty-eight years of age, an employee of TelePrompTer Corporation, asked D'Amato for the promotorial rights to the bout.

"Have you got that kind of cabbage?" D'Amato asked.

"I'll have it."

"You got it," D'Amato said.

Nobody in boxing took Rosensohn seriously. He had never promoted a bout, although he had the advantage of being completely versed in the closed-circuit telecasting of boxing. He was introduced to the press at a luncheon in Mama Leone's Restaurant, off Broadway. The food was fine. Rosensohn asserted his capabilities while the journalists ate heartily of fine Italian food. He surprised everybody by turning in a fair job as a promoter. Instead of losing $50,000, as everybody who knew about such things expected, he came through with a loss of only $3,000. Patterson came off the floor to knock out Harris in the twelfth round at Wrigley Field, Los Angeles, on August 18, 1958.

Pleased with his performance as a promoter in his first venture, Rosensohn returned to New York and later conferred with D'Amato.

"When will I get a chance to promote again?" Rosensohn asked.

"Well, I have got a lot of obligations to people," D'Amato said. "Maybe a year, maybe two years."

"Supposing I develop my own contender and bring him in, would

I then take precedence over some of those people you have obligations to?"

"If the contender is acceptable to me," D'Amato said.

"Well, let me try," Rosensohn said.

ELEVEN

WHILE ROSENSOHN was busy promoting the Patterson-Harris bout, the New York County grand jury was also learning about boxing. Late in July, Paul John Carbo, alias Frankie Carbo, alias Frank Russo, alias Mr. Gray, was indicted on a ten-count true bill charging him with conspiracy, undercover management of fighters, and unlicensed matchmaking in bouts promoted by the International Boxing Club.

In the ten-count indictment Carbo was accused of acting as both undercover manager and undercover matchmaker in the Akins-Logart bout at the Garden, the one he had discussed at great length on two occasions in Wallman's apartment.

District Attorney Hogan sent out a nationwide alarm for Carbo's arrest. The "wanted" bulletin was broadcast to every police agency in the country. It described Carbo as "Male, white, 54, five feet eight inches tall, 180 pounds, with brown eyes, gray hair, partly bald, sallow complexion, and a neat dresser." It concluded: "Warrant issued. Will extradite."

District Attorney Hogan said Carbo had last been reported in Tiajuana, Mexico. He was said to have been in the company of Al Weill.

TWELVE

THE GRAND JURY did not halt its investigation of boxing the moment it indicted Carbo as an undercover manager. For months, District Attorney Hogan attempted to bring Norris before the grand jury to testify on his association and dealings with Carbo. Finally, in November, 1958, a physician appointed by the New York State Supreme Court recommended that Norris's health would not permit him to testify.

Dr. Abram Wilbur Duryea was the physician who gave Norris the certificate of ill health. Dr. Duryea, a specialist in cardiovascular diseases and a professor of clinical medicine at Cornell University, expressed the opinion "that with the objective evidence found in this case of rather severe heart disease the emotional stress of a court appearance could readily produce another myocardial infarction which in itself could be fatal."

"Myocardial infarction" is translated as a type of heart attack.

Justice Jacob Markowitz accepted Dr. Duryea's recommendation.

Although Norris was no longer president of the International Boxing Club, he was still president of Madison Square Garden, which controlled the IBC of New York.

There had been other indictments by the New York County grand jury, but none named anybody as important in boxing as Carbo. Jimmy White was indicted for acting as an undercover manager, but the case against him was so nebulous he was never brought to trial. A few years later, the indictment was dismissed.

The grand jury also indicted a boxing judge who was accused of accepting money from Wallman to cast the right votes in bouts at Madison Square Garden, but he, too, was never brought to the bar. The indictment against him was dismissed.

Apart from Carbo, only Genovese was on the hook. Rather mildly, the grand jury had named him as the unlicensed manager in 1956 of Ludwig Lightburn, a rather unpromising lightweight who was handled by Allie Clark, a retired New York City policeman.

Genovese, the indictment stated, had collected $4,056 from Lightburn's purses.

After Genovese's conviction, and before his sentencing by Judge John A. Mullen, Genovese was described by Assistant District Attorney John G. Bonomi as "an evil and degrading influence on professional boxing for over two decades."

Genovese, Bonomi said forcefully, "collected $10,000 from Norman Rothschild, an upstate fight promoter, to stage the Carmen Basilio-Johnny Saxton welterweight championship match held on September 12, 1956, in Syracuse."

The prosecutor also cited chapter and verse regarding Genovese's activities as Carbo's bagman: "Joe Netro and John DeJohn, the licensed co-managers of former welterweight and middleweight champion, Carmen Basilio, stated to me that they paid Genovese $7,000 from the managers' share of Basilio's purses in 1956. During that year Herman Wallman, also known as Hymie Wallman, gave Genovese $1,500 from the earnings of Charlie Cotton, a prominent middleweight. In 1957, Netro and DeJohn shelled out $20,000 to Genovese from Basilio's earnings, and Wallman contributed $640 from a Cotton purse."

Basilio earned more than $500,000 in his two bouts with Robinson, in 1957 and 1958. Genovese's tribute went up in direct ratio to Basilio's purses, Bonomi insisted.

"In the past year," the prosecutor said, "Basilio's co-managers, according to their own statements, gave Genovese $24,000. That makes a grand total of $67,196 to Genovese in ring plunder during the past three years."

Everybody drew the inference that Genovese had been a collector for Carbo.

Genovese was sentenced to two years in the Rikers Island Penitentiary, but served a little more than one year. Soon after his release, he died.

THIRTEEN

CARBO WAS STILL a fugitive. The long arm of the law reached everywhere, but could not pluck him from his hiding place. Boxing people had no such difficulty. Along Jacobs' Beach it was known that Carbo was in Florida.

Basilio and his co-manager, DeJohn, were visitors in Miami Beach in January, 1959. Negotiations had begun for a third bout between Basilio and Robinson, but Sugar Ray had been demanding too much money, according to Basilio, and negotiations had reached a stalemate. One morning, while the fighter and his manager were passing the time of day in the hotel lobby, DeJohn suddenly said, "Let's take a ride, Carmen." They did.

As Basilio would describe the incident later, "We went down Biscayne Boulevard, pulled into a Howard Johnson's. We were going to get a cup of coffee, and as we got out of the car to walk across the drive a car pulled up and I had seen this fellow before— did not know him—but I had seen him. We talked to him, Johnny talked to him, and he says, 'Get in the car and we'll go for a ride.' So we got in the car, and I did not pay attention to just where we went. We went a few blocks and made a left or right turn, and we came to this house and parked in the driveway.

"We got out and walked toward the back of it and in the back was a screened-in patio. They had a swimming pool in the back and, well, we walked in and there was Frank Carbo there."

Basilio was surprised; Carbo wasn't. Basilio shook hands with Carbo, who asked almost immediately, "How are you making out with the progress in the Robinson fight?"

"Well, it looks like Robinson wants too much money, wants everything, and Carmen would not fight for less than 30 per cent," DeJohn said.

They talked for about ten minutes, according to Basilio, and as they were leaving, Carbo said to DeJohn, "Well, do the best you can in getting the percentage."

Basilio and DeJohn returned to their hotel. The fighter went to his room to see his wife Kay. He was there only a few minutes when the telephone rang. Blinky Palermo was calling.

"We're down in the lobby. Jim Norris wants us to bring you over to his house in Coral Gables," Palermo said. "He wants to talk to you about the Robinson fight."

Basilio went down to the lobby. Palermo was accompanied by Gabe Genovese. Basilio drove in their car to Norris's house in Coral Gables. Norris answered the door. The guests were taken to the swimming pool area off a screened-in recreation room. As they went through the house they saw a large, tastefully furnished living room, a splendid dining room, and then the swimming pool. In a canal running in back of Norris's house there was a thirty-six foot speedboat. When Basilio looked around him, Palermo and Genovese had disappeared.

Norris began discussing the projected fight between Basilio and Robinson. The fighter insisted he would not accept less than 30 per cent for his end of the purse.

"Well, it is going to be a tough thing," Norris said. "Because Robinson is going to want more than 40 per cent."

"I don't care what Robinson gets," Basilio said, "I have got to have 30 per cent."

Breakfast was served, and after eating Basilio and Norris played with an electrically-powered hockey game which simulated action on the ice. Unexpectedly, there was a telephone call for Norris, who spoke for a few minutes and then turned to Basilio and said, "Frankie wants to talk to you."

Basilio took the phone and talked with Carbo. Later he would say, "Carbo never made sense to me. This guy talks in circles, as far as I am concerned. And he hemmed and hawed on the telephone. He asked how I was doing talking about the Robinson fight. I said I'm asking for 30 per cent and I am not going to fight for less. He says 'Good luck' to me and that was that."

The third bout between Basilio and Robinson did not happen.

FOURTEEN

NORRIS WAS STILL AT Coral Gables on Monday, January 12, when the Supreme Court in Washington affirmed Judge Ryan's decision sundering Norris's empire. By a 5-to-3 decision, the Court held that the Norris, Wirtz, Madison Square Garden, and the various International Boxing clubs had violated the Sherman Act by conspiring to control the promotion of world championship bouts throughout the United States.

Judge Ryan had ordered Norris and Wirtz to resign their positions with the Madison Square Garden Corporation, to sell all their Garden stock within five years, and to dissolve the International Boxing Club of New York, Inc. and the International Boxing Club of Illinois, Inc. Ryan's decree had also restricted the Garden and the Chicago Stadium, which Wirtz and Norris owned, to the promotion of no more than two championship bouts a year for five years.

Gibson was in London when the Supreme Court decision was announced. He had gone there to see Henry Cooper, a London plasterer, fight Brian London, a pudgy brawler, for the British Empire heavyweight championship. Cooper was the winner.

In London, Gibson said, "The International Boxing clubs have no alternative but to comply with the Supreme Court decision ordering dissolution. When I return to New York tomorrow, I shall see our counsel to decide what to do. I do not think the court intended to stop boxing or televised boxing, but rather to separate the New York and Chicago operations."

Justice Tom Clark wrote the prevailing opinion. He addressed himself to the defendants' claim that Judge Ryan's decision was "punitive, oppressive, and unnecessarily severe."

Justice Clark said that narrower curbs on the defendants would have defeated the government "in its effort to free the professional boxing business of monopoly." The government, he wrote, "would have won the battle but lost the war."

Justice John Marshall Harlan, writing for the minority, called the "drastic remedy" of divesting Norris and Wirtz of their stock in

Madison Square Garden unsupported by the record in the case. He called the dissolution of Norris's clubs a "punitive" measure.

There was widespread speculation concerning the future of Norris and Wirtz in Madison Square Garden. While they had five years in which to sell their stock in the Garden, they were under orders to break up the boxing clubs immediately. They were unhappy, and in Coral Gables the splendid house on Granada Boulevard was under a pall. Norris and Wirtz held a meeting there and decided to get out of the Garden as quickly as they could dispose of their holdings.

One weekend Norris received a call from Tom S. Gallery, who was director of sports for the National Broadcasting Company. Gallery asked Norris if he would be interested in making a deal with the Graham-Paige Corporation, of which Gallery's friend, Rear Admiral John J. Bergen, USNR, retired, was chairman of the board.

"Have him call me," Norris said.

"He'll be in touch with you," Gallery replied.

Within weeks a deal was closed. The Graham-Paige Corporation paid the Norris and Wirtz interests $3,948,300 for·their holdings in the Garden. Their 219,350 shares represented 40 per cent of the shares issued by the Madison Square Garden Corporation.

The value of the 219,350 shares was carried on the books of Madison Square Garden at $1,723,580, but the stock had increased in value while Norris and Wirtz controlled the Garden. The price of each share they sold to Graham-Paige came to about $18.23. On the day of the sale, the stock closed at $16.75 on the New York Stock Exchange. The value of Graham-Paige stock rose 50 cents to $3.00 each on a turnover of 116,100 shares.

Judge Ryan did not concern himself with these financial matters. On February 18, 1959, he approved the sale to the Graham-Paige Corporation. Norris's time at Madison Square Garden was at an end.

The "new people" at the Garden immediately organized Madison Square Garden Boxing, Inc., and they continued the production of Friday night bouts, which were telecast by the National Broadcasting Company. In Chicago, Norris organized the National Boxing Club, which presented boxing on TV Wednesday nights. Markson was named general manager of boxing at the Garden; Gibson assumed a similar role at the Chicago Stadium.

Inevitably, sports writers began referring to Norris's new boxing club as "NBC," just as they had called the International Boxing Club "IBC." The National Broadcasting Company asked Norris to change the name of his new corporation. It became the National Boxing Enterprises. It was, in a sense, stillborn.

FIFTEEN

J OE LOUIS, whose resignation as heavyweight champion in 1949 had started it all, stood by and wondered. Some years earlier he had sold out his interest in the Norris empire in exchange for an income of $20,000 a year, paid in equal parts by the International Boxing Club of New York and the International Boxing Club of Illinois. Now, it was a new deal.

On March 20, 1959, almost ten years to the day after the announcement of Louis's abdication and the formal organization of the boxing conspiracy, Markson wrote a letter. It was addressed to Mr. Joe Louis, 1711 Wellington Road, Los Angeles, California. It said:

Dear Joe:

As you must know, the Supreme Court decision in the government's antitrust case against the International Boxing Club, the Garden, etc., made it necessary to separate completely the operations of Madison Square Garden and the Chicago Stadium. We learn that you are to be associated with the National Boxing Enterprises. Our lawyers tell us that we are not permitted to carry you on our payroll at the same time. We are sorry that this is so, Joe, but maybe sometime in the future we'll be able to use your services again without breaking any of Uncle Sam's laws.

With kindest personal good wishes.

> Sincerely yours,
> HARRY MARKSON
> Managing Director, Boxing

Once again, Louis was cast among the lions.

SIXTEEN

I N APRIL, 1959, District Attorney Hogan was still looking for
Carbo. Boxing men knew the fugitive had transferred his hideout
from the Miami area to New Jersey, but nobody was talking.

At that time, DeJohn was invited to Philadephia to discuss a
possible match between Basilio and Joey Giardello, a trouble-ridden
Philadelphia middleweight who was managed by one Anthony
Ferrante. DeJohn accepted the invitation.

In Philadelphia, DeJohn and Ferrante discussed the match.

"I don't think Carmen would be sold on a match like that,"
DeJohn told Ferrante. "We are looking to fight Gene Fullmer because we can't make the Robinson fight."

"Well, all right, you can go and talk it over with Carmen and see
what he has to say."

Then, unexpectedly, Ferrante said, "How about going over to the
race track with me? We can get some action. It's Garden State, you
know."

DeJohn agreed to go with Ferrante. On the way to the track
Ferrante stopped his car in front of a house on Crystal Lake Terrace,
in Hayden Township, just outside of Camden, New Jersey.

"Come on in," Ferrante said as he left the car.

DeJohn followed. Inside, he was greeted by Carbo.

"How are you?" Carbo said. "What are you doing?"

Surprised, DeJohn could not manage an answer. He looked
around. Palermo was present. They talked about boxing and baseball and horse racing, and then DeJohn and Ferrante went to the
race track. DeJohn won a few bets.

So did Lieutenant George Salayka and three other detectives from
Hogan's office, on May 29, about a month after DeJohn's unex-
pected confrontation of Carbo. Forty-five minutes after midnight
on that date, Salayka, his three detective companions from New
York, and New Jersey State troopers surrounded the house in which
DeJohn had talked with Carbo.

When Salayka, at the front door, announced that the house was surrounded, Carbo, who was fully dressed, bounded out of a rear window and fled into the arms of two detectives with drawn guns. He surrendered meekly and one of his captors described him as "mild-mannered, polite, and soft-spoken." He had $2,800 in cash in a trouser pocket.

In New York, District Attorney Hogan happily announced Carbo's arrest. Carbo fought extradition, but while he was in jail in New Jersey a new blow hit him from an unexpected direction.

SEVENTEEN

VIRGIL AKINS defended the world welterweight championship against Don Jordan in the Olympic Auditorium in Los Angeles on December 5, 1958. Akins's co-manager, Glickman, the celebrity of the testimonial dinner at Norris's Bismarck Hotel earlier in the year, had told the grand jury in New York that he wanted to get out of boxing, but he had remained in it because he was, to his surprise, the manager of a world champion and hoped to recoup some of the financial losses he had endured in the game.

His losses were substantial. Glickman had been involved with Palermo in the management of Johnny Saxton and had, back in 1954, put up a $40,000 guarantee to get Saxton a welterweight title bout with Kid Gavilan. The bout had been a notorious hoax, and Gavilan, who was adjudged the winner by most of the reporters at ringside, lost his championship. The outcry was great, and charges of gangsterism in boxing were heard everywhere.

Four years later, Glickman was disillusioned with boxing. Somebody had sold him a bill of goods, and he had invested some $140,000 in an arena in South Florida that had proved a failure. He lost the entire investment. In addition, his prosperous manufacturing business was on the verge of liquidation. Boxing, he would say later, "wound up destroying me."

He had testified before the grand jury in New York that he had once loaned Carbo $10,000 without a cent in collateral. He told the jurors he had arranged to get the $10,000 in cash from Yawitz, the St. Louis druggist who was his partner in the management of Akins.

"Well, as near as I can recall," Glickman had testified, "Yawitz came into the office, my office, and this other party came into my office, and I gave him the money, and he took it away, and I verified later that Frank Carbo received it. That's the whole thing."

"Who was the party who came into the office?"

"He identified himself as Mike."

"Did he tell you who the $10,000 was for?"

"He didn't know what he was getting or anything else. He identified himself as Mike and got the money in a sealed envelope. I verified later with Frankie that he received it."

"He told you that it was money that Frank Carbo wanted, is that right?"

"I don't remember what he said. He said he was from him, yes."

"You never saw that person before. Is that right?"

"No, I saw him down in Florida."

"Do you know who that person was?"

"Mike."

"Mike who?"

"I don't know. It sounds funny."

"Do you know where he lives?"

"I think he lives in Chicago."

"Do you know what his business is?"

"No."

"Did you hand him $10,000 in cash?"

"That is right."

"Can you describe this fellow Mike?"

"About five feet ten inches."

"How old a man was he?"

"About thirty."

"What color hair?"

"Curly hair. Sometimes it is impossible to remember a face and try to remember a face. I saw him many times in Chicago and I saw him down in Florida."

"Is he a friend of Carbo's?"

"I don't know. I imagine he is."

Glickman was; he waited, by his own admission, a year and a half to get his money back in two installments, one of $3,500, the other of $6,500.

Carbo, Glickman admitted, had been the go-between in making the Akins-Logart bout, the one in which Akins had surprisingly and suddenly knocked out Logart. He testified that Carbo had informed him that Akins' purse for the bout with Logart would be $20,000.

"Carbo called me one time," Glickman testified, "and told me that we are—we're going to get $20,000. I said, 'Swell, good, I am happy.' Where he got it from or what, I hoped it was from the horse's mouth. The next day or two days later I did get the call we were going to get $20,000, so I accomplished my purpose."

That call was from Jim Norris.

Akins' bout with Jordan was a dismal affair. Akins was the favorite at odds of 3 to 1, but he lost without making a stand. Instead of punching, he wrestled with Jordan and lost points for hitting low. When the bout was over, Jordan was declared the winner.

Sports Illustrated took note of the strange event. "There will, of course, be a return bout and it probably will be in Akins' home town, St. Louis." The magazine concluded. "That may give a clue as to whether Akins has set out on the win-lose, win-lose road that Jimmy Carter took in the lightweight division."

The consequences of Akins' unexpected defeat were even more shocking than anybody suspected.

EIGHTEEN

BILL ROSENSOHN's appetite for boxing was whetted by his role as entrepreneur in the Patterson-Harris bout. It was in his commercial blood. On September 14, 1958, Ingemar Johansson, a Swedish heavyweight who was unbeaten and unfamiliar to American fight fans, fought Eddie Machen, the leading heavyweight contender, at Goteborg, Sweden. Enterprisingly, Rosensohn flew to Sweden to see the fight.

Johansson knocked out Machen with a right-hand blow to the jaw in the first round. Rosensohn, who was perhaps the only American fan among the 55,000 persons in the stadium at Goteborg, was overjoyed. He had made certain of one point before going to Sweden: Johansson was not tied up to Norris or to the International Boxing Club in any way. Such nonalliance was a prior condition invoked by D'Amato before he would consider any opponent for Patterson.

Minutes after Johansson's victory, Rosensohn was in conference with the winner's adviser, Edwin Ahlquist, who also doubled as promoter. Before long, Rosensohn had paid Johansson $10,000 for a forty-day option on his services. All he needed to do now was to get D'Amato to sign for a bout between Patterson and Johansson, the signature to be obtained within the forty-day option period.

The next day Rosensohn flew back to the United States and presented himself to D'Amato, who greeted him warmly. Then, as the days passed, D'Amato ignored the young man. The manager said he was now considering a match between Patterson and Nino Valdes.

Rosensohn was frantic. He told D'Amato, "Cus, look what's going to happen now. I have only got ten days left before my option on Johansson runs out. If I don't sign—if I don't get Patterson to sign up—or, in effect, if you sign for Patterson, I am going to lose the Johansson deal."

"Well, I didn't tell you to sign that option," D'Amato said. "That's your problem."

On the way out of D'Amato's office one day, Rosensohn ran into Charles Antonucci, alias Charley Black, a former second-rate bookmaker who was D'Amato's confidant. Rosensohn blurted out the story of his troubles.

"Well, maybe Tony Salerno can help you," Black said.

"I'd like to talk to him."

"Why don't I bring him over to your apartment tomorrow?"

"All right," Rosensohn said.

The next day Salerno turned up at Rosensohn's apartment on Central Park West. They talked, and Salerno said he was interested in the proposed deal and would try to help Rosensohn.

Four days later, after another fruitless appeal to D'Amato, Rosen-sohn told Black, "Charley, I guess you had better bring Salerno over."

Black was prompt. The next morning he had Salerno at Rosen-sohn's apartment once again.

"Well, now, tell me what is your deal?" Rosensohn asked.

"Well, we would like to . . . I would like part of the promotion."

"What do you call 'part'?"

"Well, I'll make a fair deal with you. I'll put up all the money that the promotion needs, and I want a third of the profits."

"Will I get an agreement for the fight before the forty-day period expires?"

"Don't worry," Salerno said.

On the way out, Salerno turned to Rosensohn and said, "What are you going to do for my friend Charley?"

"Charley is your friend and you take care of him."

"Oh no, Charley is Cus's friend. I think you ought to take care of him."

"How should I take care of him?"

"Well, I think Charley ought to get at least the same as I have."

Rosensohn couldn't argue. His back was to the wall. Not only was he aware of Salerno's financial reliability but he knew that Salerno's connections assured him of the promotional rights to the title bout. He had met Salerno some years earlier through Gilbert Lee Beckley, the bookmaker who had been Carbo's neighbor at the Palmer House in Chicago the week of the Basilio-Robinson bout. Rosensohn had been a steady customer of Beckley's.

Salerno, who was also known as Anthony Russo to the New York City Police Department, had influence in the underworld utterly out of keeping with his criminal record. He had been arrested only once, in October, 1935, for bookmaking and had paid a $100 fine in the Court of Special Sessions, hardly enough of a dossier to equate him with the other hoodlums who wandered into the boxing busi-ness. Yet he was able to achieve Rosensohn's purpose. He delivered the fight.

Patterson fought Johansson under the promotion of Rosensohn Enterprises, Inc., at Yankee Stadium on June 26, 1959. Johansson floored Patterson seven times and scored a knockout in the third round in a startling upset. Although it rained most of the day, the bout drew $470,000 at the gate, a fair figure but not enough to make the promotion profitable. The loss came to $70,000.

Everybody but Rosensohn was unhappy. He looked forward to promoting the return bout between Johansson and Patterson, but instead of staying in New York to tie up loose ends he went off to California for a vacation. Upon his return, he received a telegram from Vincent J. Velella, Salerno's lawyer. The telegram informed Rosensohn that he was not to take any action in behalf of Rosensohn Enterprises, Inc.

"As majority stockholder, director and counsel of Rosensohn Enterprises," the telegram said, "I must remind you that no deal, commitments, or other arrangements are to be made by you with respect to the forthcoming Patterson-Johansson return bout without proper consultation and appropriate approvals from Rosensohn Enterprises, Inc."

Rosensohn was angry. He was aware that the promotion had lost money, because D'Amato had insisted that the promoter could retain 50 per cent of the net gate only, without any recourse to any of the receipts from the closed-circuit television, which provided a large pot of gold for Patterson, D'Amato, and TelePromTer, Inc.

Actually, Rosensohn had been caught with his plans exposed. In California he had indeed discussed with Gibson an amalgamation of interests with National Boxing Enterprises, Norris's new organization. Velella's telegram had put a crimp in his plan. He called Gibson in Chicago, and Gibson urged him to come to Chicago and talk with Norris, who wasn't letting go.

NINETEEN

BY 1959, Jackie Leonard had been in the fight business for many years. His real name was Leonard Blakely, but he had fought as "Jackie Leonard" and had retained the name after retiring from the ring. He was forty-two years old, married. He had a home in Los Angeles, a swimming pool, and troubles.

No man can point back to a precise moment and say his troubles began then, but perhaps Leonard could cite March 25, 1958, as the beginning of his ordeal. Leonard was then the matchmaker of the Hollywood Legion Stadium, where boxing was conducted under the auspices of Hollywood Post 43.

On that day in March, 1958, Leonard was in Chicago to attend the second bout between Basilio and Robinson. He encountered Norris, who told him that Carbo wanted to see him. Leonard did not attempt to communicate with Carbo, but later in the day he received a call from Al Weill, who came to Leonard's hotel and then accompanied him to the Palmer House, where Carbo was staying.

In Carbo's suite, Leonard was to testify in a federal court later, "they held trial for me more or less." The trial took place because Leonard, in Carbo's opinion, was not giving fighters managed by Weill enough work at the Hollywood Legion Stadium.

Several months later, Gibson went out to Hollywood and stayed at the Hotel Roosevelt, where he held a meeting with George Parnassus, and Cal and Aileen Eaton, all of whom were associated in the promotion of boxing at the Olympic Auditorium in Los Angeles.

At the time, the Hollywood Post 43 of the American Legion was eager to separate itself from the promotion of boxing at the Hollywood Legion Stadium. Gibson, Parnassus, and the Eatons, man and wife, discussed the possibility of taking over the Legion Stadium. At this time, Gibson was president of the IBC of New York, Norris's successor. He was eager to assure a steady source of bouts for the two weekly television bouts packaged by the IBC.

Typically, no direct approach was made to the Legion by Gibson. Instead, Bill Daly was called in to help out. Daly was friendly with Edward Underwood, who was the Legion's man in charge of boxing, and Daly was asked by Gibson and Parnassus to call Underwood and recommend a change in management to the IBC-sponsored group.

Daly's friendship with Underwood apparently was convertible into a lease. It was decided that Leonard would become the president of the new club, which would be called the Hollywood Boxing and Wrestling Club. Five shares were issued, nominally to Leonard, who pledged them as security for a loan of $28,000 from the IBC and $10,000 from George Parnassus.

When the loans were paid off, according to the program, the stock would be shared equally by Gibson, Norris, Parnassus, Daly, and Leonard, who would be the matchmaker under Parnassus' direction. The California State Athletic Commission later approved Leonard's application for a license to run boxing and wrestling at the Legion Stadium without being informed that Daly, for one, was a member of the combine.

Some time earlier, Leonard had become associated with Donald Paul Nesseth, a dealer in used cars, in the management of Don Jordan, a Los Angeles welterweight. Nesseth had encountered trouble getting nationally televised matches for Jordan until Leonard had interceded with Gibson. Then, in rapid succession, Jordan fought in three televised bouts and became a contender for the world welterweight title. His reward was to be a bout for the championship with Akins.

On the morning of October 23, 1958, Leonard, accompanied by Nesseth, went to Parnassus' office in the Olympic Auditorium in response to a summons from Gibson, who said he wanted to discuss with them the projected bout between Akins and Jordan.

Before going to the Auditorium Gibson had called Palermo at the Bismarck Hotel in Chicago. While Gibson, Nesseth, and Leonard were talking about the title bout in Parnassus' office, Gibson was called to the phone. Gibson spoke to the person on the other end of the line, then turned to Leonard, and, the federal government would contend later, said, "Blinky wants to talk to you."

Leonard took the phone.

"Hello," he said.

"Hello, Jackie," Palermo said.

"Yes," Leonard said.

"Do you know we're in for half?"

"Half of what?" Leonard asked. "I don't know what you are talking about."

"We are in for half of the fighter or there won't be any fight."

"This is the first I have heard of it. I don't know what you are talking about."

"Didn't Truman [Gibson] explain everything to you?"

"No. This is the first time I ever heard anything about it."

"Well, there won't be any fight unless we are in for half. You better talk to Mr. Gibson and get back to me."

"That is what I will have to do. I don't know anything about it. This is the first I heard of it."

"Well, I am at the Bismarck Hotel in Chicago. You go talk to Truman and call me back."

Leonard hung up and asked Gibson and Nesseth to step into the hallway just outside of Parnassus' office. He told them of Palermo's demand for a 50 per cent interest in Jordan in the event Jordan won the championship from Akins.

"There won't be any of that," Nesseth said, his bespectacled eyes flashing.

"Well, gee, I'm sorry," Gibson said. "I should have told you, but I had so many things on my mind, pressing my mind, I forgot to. We better not discuss this here. I don't want George Parnassus to know about it. Meet me at the Ambassador in a few minutes and we will go on further with the discussion."

Later that afternoon Leonard and Nesseth conferred with Gibson in a bungalow suite at the Ambassador Hotel. Warren Wayland Spaw, who had boxed as "Jackie McCoy" and who was now associated with Nesseth in the management of Jordan, was also present.

During the conversation, according to Leonard, Gibson told the others that he had learned in Chicago that Carbo and Palermo controlled Akins. Leonard insisted Gibson told them, "You know how

Carbo and Blinky are. . . . They want all of everything before you can get a welterweight title fight. . . . You should go along with this thing, and I will straighten them out when I get back to Chicago. . . . I am going back tomorrow and straighten this thing out."

Nesseth and Leonard insisted it would be dangerous to feign agreement.

Leonard would testify later, "Truman says, 'They wouldn't resort to violence or anything like that, so severe.' Besides he would take care of that, that kind of stuff went out with high-button shoes. Truman said, 'Well, go along with it.' He said, 'It has been done before. That is the way the welterweight and lightweight title has been worked since Carbo and Blinky got into the picture.' "

Just before the meeting ended, Nesseth would say under oath later, "Truman prevailed upon Leonard, finally, to go ahead and tell them, 'Yes, and when I get in Chicago I will straighten everything out so there won't be any problems,' and he said, 'It won't cost you any money. I will take care of that and there won't be any problems.' "

Finally, Leonard went to a pay phone in the lobby of the Ambassador Hotel and called Palermo in Chicago. Palermo insisted that he would call Leonard back from a pay phone. In a few minutes, he was again talking with Leonard, who reported:

"I talked to him there, and I told him that I thought things would be all right. He says, 'What the hell do you mean, think?' He says, 'You either know whether they are all right, you can handle the situation, or you can't handle it.' He said, 'Truman told us before he left Chicago that everything was all right, that he had already talked to you out there.'

"I told him this was the first we had heard about it. I thought everything would be all right.

"He said, 'I don't want no thinks. Can you handle it or can you not? Otherwise there won't be any fight, we are going to pull out.'

"I told him, 'Truman told us there is a contract.'

"Blinky said, 'There is no contract on the fight. I told him that before he left Chicago for Los Angeles, there is no contract.' There would be no fight unless we would handle the situation the way he wanted it, by giving up half the fighter.

"I said, 'All right then, you have got a deal.'

"He said, 'All right then, you have got a fight.' "

Upon his return to Chicago, Gibson was visited by Glickman, who now demanded a guarantee of $40,000 in Akins' behalf instead of 40 per cent of the net gate. When a dispute developed, Palermo announced to Gibson that he owned a "piece" of Akins.

When Jordan unexpectedly defeated Akins to win the 147-pound championship on December 5, 1958, the IBC had to pay the defeated fighter the $40,000, which came to $13,000 more than 40 per cent of the net gate.

Gibson was sanguine about the future. Leonard said he told him, "At least Jordan has to do it twice."

TWENTY

LEONARD WAS HAVING difficulties at the Legion Stadium. He was unable to obtain attractive matches and Palermo prodded him to go to Miami Beach to see Norris and register a complaint. He also heard from Daly, who promised to help him out of his financial difficulties by sending him some money. Christmas was coming, and Leonard was unhappy over the bleak prospects for the holiday season.

Just before Christmas, Palermo called Leonard and told him that he had talked with Daly and a sum of money was being sent to Leonard. The day before Christmas, 1958, Leonard received a money order for $1,000 from Western Union. The money order had been purchased in Philadelphia, ostensibly by somebody who had made the application in the name of "William Daley." Nobody at the time took note of the misspelling of "Daly." The very next day, Leonard heard from Palermo: Wouldn't Leonard want to come to Miami Beach to tell Norris that Gibson and Parnassus were imposing weak matches on the Legion Stadium?

Leonard said he would like to make the trip, but couldn't because he had no money and couldn't get a reservation on a plane during the year-end holiday rush. Palermo rejected the first part of the excuse. He pointed out that Leonard had received a Western Union money order for $1,000. When Leonard asked Palermo how he knew about the money, he said he had sent it. This should have been obvious: Palermo lived in Philadelphia, while Daly lived in Englewood, New Jersey, some ninety miles from Philadelphia.

On January 5, 1959, Leonard arrived in Miami. He was met at the airport by Palermo and a crony, one Abe Sands, who was introduced to Leonard as "Mike." Later it would be inferred that "Mike" was the same man who had picked up the $10,000 Glickman had "lent" to Carbo.

They all drove to the Blue Mist Motel in Miami, where Palermo had registered that afternoon as "George Tobias, 1620 Wood Street, Carbondale, Pennsylvania." Each man had his own room. The next morning Leonard was told that Norris was not in town. He had been called away by business connected with the Chicago Black Hawks, his hockey team.

Curiously, Palermo also said they would have to move from the Blue Mist Motel because he had become involved in an argument with the manager the previous night. Palermo and Leonard packed and moved to the Chateau Resort Motel, where Palermo registered as "Lou Gross, 1620 Wood Street, Lehigh County, Pennsylvania." Unimaginatively, Leonard wrote "Jack Leonard" on the register.

While the two were having breakfast in the Château Resort coffee shop, "Mike" returned. He was accompanied by Carbo, who turned angrily on Leonard and said, "If you had been here yesterday you would have seen the whole mob out at Mr. Norris's. Now you missed him. He won't be here today. He had some business to attend to. But . . . I will handle it for you."

They returned to Palermo's room, where Carbo challenged Leonard. He wanted to know whether Leonard could control Nesseth.

"Can you or can't you?" he demanded.

Blinky interrupted. He explained that he was determined to force Jordan to fight Garnet ("Sugar") Hart, a Philadelphia welterweight. He said he had taken over "control" of Sugar Hart's management the night before and was in a good position with the fighter because Hart had defeated Ralph Dupas the week before to become the foremost contender for the welterweight championship.

Leonard said, "Nesseth won't go for it. He can make a lot more money fighting easier fights than Sugar Hart."

"He has got to," Palermo said. "The only reason I got control of Hart is by telling the manager I would get a title for him. What the hell is the difference? A fighter wins the title, and Nesseth gets 15 per cent of Hart. That is the way it works."

Carbo said he was not interested in money for himself but was concerned with Palermo's financial position. "As long as these fellows are making money," he said, "I don't have to be doling out money to them."

Just then, two other men entered the room. They were Chris Dundee, a former manager who had been promoting bouts at the Miami Beach Auditorium, and Genovese, who was on his way to jail in New York as an "undercover manager."

Carbo and Dundee walked out of the room, but Genovese remained with Palermo and Leonard. Genovese told Leonard he was pleased to see that he had joined the "family" and he described Carbo as "a great guy."

"You should be getting good television fights now, with Frank helping," Genovese said. "He'll tell Gibson to give you the fights."

A while later, after Carbo and Dundee had reentered the room, Genovese and Dundee left. Leonard said he would like to take a walk. Carbo ordered him to stay. Neither Carbo nor Palermo ever permitted Leonard to be alone for a moment while he was in Miami.

That night Palermo and "Mike" drove Leonard to Joe Sonken's Gold Coast Restaurant and Cocktail Lounge for dinner. During the meal, Palermo and Carbo went off to a corner of the restaurant. They exchanged money. On the way to the Greater Miami Airport, Palermo stopped at an apartment a short distance from the restaurant. Carbo and a woman were there. Palermo and Carbo went into a bedroom, and when they rejoined the others in the living room Carbo asked Leonard:

"Are you sure you can handle everything all right now?"

"I'll try." Leonard said.

"God damn it, don't *try*. You are going to do it, aren't you? You are the man we are looking for and you are the man responsible out there. This is your baby; you are the one that is going to handle the thing."

Leonard was frightened by the possibility of physical and commercial harm.

Back in Los Angeles, Leonard learned that Jordan would engage in a nontitle bout with Alvaro Guiterrez at the Olympic Auditorium on January 22, 1959. Leonard asked Gibson who was going to pay the money Carbo and Palermo expected to receive from Jordan's purse. He was told not to worry about it because, if any money had to be paid, Gibson would take care of it.

"In the meantime," Leonard would testify later, "I heard from Blinky two or three times, wanting to know if everything was all right, and Truman told me to keep telling him everything was all right, so I kept telling him everything was all right. And it was sometime prior to the fight, sometime around the 16th or 17th of January, that Blinky told me where to send the money to, Philadelphia. . . .

"He told me to send it to a woman by the name of Clare Cori and he gave me her address in Philadelphia and I wrote it down."

Clare Cori was Palermo's wife.

TWENTY ONE

JORDAN RECEIVED $12,500 plus expense money for knocking out Alvaro Gutierrez in three rounds on January 22, 1959. Palermo called Leonard to find out when his share of the purse would be forthcoming. Leonard appealed to Gibson, who assured him that payment would be made.

Five days after Jordan's bout with Gutierrez, Leonard, Nesseth, and McCoy met Gibson in his suite at the Ambassador Hotel on Wilshire Boulevard in Los Angeles. While they were there the telephone rang, and Gibson answered it. He spoke for a few minutes and hung up. He told his visitors that the caller was Palermo, who asked to talk with Leonard or Nesseth. Gibson said he had told Palermo neither one was in his suite.

Nesseth and Leonard went out together and drove to Leonard's home, where they found a message to call Palermo at the "Palermo hotel back east." Leonard had two telephone numbers for Palermo, both in the Philadelphia area. One was Hilltop 9-1585, the other Fulton 9-2664. The Fulton number was in the name of Felix Corey at 1350 South Grove, Philadelphia. Felix Corey was the father of Clare Cori. The Hilltop number was installed under the name of Mrs. Margaret Dougherty at 211 South Lynn Boulevard, Highland Park, Pennsylvania. Leonard had been instructed by Palermo to call him person-to-person as "Mr. Badone" or "Mr. Tobias," or to call him station-to-station. Leonard and Nesseth made the call from a phone booth.

Palermo answered the phone at 5:23 P.M., California time, and the call lasted five minutes, fifty-three seconds. Blinky was angry and screamed about Leonard's duplicity. He burdened Leonard with a double-cross. Leonard explained that he had seen Gibson earlier, and that Gibson had promised to send the money. Leonard heard a voice in the background say, "Give me that phone." It was Carbo, who shouted, "You son-of-a-bitching double-crosser. You are no good. Your word is no good. Nothing is good about you. Just because you are two thousand miles away, that is no sign I can't have you taken care of. I have got plenty of friends out there to take care of punks like you. The money had better be in."

Leonard, by his own description, "was trying to get a word in edgewise, to tell him the money would be sent the next day. He wouldn't let me say anything, he was just cursing and hollering at me and saying there would be somebody out here to take care of me, and if that money wasn't there right away somebody would be looking me up."

During the conversation, the operator demanded more money for the charges. Nesseth obtained ten or twelve additional quarters. The call cost eighteen quarters, three dimes, and two nickels.

Several days later, Leonard talked with Gibson and told him of the telephone conversation with Palermo and Carbo. Gibson promised to send $1,800 to Leonard immediately, but by February 6 nothing had been done. Leonard called Gibson at Madison Square Garden, where Norris was in the process of selling out to the Graham-Paige Corporation. He again asked Gibson for the $1,800, which was 15 per cent of Jordan's proceeds from the bout with Gutierrez. Gibson told him to withdraw the $1,800 from the boxing club in which they were associated.

Leonard explained that Gibson had instructed James Ogilvie, the club's bookkeeper, not to give Leonard money without Gibson's approval. Gibson said he would call Ogilvie and grant his permission. The call to Ogilvie was made some days later, and Gibson requested that Ogilvie write a check to "cash" for $1,800 and give it to Leonard, who would reimburse the Hollywood Boxing and Wrestling Club. Not once during the call did Gibson mention a proposed bout in Porterville, California, which was the explanation Gibson later caused to be written into the Chicago Stadium Corporation's books to explain the issuance of a check for $1,800 to Leonard.

Meanwhile, in accordance with instructions from Palermo, Leonard mailed a check for $1,725 payable to Clare Cori to her in Philadelphia. He sent the check by registered mail and requested a receipt. Protectively, he had dated the check back to January 27. When Palermo called him on February 6 to ask why the money had not arrived, Leonard lied. He said the check had been mailed on January 27, but the letter had been returned because his son, who had posted the letter, had forgotten to put a stamp on the envelope.

Ogilvie issued the check soon after receiving the request from Gibson. A few days later he received a check for $1,800 drawn by Gibson on the Chicago Stadium Corporation's account and payable to Leonard. The requisition described the purpose of the check as "Advance, Promoter's share of April fight, Porterville, California." This entry was in Gibson's handwriting. As of September 30, 1959, the $1,800 was written off the books of the Chicago Stadium Corporation as an "uncollectible bad debt."

The check for $1,725 that Leonard mailed to Clare Cori was collected by the First National Bank, Hollywood, Florida. It bore the prior endorsements of "Clare Cori" and "Joe Sonken." The check had been cashed by Sonken, who charged Palermo $25 for the service. He did this by depositing Leonard's check in his own account and then issuing his own check to a fictitious person called "Carmen Cosara." Sonken owned the restaurant to which Palermo had taken Leonard for dinner during the Californian's command visit to Florida some weeks earlier.

Palermo wasn't happy with the transaction. He telephoned Leonard in Los Angeles and railed at him for sending a personal check. He demanded that money orders be used in the future. Later, he had a change of heart. He assured Leonard he would ask Carbo to intercede with Norris so that Leonard's club in Hollywood might obtain nationally-televised bouts. In these calls, Palermo referred to Carbo as "The Man" or "The Gray."

Jordan was booked to fight Akins in a return bout in St. Louis on April 24, 1959. Two weeks before the match he received word from Leonard that Palermo wanted to see him in East St. Louis when Nesseth arrived in St. Louis for the bout. Palermo also was eager to have Leonard come to St. Louis for the bout. Leonard said he had not planned the trip.

"Jesus, you got to be here," Palermo screamed. "You have got to settle this thing. You have got to give us some money, and I want him to fight Hart."

"Well, Jesus, I told you before that I didn't know about Hart. I am almost positive that Nesseth will never fight Hart."

"Well, he is going to have to fight him."

"What are you doing, taking over complete possession of Jordan?"

"In a way, yes. We want to know who he is fighting for, who he is fighting, what he is fighting, and we have got to give the OK. Carbo told you that in Miami, that if you are going to work with us you have got to go all the way with us or you won't get any help out there."

TWENTY-TWO

LEONARD FIRMLY REFUSED to make the trip, and when Nesseth arrived in St. Louis on April 14 his partner was not with him. The manager was on his own. He stayed at the Kingsway Hotel, where most of the fight crowd congregated, and on the night of the fight went to the St. Louis Arena, which was owned by Norris and Wirtz, accompanied by Sgt. Edmond Moran, who was head of the hotel squad of the St. Louis Police Department.

Moran observed that Palermo was in the arena and saw him confer with Glickman, Akins' manager, in the challenger's corner during the fight. Jordan again defeated Akins and retained the world welterweight championship.

The next day, Palermo showed up at the arena accompanied by Glickman. They entered the office of Sam Muchnick, a St. Louis resident who had promoted the bout. Glickman asked Muchnick for a report on the gate receipts. Each fighter was to be paid 30 per cent of the net gate plus $15,000 from the television receipts, which had come to $55,000. Muchnick handed the statement to Glickman.

Palermo asked Muchnick if he had heard about money that was owed to him out of Jordan's purse.

"No, sir, I didn't," Muchnick said.

Glickman called his lawyer, Morris Shenker, who then spoke to Palermo. Blinky hung up the phone and said, "I have got to leave. Mr. Shenker told me to leave."

Later that morning, Palermo went to the Kingsway Hotel. Nesseth was visiting in the room of friends, Don Chargin, a fight promoter from Oakland, California, and Harvey Livingston, of Hayward, California, an auto tire dealer who also managed Johnny Gonsalves, a lightweight contender.

Palermo called Nesseth on a house phone and Nesseth invited him up. Immediately, Nesseth called Muchnick, who then called Sgt. Moran at his home. Sgt. Moran immediately called Nesseth, who engaged in quiet conversation with him while Palermo, Chargin, and

Livingston were in the room. When he hung up, Nesseth went into an adjoining bedroom with Palermo.

"You know why I am here," Palermo said.

"Yes, I know why you think you are here."

"I want my money. . . ."

Nesseth denied owing Palermo any money.

"Well, you paid me the last time," Palermo said, obviously in reference to the money received from Leonard.

"I have never paid you a cent and I don't intend to," Nesseth said firmly.

Nesseth retraced all the events of recent months. He said he didn't care whether Gibson paid Palermo $10,000 each time Jordan fought; he wasn't going to give Palermo a cent.

"Well, we better call Truman about this." Palermo said.

"Truman doesn't owe me any money and I am not going to call him."

Palermo demanded that Nesseth go to Chicago with him and confront Gibson. The manager refused.

As Palermo was leaving he said, "Well, I am going to be out on the Coast, and we are going to have a meet."

"Well," Nesseth said, "I told you I met you this once to explain my situation and the truth of the matter, and I don't want to meet you on the Coast or anywhere."

Minutes after Palermo's departure, Sgt. Moran arrived at the hotel, and Nesseth told him of Palermo's demands. The detective assured Nesseth that Palermo would not trouble him as long as he was in St. Louis.

Upon leaving Nesseth's room, Palermo went to a telephone and called Leonard in Los Angeles.

"What the hell is going on?" Palermo demanded.

Leonard told him that Nesseth was his own master.

"Well, I will be out on the Coast to see you," Palermo said menacingly.

"There is no use coming to the Coast to see me, you are still going to have to see Nesseth whether you are here or there," Leonard said.

"I am coming out, and I will see you in a few days."

Three days later, Gibson phoned Leonard at the Hollywood

Legion Stadium. Gibson told Leonard he was going to pay "those people" their share of Jordan's purse from the return bout with Akins because he had promised to do so.

Palermo also called Leonard that day, and some hours later, after Nesseth had come to Leonard's office, there was another call. Leonard answered, and the caller said. "Hello, hello, hello. You know who this is?"

"Yeah, I know who this is."

It was Carbo. He called Leonard a double-crosser and said that he would gouge Leonard's eyes out if he were there.

"We are going to meet at the crossroads," Carbo warned Leonard. "You will never get away with it."

Leonard turned pale. He ran across the hall to a ladies' room that he used during the day as a men's room and vomited.

"I have never seen anybody more shaken up than he was at that time," Nesseth said later.

Within five minutes, the phone rang again. It was Palermo. Leonard told Palermo of Carbo's call.

"Well, Jesus, he was right, wasn't he?" Palermo demanded. "What do you think you got coming? You are nothing but a double-crosser. You had it coming. Anything he said, you had it coming."

Palermo said less than cryptically that he was coming to the Coast to see "some people" who would come to see Leonard.

Further shaken, Leonard returned to his home in Van Nuys, outside of Los Angeles, only to receive another call from Palermo, who wanted to know if Leonard had cooled off.

"Jesus, there is no use being like that," Palermo said. "After all, maybe the guy shouldn't have called like that."

Palermo explained that "they have had that account a long time and you people out there are double-crossing him." The reference was to Carbo's control of the welterweight championship. "Now," Palermo continued, "we might as well be like gentlemen and not be mad. I will be out there to talk to you."

"There is no use in coming out here, I am fed up with all of you," Leonard said. "See Nesseth."

"I can't see Nesseth unless he sits down and talks to me," Palermo said.

"You will have to take care of that, there is nothing I can do about it," Leonard responded angrily. "Nesseth doesn't want to talk to you, and if you want to talk with him, you will have to make your own contact with him."

"Well, I will be out there in a few days and we are going to look you up," Palermo said threateningly.

Now, it seemed, the phone lines across the country really began singing. During business hours on April 29, 1959, three calls were made from the Chicago Stadium to the Hollywood Legion Stadium. Gibson also received a collect call from Philadelphia from a person named "Frank." It was either from Carbo or Palermo.

That evening the wires still hummed. At 7:20 P.M. Philadelphia time, Palermo called Gibson collect at Gibson's home in Chicago. The call lasted four minutes, thirty seconds.

At 10:58 P.M., Philadelphia time, Leonard received Palermo's call at his home.

Seven minutes later, Gibson, at home, received another call from the home of Felix Corey, Palermo's father-in-law. The call lasted three minutes, eight seconds.

At 11:25 P.M. twenty minutes later, Daly called Leonard from his home at Englewood, New Jersey. This call lasted five minutes, twenty-seven seconds.

Thirty minutes later, there was still another call to Gibson from Felix Corey's home.

The next day, the telephone people were still reaping a harvest. At 10:01 A.M., Chicago time, Gibson called Leonard at Leonard's home. The call lasted six minutes, forty-six seconds.

There were four other calls that day from the Chicago Stadium to the Hollywood Legion Stadium. The record shows they lasted a total of about twenty minutes, an average of five minutes a call.

At the Hollywood Legion Stadium, Leonard was in financial difficulty. Parnassus and the Eatons, the promoters of boxing at the Olympic Auditorium, now withdrew their $20,000 surety bond which guaranteed the Hollywood Boxing and Wrestling Club's financial integrity to the California State Athletic Commission. Without the bond, the Hollywood club could not remain in business.

TWENTY-THREE

ON HIS WAY TO Los Angeles to see Leonard, Palermo paid a social call in Chicago. He registered at the Bismarck Hotel on April 30 and charged his room to the International Boxing Club, which was no longer in existence, having been succeeded by then by the National Boxing Enterprises, Norris's new corporate name.

The day Palermo came to Chicago, Gibson phoned Leonard in Los Angeles and offered to put additional capital into the Hollywood Boxing and Wrestling Club, if Leonard would persuade Nesseth to approve a welterweight championship bout between Jordan and Hart, the fighter Palermo claimed he controlled. Later that day Gibson held a conference in the lobby of the Bismarck Hotel with Palermo and Marty Stein, Hart's manager-of-record.

Palermo was so eager to get to Los Angeles that he failed to check out of the Bismarck Hotel after talking with Gibson and Stein. In Los Angeles, he registered at the Beverly Hilton Hotel as "George Tobias" and gave his address as "110 North Clark Street, Chicago," the address of the Cook County Building, which houses the various offices of the county government.

Carbo's "friends on the West Coast" now joined the conspiracy openly.

TWENTY-FOUR

PUCCINI'S RESTAURANT in Beverly Hills was the scene of a "meet" on Friday night, May 1. Palermo played host to Louis Dragna, a handsome, balding Los Angeles ruffian who was well known to the local police. At dinner, Palermo suggested to Dragna that he call on Leonard. Dragna suggested that Palermo get in touch with him after the weekend. Palermo needed activity. Nervous, impatient, he telephoned Leonard either on Saturday or Sunday and asked him to come to see him at the Beverly Hilton.

"Well, Jesus, it is late," Leonard said. It was 10 P.M. "I have the wife and kid here," Leonard moaned.

"Bring them with you and they can wait in the lobby," Palermo insisted.

Leonard, his wife, and their child drove to the hotel. Mrs. Leonard and the child stayed in the car in the hotel parking lot; Leonard went into the hotel. In the lobby he was greeted by Palermo and Joe Sica, another Los Angeles tough guy. The trio took the elevator to Palermo's room.

Sica opened the proceedings. "I am surprised at you. You got yourself in a hell of a jam here, with good people and doing a thing like this."

Leonard attempted to explain that he was caught in the middle, that Nesseth was balking, and that Gibson had misled everybody by insisting he could take care of everything.

Sica said, "Leave him out. We don't want to hear nothing about Truman Gibson."

Blinky said, "I don't want to hear anything about Gibson, he has nothing to do with this. You are the man we are holding responsible."

"I want to hear your story and I want to hear Blinky's," Sica said.

When Leonard attempted to relate his side of the controversy, Blinky shut him up. He wanted to tell his story first and he did, stressing Leonard's assurances to Carbo that everything would be all right.

Leonard was impatient. "Jesus, I told you that Truman was in the middle of this thing," he said, interrupting Palermo.

"I told you to shut up and sit down," Palermo screamed. "We are not going to talk about Truman. We are talking about you and your part in this thing."

Sica listened to Palermo's version of the plot and then turned his attention to Leonard. He told the promoter he had been a friend of "The Gray" for many years, and that Leonard was in serious trouble and could get hurt.

Palermo blurted out a list of complaints: his neck was in a noose, he said, because Carbo had taken his word that money would be forthcoming; Gibson was in the "middle" because he had insisted all along that everything would be all right; Leonard was in difficulty because he had informed Carbo that he would handle Nesseth.

"What the hell are we going to do to straighten this thing out?" Palermo demanded. "We got to do something. I can't go home like this."

"There is nothing I can do," Leonard said. "I just don't know what to tell you. You are going to have to talk to Nesseth."

"Jesus Christ, get hold of Nesseth," Sica shouted.

"It is late at night," Leonard said. "I can't get hold of Nesseth."

"Doesn't he have a phone?" Sica asked.

"He has got one, but I don't even have the number. Can you see him tomorrow?" Leonard requested patiently.

Sica said, "Drag him in, go out and grab him by the neck and get him out of bed and shake him and get him in line."

"Well, I can't do that," Leonard said.

"Can't you whip him?" Sica asked.

"It isn't a question of whipping him," Leonard said. "I don't know whether I can whip him or not but I am going on doing business with him again."

"Well, look, Jackie, you made a choice. It is a question of either you or Don Nesseth is going to get hurt. Wouldn't you rather go grab him by the neck and straighten him out, than for me to go back and tell 'The Gray'? You try it, you are all right, but it is Nesseth that is no good. The way it is now, you and Blinky have both got your necks in a sling. Something has got to be straightened out. If you have to, go and beat hell out of Nesseth. If you need help, we will go with you and help you drag him out of bed."

Leonard pleaded a pacific outlook. He said he would not assault Nesseth. He got up and edged his way to the door. Sica said, "Are you going to see this guy in the morning and straighten things out?"

"Well, I am going to try."

"Try, hell," Palermo said. "You are going to straighten it out. I can't go home like this. I am in a hell of a jam with 'The Gray.' "

Leonard walked out.

TWENTY-FIVE

TWO DAYS LATER, on a Sunday, Leonard met with Nesseth and McCoy at the Hollywood Legion Stadium. A call was placed to Gibson in Chicago. It lasted nineteen minutes, four seconds. Nesseth did the talking.

He told Gibson of the threats to Leonard's and his life and urged him to inform "your boss" of them.

"When you say my boss, you mean Mr. Norris?" Gibson demanded.

"Of course I mean Mr. Norris," Nesseth said.

"Well, I am not threatening you," Gibson said quietly.

"No, you have never threatened me, but these other people are."

"Well, all the pressure can be relieved, and you can also do your own Jackie Leonard a favor by saving his club, if you will just agree to fight Sugar Hart."

The next day, while Nesseth was in Leonard's office, Palermo and Dragna walked in. Palermo said, "I want to talk to you."

"Well, I don't want to talk to you," Nesseth said. He walked out. In the street, he made a decision. He went straight to a telephone and called the Los Angeles Police Department. The next day he was given police protection.

When Nesseth walked out on Palermo and Dragna, he left Leonard holding the bag.

Palermo said, "Jesus, I want to talk to that fellow," referring to Nesseth.

"Well, you are going to have to get with him and sit down and talk to him," Leonard said.

"How in the hell am I going to do that? What am I going to have to do, grab him and shake him and set him down?"

"I don't know how you are going to talk to him. No use talking to me. You are going to have to talk to Nesseth."

The next day Leonard received notice from the Legion Post that his lease on the Stadium would be terminated in five days. The same

214

day Leonard received several telephone calls from Palermo and Sica at his home. They urged him to come to a restaurant at which Palermo, Dragna, and George Raft, the Hollywood actor, were waiting for him. "Let's see if we can straighten it out," Palermo said.

Back in Chicago, Gibson was growing apprehensive. He called Palermo at the Beverly Hilton Hotel and urged him to leave Los Angeles. Gibson also spoke on the telephone with Daly, who was at his home in Englewood, New Jersey. He arranged to meet Daly in Los Angeles six days later to discuss the "crisis" at the Hollywood Legion Stadium.

In Los Angeles, Leonard visited the headquarters of the Los Angeles Police Department. Later the same day he was accompanied by Sergeant Conwell Keeler, of the Los Angeles police, to his home in Northridge. Keeler connected a tape recording machine which employed an induction coil to Leonard's telephone receiver. That evening Palermo phoned Leonard.

Leonard told Palermo that he could not get Nesseth to sign Jordan for a bout with Hart, but that he was confident that he would get Nesseth to agree to a fight between Jordan and Del Flanagan, a boxer from Minnesota who was managed by Glickman, Carbo's friend.

"That's very good," Palermo said. "That will get you and me off the hook."

The next morning, Sica was waiting for Leonard in the promoter's office at the Hollywood Legion Stadium. Sica was nervous. He inspected the room suspiciously, as though he were searching for concealed microphones. He found nothing.

During the morning they were joined by Nesseth, McCoy and Palermo. Sica demanded a resolution of the controversy in order that Palermo might return to Philadelphia. He reviewed the circumstances in which all concerned found themselves and stressed that when Jordan was given the opportunity to fight Akins for the championship Leonard "dealt with some other people, and by dealing with these people, there were certain commitments made . . ." He went on, "Now, when you fellows got lucky and you won the title, there were certain things that were supposed to be fulfilled."

Nesseth said he was a free agent. He explained that Jordan would not fight anybody selected by Palermo or Carbo. He insisted he had worked hard over a two-year period grooming Jordan for the title.

"Well, do you think you got the title fight on your own?"

"Yeah, I think I got—I think I got the title fight. As far as I am concerned, I got it on my own," Nesseth insisted.

"You did like fun get it on your own," Palermo said.

Nesseth announced he was annoyed by the many telephone calls to Leonard.

"I'd like to make one thing clear right now," he said, "that I don't think all these phone calls and all this harassment are necessary, do you?"

"No, no, I don't agree with that," Palermo said. "I don't agree with that. I don't agree with that at all. You're right. That's out. There ain't going to be no harassment, that's out of the question."

A moment later, Sica said, "Well, let's go, Frank. Jackie, you got yourself in a hell of a spot with this thing. It's terrible. How could you let people double-cross other people? That's all it is."

Now Palermo turned to Nesseth. He asked Jordan's manager if anybody had been told of Palermo's visit to him at the Kingsway Hotel in St. Louis the day after the Jordan-Akins bout the previous April.

"Did you tell anybody about the St. Louis thing at all?" Palermo demanded.

"Tell anybody what?"

"About I was in St. Louis with you."

"Sure. I didn't tell anybody, they told me."

"Who's that?"

"People."

"People told you that? How in hell would they know it?"

"Well, it's a guy came up to my room five minutes after you left."

"Who was that?"

"A cop."

"Oh, a cop?"

"Yah."

"Did you tell him what we talked about?"

"Yah, I told him what we talked about."

"You told him about the 15 per cent, too? You didn't tell him about the 15 per cent, did you?"

Just as Sica and Palermo were leaving, Sica leaned over and whispered into Leonard's ear, "Jackie, you're it."

He didn't know the room was "bugged."

TWENTY-SIX

PALERMO DECIDED to return to Philadelphia. He went to the Los Angeles International Airport to catch a plane and strode to a newsstand adjoining Mike Lyman's bar. He picked up two magazines devoted to sports and a couple of packages of gum. The cost of all the items came to eighty cents. Going toward the cashier, he picked up a package of peanut butter crackers. Then he paid the cashier—for the crackers only. A policeman in plain clothes had been tailing him. He arrested Palermo as a petty thief.

In Municipal Court, Blinky appeared before Judge Delbert E. Wong and was held in $500 bail for a jury trial. He made bail and left town, but not before Police Captain James D. Hamilton had the pleasure of talking with him.

Palermo told Captain Hamilton he was in Los Angeles on a social visit and that he had never heard of Dragna or seen Sica during his visit.

When he was at last placed on trial in Los Angeles, it was not on a charge of stealing eighty cents' worth of magazines and chewing gum.

TWENTY-SEVEN

IN JULY, 1959, Norris met with Rosensohn and Gibson in his Lake Shore Drive apartment in Chicago. Although Rosensohn had lost his position in Rosensohn Enterprises, Inc., Norris apparently believed the young man had a future in boxing. Of his own position in the game, Norris was less certain.

During the meeting, Gibson outlined a plan for a world-wide promotorial combination which would include Norris, Rosensohn, Jack Solomons of London, who was then Europe's premier promoter, Edwin Ahlquist, Johansson's advisor, and Johansson himself. Rosensohn was to be president of the agglutination of promoters at a salary of $100,000 a year and was to receive a five-year contract.

There was a real problem confronting Norris: how could he involve himself in an international boxing combine when he had only recently been enjoined by a federal court from engaging in the boxing business anywhere in the United States but at the Chicago Stadium?

During the meeting, Rosensohn was overcome by an idea. He still held a minority interest in Rosensohn Enterprises, which held the contract for the return bout between Johansson and Patterson. Why not sell the stock to Norris? He made the suggestion.

"What do you want for it?" Norris asked.

"Well, I will be very happy to sell my one-third interest for $25,000."

"All right, fine," Norris said.

Rosensohn was pleased with himself. He was aware that the stock was not worth very much to him because of the way he was being pushed around by Salerno and Velella. He also knew that Norris knew his way around such people as Salerno and Velella. And, by this ownership, Norris believed, he would not be going counter to the antitrust verdict.

The next day Rosensohn received bad news. Gibson informed

him that the deal was off; it had been vetoed by Wirtz, who opposed Norris's affiliation with Salerno and Velella.

"Well, he has already made the deal," Rosensohn told Gibson. "He cannot welsh on a deal that he has made."

'Well, you had better speak to Mr. Norris," Gibson said.

Rosensohn did.

"I do not understand this," Rosensohn told Norris. "You have already made a deal with me and today you tell me that your partner says 'no.' I do not understand. Don't you have authority to make a deal?"

"It is not the money that bothers me," Norris explained.

"Well, money bothers me," Rosensohn said.

It was suggested that the Chicago Stadium Corporation lend the $25,000 to Rosensohn, with the stock being put up as collateral. When and if the stock was sold, Rosensohn was to repay the $25,000. If the stock were sold for more than $25,000, the Chicago Stadium Corporation would receive half of Rosensohn's proceeds above $25,000.

Some weeks later, on August 3, Rosensohn again saw Norris and Gibson at Norris's Park Avenue apartment in New York. A telephone call was made to Solomons in London, and arrangements were made for a meeting the very next day at the Hotel George V in Paris.

In Paris, Rosensohn was an active young man. His dark features were brightly lit in the presence of the company he was keeping. He held separate meetings with Johansson and Ahlquist on one hand, and with Ahlquist, Solomons, and Gibson on the other; and all through the day he was wondering about District Attorney Hogan back in New York.

On July 22, Rosensohn had gone to the District Attorney's office in New York and had poured out his heart to Mr. Bonomi. He told the story of Salerno, Black, and Velella, and of his ouster from control of the company bearing his name. He said he had been surprised when Velella, who had first appeared as Salerno's lawyer, suddenly turned up as owner of both Salerno's and Black's stock in Rosensohn Enterprises, Inc.

The District Attorney's office, concerned with Rosensohn's safety, assigned police protection to him until his departure for the Paris conference.

Now, in Paris, Rosensohn was pleased with himself. He was wheeling and dealing with important people and seemingly was on the verge of a coup. He went down to Cannes, in the south of France, and gambled for a while. By August 20, he was in London, where he encountered Jim Norris, who was on a pleasure trip to England.

The meeting was an unhappy one. The conversation concerned itself with Johansson, who had been so buoyantly involved in Rosensohn's plans short weeks before, only to give *Life* magazine an exclusive story in which he excoriated Norris, Rosensohn, Gibson, and Solomons as promoters for whom he would not fight under any circumstances.

Rosensohn, whose dream of empire was all but over, still had in his name the minority stock in Rosensohn Enterprises, Inc. So long as Velella had controlling interest, Rosensohn's stock was worth only the amount he could obtain through its sale. As it happened, he had forced just such a turn of events by informing the District Attorney's office of his involvement with Salerno, Black, and Velella.

The consequential investigation before a grand jury in New York County resulted in Velella's indictment for perjury. Later, the lawyer was cleared of the accusation, but it was impossible for him to continue in control of Rosensohn Enterprises, Inc. The stock he held was sold to a new group put together by Roy M. Cohn, who had gained a measure of notoriety as counsel to Senator Joseph McCarthy when the late Senator was seeing Red everywhere in the land.

Cohn's company, called Feature Sports, Inc., was made up of William D. Fugazy, a travel agent, and Thomas A. Bolan, Cohn's law office associate. Also involved in the new organization was Fugazy's uncle, Humberto J. Fugazy, who had been a boxing promoter three decades earlier.

Both Velella and Rosensohn sold their stock in Rosensohn Enterprises, Inc. Rosensohn's proceeds came to $78,000, of which $25,000 went to Norris's Chicago Stadium Corporation, to which Rosensohn had pledged his stock as security for the $25,000 loan. Norris did not exercise his right to half of Rosensohn's profit, to which he was legally entitled.

The sole asset Rosensohn Enterprises, Inc., had sold to Cohn's group was a contract for the return bout between Johansson and Patterson. When the fight happened, on June 20, 1960, at the Polo Grounds in New York City, Patterson regained the heavyweight championship by knocking out Johansson in five rounds, virtually leaving him for dead.

Rosensohn was a mere spectator. Six months earlier, the New York State Athletic Commission had suspended his matchmaker's license for three years because of his failure to inform the board of his dealings with Salerno. The young man's adventure in wonderland was at an end. When last heard of, he was selling dry-cleaning equipment.

TWENTY-EIGHT

IN MAY, 1959, the California State Athletic Commission conducted an investigation of boxing. The board's action was prompted by reports of the attempt by Carbo and Palermo to muscle in on the earnings of Jordan. Leonard, on the witness stand on May 20, told a story of threatened reprisal by Carbo and Palermo if the hoodlums were not accepted as partners in the management of Jordan.

Gibson went from Chicago to Los Angeles to appear as a witness before the California board and testified that he had attempted to persuade Palermo to refrain from threatening Leonard and Nesseth.

When all the testimony was heard, the California board asked Captain James Hamilton, chief of the police intelligence unit of Los Angeles, to investigate the activities of Carbo, Palermo, Sica, Dragna, and Gibson. Captain Hamilton handed over the evidence he had obtained to the Federal Bureau of Investigation. Thereafter, the United States Attorney in Los Angeles, Francis C. Whelan, began presenting evidence to a grand jury.

Leonard felt secure because Captain Hamilton had assigned him police protection, but on June 3, 1959, just two weeks after he had told his story before the boxing board, his name hit the headlines.

That evening Leonard drove up to the garage of his home in Los Angeles, turned off the ignition, and emerged from his car. Just as he reached up to pull down the garage door, he felt a blow on the back of the head.

"The blow drove me to my knees," he remembered later. "I was hit again. I went down and while I was down, I was kicked a couple of times. I heard voices. There were two men. I couldn't tell who they were."

He had suffered a concussion of the brain.

Chief of Police William H. Parker delineated the attack on Leonard as a typical assault by mobsters, but a week later he reversed his field.

"We have carefully amassed and evaluated all known available facts," Chief Parker told the Los Angeles press. "It is the considered and unanimous opinion of our investigating officers assigned to this case that the physical facts fail to support the probability that Mr. Leonard was subject to assault as originally reported. It now appears that Mr. Leonard suffered some acute physical incapacitation of a stunning nature that produced an illusion of assault."

Leonard said, "All I know is I have a headache."

TWENTY-NINE

CARBO WAS OUT on bail and although he had not been slugged, he was in pain. An old kidney ailment was acting up, and he had gone to Johns Hopkins Hospital in Baltimore for a check-up.

In Philadelphia, Palermo was moving around as usual, free of any social encumbrances. He owned or controlled no champions, but he had a "piece" of a hard-hitting heavyweight named Charles ("Sonny") Liston and looked forward to the time when Liston would be the world's champion.

In Los Angeles, Dragna and Sica were, at last, apparently minding their own business.

Gibson was in Chicago, where the National Boxing Enterprise was still in business. On the night of September 22, 1959, he went to the home of a friend on the south side of town. The Chicago White Sox were playing the Cleveland Indians in Cleveland, and the game was on television. If the White Sox won, they would be the American League champions, and Gibson and his friend were White Sox fans. They watched the game on a television set in a room opening on a rear yard. Gerry Staley was pitching a fine game for Chicago, and Gibson was warmed by the feeling that the White Sox were on the verge of the American League championship.

Suddenly, looking through the window, Gibson noticed flashing lights. The illumination was so bright it lit up the room in which he and his friend were watching the game. Simultaneously, there was a banging on the front door. Gibson's friend rose, walked down a hall, and opened the door. He was brushed aside by several men. "We're from the FBI," one of them announced. They seized Gibson, clapped handcuffs on him, and hustled him down to the city jail. News photographers gathered quickly and got shots of Gibson wearing the bracelets.

"It was as though Dillinger were reincarnated," Gibson said later.

In Baltimore, FBI men picked up Carbo at Johns Hopkins Hospital. Palermo was arrested in Philadelphia, while Sica and Dragna were picked up in Los Angeles.

The Federal Bureau of Investigation's timetable had been read perfectly. All the arrests had been accomplished within half an hour. Only six minutes separated Carbo's arrest from Gibson's.

Earlier in the day, the federal grand jury for the Southern District of California, sitting in Los Angeles, had returned a ten-count indictment involving the five men. Carbo was named in five counts, Palermo in six counts, Sica in three counts, Gibson and Dragna each in two counts. The charges involved conspiracy to violate the federal anti-racketeering act, extortion, and conspiracy.

Gibson, who was accused of conspiracy only, was burdened by the government with using "Carbo and Palermo in the operation of his business." Conversely, the government alleged "that Carbo and Palermo used Gibson and the IBC in their extortive activity."

William P. Daly was named as a co-conspirator, but was not indicted.

The government charged that Nesseth and Leonard were "subjected to mental torment and abuse resulting from repeated economic and physical threats" from October 23, 1958, through September 22, 1959.

"When the pressure became intolerable, the terrorized victims were afforded relief and protection through the intercession of the police and the Federal Bureau of Investigation," the government contended.

The arrest of Gibson created a minor scandal in Chicago. He was, after all, a respected member of the Illinois Bar. And he had friends. One of them was Federal Judge Michael Igoe. A mutual friend called Judge Igoe and informed him of Gibson's arrest. The judge immediately insisted that Gibson be brought before him at his home. The FBI complied with the judge's request.

When Gibson came into Judge Igoe's home, he was immediately escorted into another room by the judge.

"That was a fine ball game, wasn't it?" Judge Igoe asked.

"I don't know what happened, Judge. I was occupied elsewhere."

'Well, Truman, the White Sox beat the Indians, four to two."

There were smiles.

Now the two men sat and talked like old friends while they waited for a bail bondsman and Gibson's lawyer, William R. Ming, Jr., a prominent member of the Illinois Bar, to arrive. When they did, Judge Igoe entertained a formal request for Gibson's release on bail. Gibson was released in $5,000 bail.

At their hearings, Carbo was held in $100,000 bail and Palermo, who apparently was lower on the underworld scale, in only $25,000 bail.

In Carbo's case, the bail was academic. He was already under indictment in New York County as an undercover manager and undercover matchmaker, and for conspiracy. Furthermore, he had only lately been named by the federal government in a suit aimed at recovering $750,000 in unpaid income taxes.

On October 27, 1959, Carbo went on trial in the Court of General Sessions in New York County. Assistant District Attorney Scotti —the man who had been chasing boxing villains for years—made the opening remarks to the jury in the courtroom of Judge John A. Mullen, who was known as "a tough judge."

Scotti told the jury he would prove with "devastating clarity" that Carbo had been the "underworld commissioner of boxing" and had acted as a manager and matchmaker without obtaining licenses. Scotti went beyond this. He asserted he would prove that Carbo had held "a summit meeting with Norris at which Carbo had dictated the terms."

Three days after the trial began, and soon after selection of the jury had been completed, Carbo's attorney, Abraham Brodsky, requested a conference in Judge Mullen's chambers. The judge granted the request and met with Brodsky, Scotti, and Scotti's associate, Assistant District Attorney Bonomi.

When they emerged from the conference and the court was once again in session, Brodsky rose with Carbo at his side. "Your Honor," the lawyer said, "the defendant wishes to withdraw his plea of not guilty and plead guilty to the first, second, and seventh counts of the indictment."

Judge Mullen accepted the plea. He said he would sentence Carbo four weeks hence. In boxing, many sighed with relief. Perhaps Norris was among them.

Only thirty days earlier, even after Carbo's arrest and arraignment on the federal charge, Norris and Carbo held a surreptitious meeting at Newark Airport.

Scotti was to describe the meeting later:

"On October 1, 1959, Carbo was observed riding in a white Cadillac, bearing Florida license plates, in front of the air terminal in Newark. Also seen at the time and in the same vicinty was James D. Norris riding in a blue Cadillac, bearing Illinois license plates. Frank Carbo was seen leaving the white car and entering the blue Cadillac with Norris in it. This took place at about 1 P.M. Carbo left the blue car at about 4:25 P.M. Carbo and Norris had conferred for over three hours. While we do not know what these two discussed, this lengthy meeting certainly removes any doubt, if there should be any, as to the extent of Carbo's influence among those connected with the professional sport of boxing, including, particularly, James D. Norris."

THIRTY

Whe Frank Carbo stood at last before the bar of boxing justice on November 30, 1959, it was in the courtroom of Judge Mullen. Carbo's hair was almost white. He wore a dark suit, as always, a white-on-white shirt, black elevator shoes, and a look of relief, although he was not well. He was diabetic, his kidneys were malfunctioning, and his face was earth-colored. Recent cardiographs had registered graphically the erratic movements of his heart.

Carbo's lawyer expressed his client's confidence in Judge Mullen's sense of merciful justice, and then Assistant District Attorney Scotti arose and asked permission to read a statement. Conciseness is not one of the virtues of forensic prose. The statement ran to eighteen pages.

"The evil influence of this man has for many years permeated virtually the entire professional sport of boxing," Scotti read. "I believe it is fair to say that the name of Frank Carbo today symbolizes the degeneration of professional boxing into a racket. This man is beyond redemption. He is completely impervious to public opinion."

Scotti went on and on, and he found a sense of pride in his words, perhaps even a measure of justice. He had been on Carbo's trail for years, and now, at last, he had his man nailed. It is perhaps a comforting thing to a man of the law to know that he had proved all is black as opposed to white, and that even somebody called Mr. Gray is neither half-bad nor half-good. From Scotti's point of view, Carbo was a totally corrupt person who had victimized abject stooges in boxing, even unto Norris.

Now it was Judge Mullen's turn. "You had a long and merry dance in pursuit of power in the boxing game," Judge Mullen told Carbo, "but the time has now come when the piper must be paid. You began at the age of eleven to throw your weight around in an improper fashion in school and in your neighborhood. You continued this way in the greater part of your early life till you de-

226

veloped a reputation that caused people to have a concern for not doing what you suggested. In boxing your wish was tantamount to a command performance. You had terrific, improper, and illegal influence in the fight game. You enriched yourself to a degree I can't contemplate."

Judge Mullen, who could have sentenced Carbo to three years in jail, was mindful of the prisoner's illness. He sentenced Carbo to two years in the Rikers Island Penitentiary.

Carbo's face was expressionless for a moment. Then, as he was being led away, Carbo managed a smile. He looked up at Judge Mullen and whispered, "Thank you, Judge."

THIRTY-ONE

IN WASHINGTON, meanwhile, the Subcommittee on Antitrust and Monopoly of the Committee on the Judiciary of the United States Senate was devoting its attention to boxing. Senator Estes Kefauver of Tennessee was chairman of the subcommittee.

The subcommittee had turned to New York City for its investigative strength. John G. Bonomi, the rugged, six-foot tall, 175-pound Assistant District Attorney of New York County, was named assistant counsel to the subcommittee, under Chief Counsel Paul Rand Dixon, while James P. McShane, a former New York City detective, was selected as its chief investigator.

Governor Edmund G. Brown of California had actually instigated the Senate hearings on August 25, 1959, when he asserted that boxing "smells to high heaven." The subcommittee decide to hold the hearings to determine whether federal legislation to control boxing was in the public interest.

Jake LaMotta was the first witness before the subcommittee. On June 14, 1960, he admitted forthrightly that he had taken a "dive" in the bout with Billy Fox in 1947. Bonomi, who had learned all about boxing while helping to put Carbo behind bars, had talked with

LaMotta three months earlier. Now in the caucus room of the old Senate Office Building, he was pressing LaMotta to the inquisitorial wall.

Senator Kefauver was not in the hearing room, but three other members of the Senatorial subcommittee—Philip A. Hart of Michigan, Alexander Wiley of Wisconsin, and Roman L. Hruska of Nebraska—were present.

Four months earlier, LaMotta had been questioned by Bonomi and McShane in New York City, and he had admitted that he had agreed to throw a fight with Tony Janiro, a young boxer, at Madison Square Garden on June 6, 1947, in exchange for a chance to fight for the middleweight championship, but had changed his mind when the guarantee of a title bout was not forthcoming.

He also denied, despite an earlier admission, that the names of Palermo and Daly had been mentioned in connection with an offer of $100,000 to throw the fight with Fox in the same ring on November 14, 1947.

Bonomi was determined to refresh LaMotta's memory in connection with the Fox fight by reading from a transcript of LaMotta's answers to the earlier questions.

"When did the $100,000 bribe offer take place? A few weeks before the fight itself?" Bonomi had asked LaMotta.

"It was during the training period. I don't know exactly."

"Do you recall where you were training?"

"Bobby Gleason's gym."

"That is in the Bronx?"

"Yes."

"In this case your brother, Joe LaMotta, was the one who told you about the bribe offer?"

"Yes."

"The committee has received certain information that Bill Daly and Frank 'Blinky' Palermo were mentioned in connection with the $100,000 bribe offer, is that right?"

"What offer I heard was from my brother."

"Your brother did mention Bill Daly and 'Blinky' Palermo?"

"Their names were mentioned, but I am not sure if it was in connection with the bribe offer."

"Do you recall, Mr. LaMotta, talking to me and to Mr. McShane within the past month and stating to us that your brother told you that Daly and Palermo were the ones who were offering a $100,000 bribe in the Fox fight?"

"But now that it is being taken down I want to be 100 per cent sure."

"Are you 99 per cent sure?"

"I would not swear to it, not even 90 per cent. But I want to be sure because I was not there. This is something that was said, that my brother said to me thirteen years ago. I want to be absolutely sure. I am almost sure it was said, but I am not 100 per cent sure. I told you before I want to be accurate and give somebody the benefit of the doubt to my best recollection."

"To the best of your recollection your brother mentioned Frank Palermo and Bill Daly as the persons offering the bribe?"

"I would not swear to it."

"Is it to the best of your recollection?"

"Yes, to the best of my recollection."

"You said that you told your brother that you did not want the $100,000 but you wanted a shot at the title. Is that right?"

"Yes."

"Did you tell your brother to send that message back to the people who made the offer? Did your brother go back and report what happened?"

"Yes, he said something to the effect that they would see what could be done, and I told him the same thing as in the Janiro fight, if it is OK, it has to come through somebody else. This one party has to say so."

Bonomi failed in an attempt to get LaMotta to concede that the person who guaranteed him a chance at the middleweight championship if he threw the fight to Fox was Thomas Milo, a gambling overlord whose tentacles reached out to every important mobster in the New York City area.

When Joe LaMotta was called to the stand by Bonomi, he invoked the Fifth Amendment. "I go to the Fifth Amendment on the grounds my answer may tend to incriminate me," he said again and again.

One answer stood out glaringly in the record book of boxing. LaMotta did throw the fight to Fox, which permitted Carbo and other mobsters privy to Carbo's intelligence at the time to make a "killing" on the fight. Big-time Broadway bookmakers were financially slaughtered by the action. On the day of the bout, about $25,000 worth of bets were placed on Fox with big-money bookmakers in New Jersey, Miami, Hollywood, and along Broadway. When the bookmakers attempted to "lay off" the action they had taken, they were forestalled; too late they learned that they had been "taken." Carbo made a $35,000 "killing," according to Bonomi.

LaMotta was paid off two years later, in the very first bout promoted by Norris and the International Boxing Club. The promised chance to win the world middleweight championship came his way. He knocked out Marcel Cerdan in the tenth round at Briggs Stadium in Detroit. It was more than a coincidence.

THIRTY-TWO

THE FIRST PART of the Kefauver hearings lasted only two days, June 14 and 15, 1960, and was devoted to the life and times of Jake LaMotta in the boxing jungle. During the summer, the subcommittee's staff devoted itself to the adventures of Frankie Carbo. Zealously, information was gathered everywhere in the land. By December, the subcommittee was ready to resume its hearings.

Gibson inevitably was a star witness on the opening day, December 5, 1960. He was under indictment in Los Angeles and apparently believed he could help his cause by testifying forthrightly before the Kefauver subcommittee. Obviously, the hearings could not concern themselves with aspects of the conspiracy trial pending in California, but they did touch on nearly all the principals involved. Carbo led all the rest.

Under questioning by Bonomi, Gibson linked either directly or indirectly every important manager of boxing with Carbo. He described them as being either "Carbo-controlled" or "Carbo-oriented." He was asked about Jake LaMotta.

"Was he Carbo-controlled?" Bonomi demanded.

"I would say that Jake LaMotta was very close to Carbo, and he is an example of the nature of control," Gibson testified. "We made a match between LaMotta and Robinson in Chicago where unquestionably LaMotta discussed the terms with Carbo, but insisted for a considerable period of time and held the fight up with us because of the difference over financial terms; even though he had agreed to fight, he insisted on a substantial guarantee. We insisted on a percentage, and we ended up with a guarantee and he got about $5,000 less than he would have gotten had he taken the percentage, so that he was controlled up to the extent of taking the match, but not controlled to the extent of bargaining and negotiating on terms."

"Was that the bout with Robinson in 1951 in Chicago?"

"Yes, sir."

Gibson might have told an interesting anecdote regarding that match. Carbo came to Chicago for the bout and stayed at the Drake Hotel, which was down the block, across Michigan Avenue, from the Cameo Restaurant, which Norris and Wirtz owned at the time. He was accompanied by Viola Masters, who was later to be found on the payroll of the Neville Advertising Agency, Inc., a spin-off of the International Boxing Club.

"I remember this very well," Gibson would say later. "Norris was very interested in knowing that Carbo had a good time in Chicago. In fact, he presented Viola Masters with a mink stole as a token of his affection for Carbo."

Gibson's testimony before the subcommittee traced the entire history of the IBC, especially in terms of Carbo.

"Did James D. Norris need underworld backing in order to become a promoter in 1949?" Bonomi asked Gibson.

"I have a little competence in the area of the organization of the International Boxing Club, since I took the idea to Mr. Norris and Mr. Wirtz," Gibson said. "The condition that they imposed on the organization of the International Boxing Club was that we get all of

the leading contenders signed to exclusive contracts and that we deliver them to the new corporation, which was subsequently named
the International Boxing Club, a heavyweight championship bout.
Well, in 1949, I did not know Carbo other than as a name. Norris
had nothing to do with getting the five leading contenders signed.
We paid money; we persuaded; we cajoled. Mr. Carbo had absolutely nothing to do about it, with it, and his influence had nothing
to do with it. The International Boxing Club started with the first
partially televised fight; the championship fight was the Walcott-
Charles fight in Chicago; so that I would say that we started certainly without any help, except the talk and the money that we spent
in getting these leading contenders signed."

"Did something happen along the way?" Bonomi asked. "That is,
you say that you started clean, so to speak. You did not need underworld backing. You did not need underworld influence. Mr. Norris
had a big bankroll. Now, what happened after 1949? Did the situation change?"

"The situation did not change," Gibson asserted, "except that we
were confronted with the facts of life because in New York the first
fight that we tried to stage, the Graziano-LaMotta fight, suddenly
was called off because Graziano developed an illness and we had a
picket line around Madison Square Garden, so that we became concerned with all of the elements that would interfere with our keeping our contracts: the organization of managers, the fact of Carbo's
friendship with managers over the years, which resulted in our making certain decisions of policy with respect to operating a business
that grew into a very big business."

"And was that the policy that you finally decided on—to cooperate with these underworld elements?"

"No, not to cooperate with them, but to live with them."

"Live with them?"

"Yes."

THIRTY-THREE

CARBO'S NAME was heard again and again in the hearing room. Hymie Wallman testified that Carbo had been the man who had gained employment for his fighters with the International Boxing Club. He told how Carbo had directed Billy (Dominick Mordini) Brown, Al Weill's successor as matchmaker for the IBC in New York, to "use" fighters managed by Carbo's pals. And he admitted his apartment in New York had been the place of the meeting between Norris and Carbo at which the welterweight championship elimination bout between Logart and Akins had been arranged. In a phrase, he "spilled his guts."

At one point, Wallman was asked whether he believed fights were fixed. The question was put to him by Nicholas N. Kittrie, counsel for the minority, or Republican members of the Kefauver committee:

"Did Mr. Carbo or anybody else ask you to have any of your fighters throw or fix a fight?"

"Never," Wallman replied.

"You mean nobody ever talked to you about fixing a fight, or throwing a fight?"

"No, sir; no, sir."

"You feel that your fighters, when they fought, did the best they could?"

"They fought their hearts out. Yes, sir."

"Did you ever hear of Carbo or Norris or anybody else trying to fix any other fights?"

"No, sir."

"So, actually, despite the fact that Mr. Carbo had all kinds of influence apparently in fixing or arranging for fights, that is, in helping in matchmaking and so on, once a decision was made to hold a fight, he did not interfere with the final results; he did not try to fix it in any way?"

"Well, I would think that he was the best influence in boxing for that sort of thing—to throw fights, I mean, as far as I know. I have never heard him discuss it, anything about fixings. Now, I read where Jack LaMotta and Fox and all that stuff, and I have been in the business so long I was so naïve about it that I think I lost $250 on the fight."

Bonomi, grasping the meaning of Wallman's double-talk, moved in like a tiger.

"Mr. Wallman—excuse me, Mr. Kittrie—may I just ask this question?" Bonomi asked urgently. "Mr. Wallman, do you recall testifying before the New York County Grand Jury on May 23 of 1958 and being asked the following questions?:

Question: So you are saying that in a bout involving your fighter, where you had a judge or a referee who would favor your fighter, and Carbo was in New York, you would inform him of that. Is that correct?

Answer: Yes.

Question: And you would inform him that you had an edge?

Answer: Right.

Question: Now, you know Carbo was a heavy gambler, do you not?

Answer: I know he bets baseball.

Question: What?

Answer: I seen him watching the baseball game where he is crazy.

Question: We are not talking about baseball now. We are talking about boxing.

Answer: I know he gambled on horses and everything.

Question: He bets on fights, doesn't he?

Answer: Surely.

Question: Did you tell Carbo right before the fight that—and the name is deleted from the grand jury testimony—was in there as the judge and you expected a break?

Answer: Well, he would call me at night.

Question: Who was "he?"

Answer: Carbo.

Question: Before the fight?

Answer: Yes.

Question: What would he say to you? What did he say? Never mind "would," what did he say?

Answer: What's doing tonight?

Question: And?
Answer: And I said, "Oh, I think it's pretty safe."
Question: Yes. And?
Answer: That's all. That's all that was necessary.
Question: That was enough?
Answer. Yes.

"Do you recall giving that testimony?" Bonomi demanded once again in the hearing room.
"Yes, sir," Wallman replied.

THIRTY-FOUR

NORRIS HAD BEEN resisting the Kefauver committee's effort to bring him into the hearing room. All medical records of his illnesses were marshaled against his appearance. Finally, Dr. V. J. Dorset, medical director of the United States Public Health Service, wrote to Senator Kefauver on December 8, 1960, and recommended that Norris not be asked to testify in an open hearing.

"Mr. Norris may testify before your committee at a closed hearing without undue risk," Dr. Dorset said.

Finally, that same day, the confrontation took place in executive session. Norris came into the room accompanied by Emil N. Levin, his attorney, and Senator Kefauver greeted him.

"Mr. Norris," Senator Kefauver said, "you are coming here of your own free will though, of course, a subpoena was served on you. You are willing to take the risk of any difficulty that might occur to you as a result of this executive session; is that correct?"

"Yes, sir," Norris replied calmly, and immediately proceeded to swear that his testimony would be true in all aspects.

Norris was asked whether he had a statement to make. He had. His lawyer read it. It was twenty paragraphs long and was autobiographical in the main. It traced the beginnings of Norris's boxing monopoly and conceded that he had employed Viola Masters, Carbo's wife, and Jack Kearns to insure a steady supply of fighters for the International Boxing Club's weekly television shows.

Senator Kefauver and Senator Everett M. Dirksen of Illinois led the questioning of Norris. They treated him respectfully. Senator Dirksen asked Norris whether his association with Kearns and Carbo was essential to the conduct of his business or the result of an abiding devotion to proper social conduct.

Norris was an imposing figure. His garb was conservative and tasteful, and the warmth of his personality shone through despite the harshness of the circumstances. Politely, he replied to Senator Dirksen's question.

"I have been greatly embarrassed by certain newspapermen, and people, I think they read it so often, that I have hoodlum associations," he said. "I certainly would not look at it that way. I never had a cup of coffee with Frank Carbo until I went to New York to try and run boxing. I am out of boxing now, so I mean I have no intention of ever having another cup of coffee with Carbo, and it has hurt me tremendously and embarrassed me tremendously. It has embarrassed my family tremendously."

Having said this, Norris responded to a long series of questions by the senators which indicated that he never had been in Carbo's home. Bonomi asked him, "Has Mr. Carbo ever visited your apartment in New York City?"

"Yes, sir," Norris said.

Norris went on to admit a long-standing friendship with Sam Hunt, the Chicagoan who was known as "Golfbag" because he carried his machine-gun as one might carry a set of matched irons.

"He would come up to the house," Norris said of Hunt, "and eventually, to my knowledge, got kicked out of the—whatever organization he belonged to—because he wanted to do the right thing and be a decent citizen which, of course, with his background he couldn't do, but he would have done anything in the world to have been looked upon as a decent citizen and have undone, at least, the things he had been charged with."

Norris did not define the "things he had been charged with" as murder, though he might have. In this little speech in defense of

Hunt's name he managed to demonstrate a depth of compassion which touched the senators in the hearing room.

Inevitably, the name of Morris Schmertzler, a big-time bookmaker, was invoked in the questioning of Norris. Schmertzler, who was also known as Max Courtney, had been Norris's friend for years. They had first met years before, when on-course handbooks were legal in New York racing. Courtney had operated such a book.

Courtney, like Kearns and Viola Masters, had been on the payroll of Cameo Enterprises, Inc., one of the Norris-Wirtz corporations, and had received $76,000 in salary at the rate of $2,000 per month from 1957 through April, 1960, when the Norris-Wirtz boxing enterprise had ceased to function.

In response to a question by Bonomi, Norris conceded that Courtney was employed by the Cameo company. "My understanding," Norris said, "was that he could be and would be well qualified to try and sell our library of fight pictures. That is what I think I originally suggested to Mr. Wirtz, that Max Courtney—or Mr. Schmertzler—be hired to try to do."

"Was that one of the functions of Cameo Enterprises, to sell your library of fight pictures?" Senator Kefauver asked.

"Evidently that is what it was."

"Don't you know?"

"No, I don't." Norris conceded.

The questioning turned to Carbo's involvement in the second bout between Marciano and Walcott. Gibson had testified earlier that Carbo had in fact persuaded Felix Bocchicchio, Walcott's manager, to accept the return match when Bocchicchio was balking.

"So Bocchicchio had some discussions with you in New York concerning this match; is that correct?" Bonomi asked Norris.

"Yes. He came up to Madison Square Garden, up to our office. I talked to his attorney quite a number of times. His attorney was all for his going through with the match, going through with the agreement, getting it out of the way for a good payday."

"Are you able to develop in greater detail, as Mr. Gibson, your associate, said, the fact that Carbo got Bocchicchio to come in and discuss the fight with you?"

"No; I cannot say that Carbo got him to come in. I understand what Mr. Gibson said, and possibly, not knowing about it, had some opinion on the thing, and said I could develop it a great deal further. I cannot develop it further. Now, I can assume, which I do not suppose you gentlemen want me to do, but Al Weill was very friendly."

"With Frankie Carbo?"

"With Frankie Carbo. We are talking about Marciano on one side," Norris said, "and Walcott on the other. I mean it could have come about that way very easily. I know when Bocchicchio came up to my office with his attorney for the final signing. I talked to him quite a number of times, he and his attorney. He was talking, mumbling about pressure or something like that, and I made a very foolish deal with him."

"We he mumbling about pressure from Frankie Carbo?"

"He did not say, but he was surly and I made a very foolish deal with him. I guaranteed him $250,000."

Norris conceded that he knew that Weill, who was his matchmaker, was extremely friendly with Carbo, and that Carbo had exerted his influence on Weill to make the match in 1952 between Marciano and Matthews.

"If I hadn't talked to certain people," Norris quoted Weill as saying in 1952, "I would never have taken that match for you."

" 'Certain people' happened to be one person, Frankie Carbo; isn't that right?" Bonomi demanded.

"I would assume that," Norris said.

Eventually, the questioning turned on a humorous note.

"You have a racehorse named Mr. Gray, do you not?" Bonomi asked Norris.

Norris conceded the point and added, "The sire of that horse was a horse named Gray Wing. Now, I mean, it is always thrown up to me that I named the horse after Carbo. I am not saying I didn't, but I mean there are other circumstances. The horse's sire was Gray Wing, and a great many times the way you name horses you take part of the sire's name, and part of the dam's name, and you put them together and try to get a euphonious name."

"Frankie Carbo was known as Mr. Gray in boxing, was he not?"

"Yes, sir. Some people called him that."

"Was he partly in your mind when you named the horse?" Senator Kefauver asked.

"Possibly facetiously," Norris said.

"Was he a good horse?" Senator Kefauver asked.

"He wasn't worth a nickel."

Norris left them laughing.

THIRTY-FIVE

CARBO CAME BEFORE the Kefauver committee on December 14, 1960, soon after the committee had heard Sonny Liston, who was not yet the world's heavyweight champion, insist that he was not managed by Palermo.

"Do you share, by virtue of an undisclosed contract, in the fight purses of Charles ("Sonny") Liston?" Senator Keafuver asked Carbo.

"I respectfully decline to answer the question on the ground that I cannot be compelled to be a witness against myself," Carbo replied.

It was his response to every question put to him by the committee.

Finally, realizing the futility of the questioning, Senator Kefauver said, "Mr. Carbo, we are about to excuse you and, before we do, do you wish to avail yourself of this last opportunity of answering some of these questions upon reconsideration, or upon consultation with your attorney, Mr. Brodsky? We will give you this opportunity of doing so. Do you wish to consult with your attorney?"

There was a hurried consultation between client and lawyer. Then, at last, Carbo spoke.

"There is only one thing I want to say, Mr. Senator," Carbo said.

"Yes," Senator Kefauver said expectantly.

"I congratulate you on your reelection."

There was laughter.

"Senator," Mr. Brodsky said, "Mr. Carbo has a diabetic condition, and he was wondering . . . "

"He was what?"

"If there was some orange juice available."

"Orange juice?"

"I had no breakfast," Carbo said.

"All right. We are about to excuse you, Mr. Carbo."

"I am trying to hold on as long as I can," Carbo said.

"Very well," Senator Kefauver said. "You look like a pleasant man, Mr. Carbo."

THIRTY-SIX

THE NEXT TIME Carbo stood before a bar of justice was on February 21, 1961, in the courtroom of Judge Ernest Tolin in Los Angeles. He was about to go on trial with Palermo, Sica, Dragna, and Gibson on conspiracy and extortion charges. Judge Tolin, unlike Senator Kefauver, was not moved to regard Carbo as "a pleasant man."

The federal government had named a Special Assistant to the Attorney General, Alvin H. Goldstein, Jr., to prosecute the five defendants. Almost immediately, he asked Judge Tolin to cancel the bail of the five men and to remand them to custody in order "to avoid interference by them with the orderly process of the trial."

Judge Tolin granted the motion, but changed his mind in Gibson's case and ordered his release on bail almost immediately. Twice during the trial, which lasted until May 30, 1961, and produced 7,500 pages of testimony, the defendants were denied applications to have their bail reinstated.

Gibson was uneasy in the company of the others, and his lawyers, the aforementioned Mr. Ming and Loren Miller of Los Angeles, asked the court for a separation of Gibson's case. The application for the severance was denied.

Leonard and Nesseth testified at length, and the sum of their testimony encompassed the entire case against the defendants. As the government would state later in a brief submitted to the United States Court of Appeals for the Ninth Circuit, the evidence adduced from Leonard's and Nesseth's testimony added up to this chronology:

> *January 27, 1959*: Carbo threatens Leonard's life and warns that he, Carbo, has friends on the West Coast who can enforce his demands.
>
> *April, 28, 1959*: Carbo threatens to have Leonard and Nesseth killed and reminds Leonard that he has friends on the West Coast who will do this. Leonard is so frightened by this that he vomits. *Within one week after this conversation of April 28th, the following occurs*:
>
> *April 30, 1959*: Palermo arrives in Chicago and stays at the Bismarck Hotel (owned by Norris and Wirtz) at IBC expense.
>
> *May, 1, 1959*: Palermo meets with Gibson in the lobby of the Bismarck Hotel and thereafter leaves the hotel for Los Angeles, neglecting to check out.
>
> *May 1, 1959*: Palermo arrives in Los Angeles and registers at the Beverly Hilton Hotel under the alias of "George Tobias."
>
> *May 1, 1959*: Palermo meets with appellant Dragna at Puccini's Restaurant in Beverly Hills.
>
> *May 2 or 3, 1959*: Leonard is summoned to the Beverly Hilton Hotel by Palermo where he is taken to Palermo's room and, in the presence of Palermo, threatened by Sica.
>
> *May 4, 1959*: Dragna and Palermo appear in Leonard's office at the Hollywood Legion Stadium. Nesseth walks out and goes to the police where he sees Dragna.
>
> *May 5, 1959*: Sica and Palermo endeavor to get Leonard to meet them at Perino's Restaurant in Los Angeles.
>
> *May 6, 1959*: Sica and Palermo appear in Leonard's office at the Hollywood Legion Stadium.

On May 13, 1959, according to testimony, Daly visited Leonard in the promoter's office in the Hollywood Legion Stadium. He did not know that Leonard's office was wired for sound, and that policemen were tending the equipment. However, he intuitively insisted that his conversation with Leonard take place in the hallway outside the office.

Leonard testified Daly told him he was "in a hell of a jam" with Carbo, Gibson, and Norris. He quoted Daly as saying, "I would like to straighten the thing out." Leonard promised to meet Daly in his room at the Ambassador Hotel the next morning.

The next day, May 14, 1959, was bright and sunny. Leonard arose early and went to the office of the Intelligence Division of the Los Angeles Police Department, where he was "wired" for sound. A wire-recording device with the trade name of P55 Minifon was fitted into a holster on the left side of his body. To Leonard's right side, under his arm, the police strapped a portable radio transmitter. Tape was applied to the transmitter switch so that it was held in the "on" position.

The transmitter signal could only be received by a special radio which Sergeant Conwell Keeler of the Los Angeles Police Department took with him to a room near Daly's at the Ambassador Hotel. In the room, Sergeant Keeler plugged a tape record into the receiver and made a separate recording of the conversation between Daly and Leonard. Both recordings, introduced in evidence, were played back at the trial.

The conversation in the hotel room at first concerned itself with Leonard's protest over the threatening calls he had received from Carbo. Then Daly attempted to explain, if not to justify, the reason for Leonard's and Nesseth's difficulty with Carbo and Palermo:

Daly: You see, if this geezer, this Nesseth, he shot his mouth off.
Leonard: Is that right?
Daly: He took the attitude instead of using some diplomacy he handles when he sells automobiles, used the same fucking bullshit with them, and went along with Truman to bullshit them, you know what I mean, work it out, con them, and win them over on his side. He'd 've had them eating fucking crazy to juggle opponents, did this, done that. Now he just challenged them and said, "Go and fuck yourself. You ain't going to have nothing. You ain't going to have no money. You ain't going to have no this, you ain't going to have that." Somebody must have made some kind of fucking promise. He wants to act as if he didn't know anything about it. That's what's killing them. They not stupid altogether. Jesus Christ, there was—he knew about it. He played possum until he got the title. They knew he done

it. They knew he fucked them. If he had said before the fight, "No," but makes the speeches you're making now, make them before the fight, but he didn't know, he's living in a world of his own, this kid is, and he's daffy, he don't care for nobody concerned.

Daly went on to explain the effect upon Gibson of Nesseth's refusal to accede to Carbo's and Palermo's demands upon Gibson.

Leonard: I hear Truman's really in a jackpot over this bullshit, too.
Daly: Oh terrible. He was so highly upset. Now why . . . [Unintelligible.]
Leonard: He told me he caught hell from Carbo, caught hell from Norris. He caught hell from everybody.
Daly: Yeah, yeah, he got—got in a hell of a fucking—
Leonard: He's still in the jackpot.

Then Daly introduced a note of terror. He referred to the assault on Ray Arcel in Boston some years before. Leonard asked why Sica, who was an "important" underworld figure, would permit himself to become involved in the attempted extortion.

Daly: Well, then, people in New York do them favors.
Leonard: Yeah. Then I guess Blinky's connected with what? The longshore outfit?
Daly: Yeah . . . [Unintelligible] that's one of his outfits. They're up to something with Nesseth. They'll get—throw some fucking—
Leonard: Bomb?
Daly: Bomb his porch off or something.
Leonard: You know they didn't like about Arcel. You know Arcel thought he was pretty smart, too.
Daly: Lucky thing Arcel didn't die.
Leonard: Yea. They never did get him, either, did they?
Daly: No . . . [Unintelligible.]
Leonard: Did Arcel really see him or not? He probably didn't even know what hit him.
Daly: It's like you and I talking and somebody walking over.
Leonard: Oh, Jesus Christ. When Carbo called me—
Daly: See what they do. They use a water pipe, see. You know, regular lead water pipe. And about that short. About that thick. And they just

get an ordinary piece of newspaper, see, newspaper don't show finger-prints. They they take it and they wrap it just in the newspaper, see—
Leonard: . . . [Unintelligible.]
Daly: Just an ordinary piece of paper, that's all they ever use. And you sitting in a crowd. And they try to give you two bats, and they kill you with two if they can. But they whack you twice and split your—fracture your skull, and knock you unconscious, and they just drop it. And if they drop it, they can't—and if they drop it, they can't—there's no heat. You can't—you haven't got no weapon on you. If they said you did it, what the hell, you drop it in a crowd or out in the street. They drop it immediately. After they do it, they drop it. And after they drop it, the law—they're protected by the law. They have to have witnesses. They seen them come out and that's the guy, and that's what he used.
Leonard: You know, that's what Frankie told me. He said, "We got friends out there." He said, "I don't need to even leave here." I don't know where he was at. I don't even know where he was calling from. He didn't tell me. He called direct. No person-to-person. You pick up the phone, and here he is.

Daly, as the federal prosecutor was to assert later in a brief filed in the Court of Appeals, "played the role of everybody's friend in the boxing business. . . ."
"The thrust of what Daly said to Leonard in his casual manner on May 14 is a very pointed reminder to Leonard of what he should have learned during his years in boxing: that Carbo controlled all money-making facets of professional boxing," the brief contended.

THIRTY-SEVEN

THERE WERE ten volumes of testimony. Gibson, Palermo, Dragna, and Sica testified; Carbo was mute. Nesseth withstood blistering cross-examination. And Daly, "everybody's friend," was a witness for Gibson. Of all the defendants, only Gibson was able to introduce witnesses who testified to his good character. It was unavailing.

Don Jordan also testified. Although he was the pawn in the entire conspiracy, little or no attention had been paid to him. He had held the championship from December 5, 1958, until May 27, 1960, when he lost it to Benny ("Kid") Paret. His reign had been undistinguished, and his behavior had not been a credit to boxing.

When Jordan was on the witness stand, he was asked to relate the content of a conversation with Dragna. Arrogantly and insolently he responded: "Roses are red, violets are blue; besamay kulo y alva fong ku."

No translation was provided, although the last two words, such as they were, obviously were obscene.

Jordan had been a difficult and unwilling witness under cross-examination, although he had been cooperative while testifying in Palermo's behalf. At one point he refused to admit he had testified before the grand jury, which he had done. The prosecution scored a telling blow by pointing out that Jordan's testimony in the courtroom was exactly opposite of his testimony before the grand jury.

Judge Tolin's charge to the jury was lengthy and all-inclusive. On May 30, the jury returned its verdict. All the defendants were found guilty. Judge Tolin said he would hear all motions on June 20, in advance of sentencing the prisoners. Gibson was the only one free on bail.

On June 11, unexpectedly, Judge Tolin died. Chief Judge Peirson M. Hall, of the Southern District of California, designated Judge George H. Boldt, of the Western District of Washington, to handle all matters remaining in the case. It was inevitable that all the defendants would ask for new trials as a result of Judge Tolin's death. These motions were denied.

On December 2, 1961, Judge Boldt denied all motions made by the defense lawyers and announced the sentences:

Carbo, twenty-five years in prison and a $10,000 fine.

Palermo, fifteen years in prison and a $10,000 fine.

Gibson, five-year suspended sentence and a $10,000 fine.

Sica, twenty years in prison and a $10,000 fine.

Dragna, five years in prison.

All except Carbo were released on bail. Carbo was removed to Alcatraz Prison in San Francisco Bay.

Norris heard the news at his home in Coral Gables. He felt bad. He had paid most of Gibson's legal fees, including the greater part of some $60,000 apparently extorted by one Sidney Brin, of Los Angeles, who had posed as a government agent and who had furnished forged documents purporting to show that the Department of Justice intended to dismiss the indictment against Gibson.

Later, the government would rebuff Gibson's introduction of this matter in his appeal, saying:

> Gibson repeats his charge that prior to the trial the government, to his prejudice, promised to dismiss the indictment against him. . . . The Gibson argument on this point is founded upon false hopes and forged documents. In the light of what Mr. Gibson must know concerning the authenticity of the documents, appellee wonders if he is acting in good faith when he urges this court to deal with the subject. Suffice it to say, Gibson was furnished with forged documents which purported to demonstrate the government's intention to dismiss the charges against him. These documents (a telegram falsely signed with the name of an Assistant United States Attorney; a forged letter purportedly signed by William Hundley, then Chief of the Organized Crime and Racketeering Section of the Criminal Division of the Department of Justice; and a forged stipulation to dismiss the indictment against Gibson purportedly signed by Laughlin Waters, then United States Attorney for the Southern District of California) were fabricated by a highly paid representative of Gibson and were exhibited by representatives of Gibson to an Assistant United States Attorney in an effort to obtain a dismissal from the Department of Justice. Although the forger himself denied that Gibson or his attorneys were aware of the false character of these documents, there is no doubt that both Gibson and his attorneys now know that they were counterfeit.

In due course, the forger was dealt with. He wound up in a federal penitentiary.

THIRTY-EIGHT

T HE UNITED STATES COURT OF APPEALS for the Ninth Circuit heard the appeals of all five men. Carbo, Palermo, and Dragna had based their appeal on the contention that Judge Tolin had erred in his charge to the jury regarding the use of declarations made by a co-conspirator. Sica claimed that the court had been in error when it had permitted the government to introduce into the trial the fact that Sica had lied in direct examination about the extent of his criminal record. Gibson alleged that the prosecutor, namely Goldstein, had "distorted the evidence during closing argument."

On February 13, 1963, the Court of Appeals in San Francisco handed down its decision. The court, in a seventy-five-page opinion, reversed the conviction of Dragna. It confirmed the convictions in their entirety of Carbo, Palermo, and Gibson. It confirmed only two of the three counts against Sica, whose sentence of twenty years in prison was unaffected by the decision.

Palermo and Sica were out on bail. Carbo was no longer at Alcatraz. The old prison near the Golden Gate had been abandoned by the government and Carbo had been moved to the Federal Penitentiary at McNeil, Washington. Gibson was at home in Chicago.

THIRTY-NINE

I T IS A curious thing about James Dougan Norris, about whom everybody was supposed to know everything and about whom nothing was known. It has been said that he is rich and that he looks like a man who polishes his skin in the morning. He has the appearance of stolidity, and his fine frame implies muscular strength. He has a warm smile and a modesty of dress and manner, and he has deep within him a secret: Why?

247

FORTY

IN THE EARLY PART OF 1962, Truman Gibson was about to sever all his connections with the Chicago Stadium Corporation. A meeting was to be held with Arthur Wirtz at which a financial settlement was to be made. In advance of the meeting, Wirtz sent a letter to Gibson in which he reminded Truman that there was $6,000 owing the Chicago Stadium Corporation. Gibson sat down and wrote a reply:

March 6, 1962

Dear Art:

Your letter dated February 26, but mailed without postage on March 2, greeted me on my return to Chicago from Sarasota and Bradenton, Florida, on Sunday.

Since you sent the letter to my home, I had all of Sunday to consider it. You refer to the $6,000. What about the balance which was due me but unresolved at the time of payment of the $6,000. In this connection, note the enclosed copy of the stipulation you had drawn. Note the reference to the amount. Your memory may also be jogged by referring back to the meeting in your office at the Chicago Stadium on the night of the Kennedy rally and in the presence of your partner.

So, at our meeting, add all of this and not just the $6,000 to the agenda. You measure everything in terms of money. You are probably correct since you have been so successful.

What measure do you put on a man's life? Was your shrewd bargain, when we last met, your determination?

I could not help but think then and now that I never knew Carbo before the organization of the IBC. I never cleared championships with him. I talked with him most infrequently. I certainly did not clear the Akins-Jordan fight with him. Some one did, and the fact that I didn't indicates who put me in the soup. While you are remembering things in the past, please also recollect that I didn't collect any of the profits (nor did Joe Louis, despite his agreement) from the split up IBC operations from behind a nice insulated shield.

I thought of all these things in your office. I would not have said or written them except for your last letter. So, at our meeting, let us include everything on the agenda.

In Coral Gables, Wirtz's partner, Norris, received a carbon copy of the letter.

INDEX